Madness in
MOGADISHU

Madness in
MOGADISHU

Commanding the 10th Mountain Division's Quick Reaction Company during Black Hawk Down

Lt. Col. Michael Whetstone, USA (Ret.)

STACKPOLE
BOOKS

Copyright © 2015 by Michael Whetstone

Published by
STACKPOLE BOOKS
5067 Ritter Road
Mechanicsburg, PA 17055
www.stackpolebooks.com

Printed in the United States of America

10 9 8 7 6 5 4 3 2 1

STACKPOLE FIRST EDITION

Photos by Michael Whetstone

Library of Congress Cataloging-in-Publication Data

Whetstone, Michael.
  Madness in Mogadishu : commanding the 10th Mountain Division's Quick Reaction Company during Black Hawk Down / Lt. Col. Michael Whetstone, USA (Ret.). — First edition.
     pages cm
  Includes bibliographical references.
  ISBN 978-0-8117-1573-7
1. Operation Restore Hope, 1992–1993. 2. Whetstone, Michael. 3. United States. Army. Infantry Regiment, 14th. Company C—Biography. 4. United States. Army. Mountain Division, 10th—Biography. I. Title. II. Title: Commanding the 10th Mountain Division's Quick Reaction Company during Black Hawk Down.
  DT407.42.W49 2015
  967.7305'3—dc23
                                       2014043690

To those in the arena;
Every man and woman in the U.S. Armed Forces,
Facing adversity with courage, commitment,
strength, and honor day in and day out;
And to those who gave all in Somalia.

CONTENTS

FOREWORD

The typical twenty-one-year-old in North America or Western Europe would shake their head in disbelief if they were suddenly transported back in time to the year of their birth. Cell phones were in their infancy. The technology to make them useful in areas outside of the largest urban pockets, coupled with their extremely high cost, seemed to doom them to novelty status for years to come. The vast majority of Americans didn't own a personal computer, much less know how to make it work if they did. The Internet had not yet invaded every aspect of our lives, and having a Sony Walkman with lots of cassette tapes was the gold standard for "cool" among the younger crowd.

Cable TV was the newest big thing, having made its grand debut on the world stage during the First Gulf War of 1990–1991. We largely have Ted Turner to thank for this, the eccentric, self-made mega-millionaire who just wouldn't let go of his crackpot idea for a twenty-four-hour news channel—the Cable News Network. CNN turned the Western world into insatiable news junkies and propelled a privileged few journalists to international rock star status along the way.

And so it was in the summer of 1992 when reports began to suggest that something really bad was happening in the Horn of Africa. The calamities of drought, civil war, and tribal warlord-ism had all converged on Somalia, creating a humanitarian crisis of epic proportions that was equal parts work of nature and work of man. And CNN was there to show it all to the world, live and in person, twenty-four hours a day. There was no escaping it. The phenomenon became known in certain circles as the "CNN Effect."

The world now seems to have become inured to the CNN Effect. I suppose that a constant stream of new technology and sixteen years of incessant crisis reporting have seen to that. A dozen or so cable channels are now devoted to around-the-clock global news coverage. Whether it's Bosnia, Kosovo, Rwanda, Darfur, Haiti, hurricanes, tsunamis, Oklahoma City, 9/11, or the latest murder in Anytown, USA, round-the-clock cable news exposure seems to elevate each big event to national or international importance. Subsequently, such events dominate the airwaves until ratings begin to dip, then are quickly replaced, in turn, with the next big events in the queue.

But CNN's coverage of Somalia—the first big event in the post–Gulf War era—reflected the network's view of the story's importance. Instead of simply reporting the story and moving on, CNN became the world's conscience, prodding the timid or unwilling into action. A humanitarian crisis needed fixing. Innocent Somalis were dying by the thousands and would continue dying unless the international community did something about it. Clearly, it would be up to the United States to lead this effort and to galvanize broader international support. Immediate action was needed; there was no time to waste. The message was repeated almost every hour on the hour and there was no escaping it.

This is not to suggest that the United States and its international partners blindly followed CNN's lead. However, knowledgeable analysts generally agree that the CNN Effect played a critical role in shaping the international community's intervention into Somalia and catalyzed its happening sooner rather than later. The irony of it all is that the CNN Effect was equally catalytic when those same countries began pulling the plug a little more than one year later. Yes, and CNN brought these images to the world, too. Scarcely an American alive at the time can forget the gruesome images of Somalis dancing around the wreckage of a downed U.S. Army Black Hawk helicopter and gleefully dragging the corpses of two valiant American servicemen through the streets of Mogadishu.

It's a regrettable twist of history that then-Captain Mike Whetstone never got the chance to meet U.S. Army Master Sgt. Gary Gordon or Sfc. Randall Shugart. On 3 and 4 October 1993, Mike and the 150 men of Charlie Company spent the sixteen most harrowing hours of their lives, laying everything on the line in an effort to reach their two unknown comrades before their fate was sealed. Mike and his men were real tigers that day, as indeed they were every day in Somalia. But sometimes even the best outfits are given missions that are just a bridge too far. Strangely, Mike and the rest of us only got to know these two heroes later on—after all the killing, dying, and suffering of innocents had ended. We can thank CNN for this, too.

It was my privilege to command the 2nd Battalion, 14th Infantry Regiment Golden Dragons from December 1991 to January 1994. Mike came to the battalion in January 1993 after being designated by the brigade commander, Col. William E. "Kip" Ward, to command Charlie Company. In all honesty, Mike really wasn't the officer I wanted to command this company. Coming from the brigade staff, he was somewhat of an unknown—not yet one of "my" guys.

The Army entrusts brigade commanders to choose those officers who should and should not be company commanders, as well as the specific companies within the brigade that they will command. Battalion commanders sometimes view this as unfair because they usually think they know better. But the system is a good one. Given their greater experience and broader view, brigade commanders are more apt to see the diamonds in the rough that younger battalion commanders might miss. Orders being orders, I saluted Colonel Ward's decision, passed Mike the guidon, and immediately began to give him the "special treatment" to see whether he could measure up to my standards and had what I thought it took to lead.

With the benefit of age and 20/20 hindsight, I confess that I didn't give Mike the fairest of shakes during his early months in command. Battalions are the Army's basic building block formation, and good battalions are real families in every sense of the word. The battalion commander is the father: a lieutenant colonel with typically sixteen to eighteen years of commissioned service. The Battalion command sergeant major, executive officer, and operations officer (the latter two being majors) are the eldest sons and play critical roles in running the outfit. Four or five company commanders, captains all, are the mid-tier sons, and lieutenants are the pups. Put simply, the better the battalion, the tighter the family. We Golden Dragons thought of ourselves as a very good battalion and had an extremely tight family. And Mike, the outsider, had come to us against Dad's wishes.

After the first two or three months, I had my doubts that Mike would ever develop into the kind of leader I wanted commanding one of my companies. Infantry company command is one of the toughest jobs in the Army, and it takes a special kind of man to excel at it. The person has to be tactically and technically competent; physically and mentally tough; personally courageous and compassionate; willing to listen to more experienced people in his sphere regardless of their rank; and coachable from above. Infantry company commanders must be firing on all cylinders from the moment they take command, and there is little margin for error. A hundred and fifty pairs of eyes study their every move every hour of the day, watching for the mistake or lapse in judgment that could cost their lives. The pressure that company commanders put on themselves to make every move the right move is unrelenting.

I can't recall any epiphany moment or event that sparked Mike's metamorphosis into a great company commander, but after those few initial rough months everything seemed to go Charlie Company's way. Mike was everywhere at once and on top of everything; no detail was too small to escape his keen eye. The company excelled in all of our toughest training events, and I could see the soldiers' confidence in Mike's leadership abilities grow with each success. And the more confidence the soldiers had in Mike, the more he had in himself. The company developed a pride and quiet confidence in itself that was palpable. I had to admit it—Colonel Ward had been right. The diamond in the rough now shone brilliantly, and Mike was squarely one of "my" guys. Little did any of us know in the spring of 1993 just how important all this was to become a few months later.

The chapters that follow do well in chronicling Mike's time in combat command. His description of the events and emotions we experienced as a unit in Somalia are accurate and unembellished. For me, his story has a twofold meaning. First, it provides historical context to a chapter in the 14th Infantry Regiment's history that has particular relevance both to those of us who lived it and those who follow in our footsteps. Second, it's the story of a young officer's personal journey toward finding the truth of what command in combat truly meant to him. Each of us who have the privilege of leading men in the life-and-death struggle of combat makes this journey in our own way. This is Mike's story.

Mike was the coolest commander under fire I've ever known, making all the right moves at just the right time with ice water running through his veins. Two Golden Dragons made the ultimate sacrifice in Somalia. Thirty-three others were wounded. Some still bear the weight of a lifetime in a wheelchair or without limbs. About half of these casualties came from Charlie Company. The battalion also had four soldiers who received Silver Stars for valor. Three of these soldiers came from Charlie Company. One of them was Mike.

I hope that one day CNN will see fit to give these heroes and their comrades the recognition they deserve for the countless sacrifices they made on the streets of Mogadishu during the African autumn of 1993.

—*Brig. Gen. William C. (Bill) David, USA (Ret.)*

"It is not the critic who counts; not the man who points out how the strong man stumbles or where the doer of deeds could have done better. The credit belongs to the man who is actually in the arena, whose face is marred by dust and sweat and blood, who strives valiantly, who errs and comes up short again and again, because there is no effort without error or shortcoming, but who knows the great enthusiasms, the great devotions, who spends himself for a worthy cause; who, at the best, knows, in the end, the triumph of high achievement, and who, at the worst, if he fails, at least he fails while daring greatly, so that his place shall never be with those cold and timid souls who knew neither victory nor defeat."

—THEODORE ROOSEVELT

PREFACE

ine was the typical upbringing of Navy brats around the world: tours in Alaska and Hawaii; coast-to-coast road trips between stateside bases when Dad was reassigned yet again; multiple schools in numerous states; and the usual mundane existence common to childhood. College was a ten-year thread woven into the fabric of a life that by then included marriage to my high school sweetheart, two beautiful children, and a hitch as an enlisted Marine that led to my choice of the military life as the career for me.

Graduating number two in the University of Alabama's Army ROTC Class of 1985 earned me the right to choose a Regular Army commission and Infantry as my branch. Jump School, Ranger School, the Infantry Officer Basic and Advanced Courses, and assignments to various company-grade leadership and staff positions at Fort Carson, Colorado, and in Germany (Baumholder and Kaiserslautern) ultimately led to my arrival at Fort Drum, New York.

And Fort Drum led to Mogadishu, Somalia.

Before Somalia, I was like all untried infantrymen, secretly hoping for the chance to prove myself. I trained hard to be ready for the day when I would lead men in the ultimate male endeavor: closing with and destroying the enemy.

Ever since I can remember, I wanted to lead men in combat. But a major frustration of my military life and professional education was that the secrets of the profession always seemed to be just beyond my reach. Many of my superiors didn't want to teach the secrets for fear of losing their "knowledge is power" edge. And many of my peers thought they had discovered the secrets by living through demanding training experiences at the National Training Center (NTC) or by being really close to the commander.

They were wrong. The people who actually revealed combat's truths were men and women I never met, but whose combat experiences I had read about. Those who have been there yearn to tell those that follow in their footsteps about the horrors of war and the effects of combat on themselves and the troops in their care.

During my readings about great leaders and their impact on the men they led, I found myself wondering whether I could ever measure up to the likes of such dynamic leaders as Joshua Chamberlain, the Duke of Wellington, George S. Patton, Lawrence of Arabia, and Erwin Rommel, chief among those I most admired in my youth. After living through a miniscule fraction of what they experienced, I am in awe.

Success does not come by one's own making. It emerges from the efforts of family, teachers, instructors, leaders, and mentors.

Reflecting back, I thank God and many personal and professional guides throughout my life. First, my family—my parents, Marcus and Rosemary, who raised me, watching me grow into the man I am today; my wife, Pam, and our kids Michael, Michelle, Mikki, Mimi, Mitchell, and Miller, who are the lights of my life and who put up with all the deployments, near tragedies, and tedious operations that came with a career in the Army. I am blessed with a great and selfless family that takes the hardships in stride and backs me with all their souls. A man could ask for no more.

The professionals who went the extra mile to show me the way include Marine Corps Drill Sergeants Gray, Reyes, and Wilson, and Corporal Simione; all the Airborne Black Hats and Ranger instructors; General David, General Ward, General Tooley, Colonel Wood, Colonel Sikes, Major Winkler (my Small Group Instructor at the Advanced Course); Miss Alise Harrison, my third-grade teacher in Lynwood, California, who taught me how to read about my boyhood heroes; and Gordon Armstrong and Brittany Stoner, who made me work at the words and forced this project to completion. Without these people in my life, I never would have accomplished my dreams. They set the highest and toughest standards, and for that I will be forever grateful.

For me and many others, our various mentors were the toughest to please. Universally uncompromising, they resolutely forced us over the top of the next obstacle when we thought we couldn't go on. They believed in us; taught us to achieve in the darkest of hours, even when faced with seemingly overwhelming obstacles; instilled in us the grit to succeed against all odds; and fully prepared us to lead in dire times. This story is as much theirs as it is mine.

INTRODUCTION

Somalia is a parched, largely pastoral country with grasslands that extend along the mid-eastern coast of the area known as the Horn of Africa. Colonial intrigue, imperialist duplicity, corruption, subversion, and military intervention have marked Somalia's troubled history and left it, at best, a hollow state and, at worst, the defining example of pure anarchy.

Somalia continues to struggle with internal conflict and crushingly poor social and economic conditions for the people that live within its borders. Since decolonization in 1960, no real centralized authority has existed in Somalia. To this day, the country is divided into warring factions based on clan alliances and opportunity. In 1969, through military force, Mohamed Siad Barre became Somalia's leader. Following a long and complicated regime, Barre was overthrown in January 1991 by a coalition of opposing clans known as the United Somalia Congress (USC). Shortly after the revolution, the USC polarized into two factions, one led by Ali Mahdi and the other by Mohamed Farah Aidid, and once again took up arms. The ensuing inter-clan civil war caused the destruction of vast areas of Somali agriculture, the ruination of local economies, and—combined with a devastating drought—extensive and tragic countrywide starvation, which captured the attention of the global media for months. This widespread human tragedy eventually brought about military and humanitarian action, particularly from the United States.

In Somalia, one of the main sources of power has been the control of food. Either grown and kept from the population or hijacked from aid sources, food has been used as a weapon. Repeatedly, hijacked food was used to secure the loyalty of clan leaders and exchanged with other state or non-state actors for weapons. Because up to 80 percent of internationally provided food was stolen, between 1990 and 1993 over 300,000 Somalis were estimated to have died of starvation.

With the growing pressure of international intervention looming, a ceasefire signed by opposing clan factions allowed United Nations military observers into Somalia in July 1992. By August 1992 Operation Provide Relief, with the full backing of the United Nations under the moniker UNOSOM I, officially began to provide humanitarian relief to the people of Somalia. This fledgling mission was considered a failure as food and supplies were hijacked at the seaports and airports or while en route to needful destinations.

As tension mounted in the major ports of Mogadishu, Marka, and Kismayo, the U.N. asked member nations for security assistance. In December 1992, in one of his last acts as president, George H. W. Bush proposed to the U.N. that the United States should lead a force into Somalia to intervene in the human tragedy unfolding in the media every day. When the U.N. accepted this offer, more than 20,000 U.S. troops, including U.S. Navy SEALs, U.S. Marines, and the U.S. Army's 10th Mountain Division, were deployed to Somalia. The objective of the intervention, named Operation Restore Hope, was to rapidly secure the fragile trade hubs and routes in Somalia so that food could get to the populace, especially in the rural villages.

In January 1993, President Clinton was inaugurated and immediately stated his desire to scale down the U.S. presence in Somalia and let U.N. forces take over. After negotiation and consensus, the U.N. officially took over the operation in March 1993 and renamed the mission UNOSOM II. With a smaller U.S. presence serving as the U.N. Quick Reaction Force (QRF), the original objective of the U.N. mission became the promotion of "nation building" within Somalia and the disarming of the Somali people. UNOSOM II stressed restoring law and order, assisting with the establishment of a form of representative government, and improving the infrastructure. By June 1993, only 1,200 U.S. troops, mostly the QRF and support organizations, remained in Somalia.

On 5 June 1993, twenty-four Pakistani soldiers on a routine inspection of a Somali arms weapons storage site were ambushed, killed, and mutilated, causing the U.N. to vote an emergency resolution to bring those responsible to justice. While not specifically stated, warlord Mohamed Farah Aidid and his followers were believed to be responsible. On 19 June 1993, Adm. Jonathan Howe, U.N. Special Representative for Somalia, ordered Aidid's arrest and offered a $25,000 reward for information leading to his capture. At this time, Admiral Howe also requested a counterterrorist task force for Somalia.

Between 12–16 June, U.S. and U.N. troops began attacking targets in Mogadishu related to Aidid. After receiving refusals to comply with surrender orders, and following a brief reprieve, U.S. Cobra helicopters attacked a house in Mogadishu where clan leaders were meeting on July 12. They destroyed several buildings, and many Somalis, including clan leaders, were killed. Four Western journalists who went to investigate the bloody scene were subsequently beaten to death by a mob of Somalis bent on revenge. On 8 August, shortly after a QRF rotation and relief in place, four U.S. military police were killed when a remote-controlled land mine was detonated by Somalis. The escalation continued, with six more U.S. soldiers wounded two weeks later.

On 29 August, Task Force Ranger flew into Mogadishu, led by Gen. William Garrison and consisting of over 400 elite troops from Delta Force, the 3rd Ranger Battalion, and the Special Operations Aviation Regiment (SOAR). Their mission was to capture Aidid, not kill him. In a parallel diplomatic maneuver, the Clinton Administration began a secret plan to negotiate with Aidid in September. U.S. military commanders in Somalia were not apprised of the diplomatic effort. Further, in September U.S. Defense Secretary Les Aspin denied a request for armored reinforcements made by the Deputy Commander, UNOSOM, U.S Maj. Gen. Thomas Montgomery. The situation continued to escalate until, following three major firefights involving the 10th Mountain's QRF and several highly successful raids by Task Force Ranger, Mogadishu was a powder keg just waiting to blow.

On 3 October 1993, Task Force Ranger conducted a raid near the Olympic Hotel in the Black Sea area of Mogadishu in an effort to capture several of Aidid's highest-ranking lieutenants. This led to an eighteen-hour battle between the Somali National Alliance (Aidid's main force) and Task

Force Ranger. From this battle emerged the QRF tasking to rescue the beleaguered survivors of the raid and two downed Black Hawk helicopters, as well as a casualty count of eighteen U.S. soldiers dead and eighty-four wounded. Americans awoke to televised images of U.S. soldiers being dragged through the streets of Mogadishu. More than a thousand Somalis also died, although an official number has never been released. At the time, this battle was the longest and bloodiest battle involving U.S. troops since the Vietnam War.

On 7 October, President Clinton abandoned the hunt for Aidid and sent U.S. representatives to resume negotiations with clan leaders. CW3 Michael Durant, pilot of the ill-fated Super 64 Black Hawk helicopter captured during the battle, was returned, and an official truce was set in place.

Two weeks after the Battle of Mogadishu, in a handwritten letter to President Clinton, General Garrison took full responsibility for the outcome of the battle. He wrote that Task Force Ranger had adequate intelligence for the mission and that the objective of capturing the targets was accomplished. The battle was not lost.

What began in December 1992 as a humanitarian mission to provide relief to the starving people of Somalia effectively culminated with a firefight during the Battle of Mogadishu. By March 1994, when all U.S. troops were withdrawn from Somalia, more than 20,000 U.N. troops remained. Shortly thereafter, all remaining U.N. troops were withdrawn, officially ending UNOSOM II. Subsequently, Somalia spiraled into anarchy and chaos. Today, the country is a warren for pirates, terrorists (including al-Shabab, now merged with al Qaeda), and the home of African Union peacekeeping soldiers trying to deal with the madness that is still Mogadishu.

The preceding text lays out the essential facts. What follows is the in-depth point of view and experiences from one individual, a U.S. Army commander who led his company in the thick of the fighting. Leadership in combat is a lonely, yet totally fulfilling experience that should be shared, especially if everything went right. What made a good unit function well as an effective team is far more important than just the telling of a good story. I was blessed to lead such a unit. We succeeded when it mattered and accomplished this difficult mission because we thoroughly trained beforehand to function efficiently in a state of chaos, then efficiently applied that training in the daily execution of critical tasks when placed in the expected chaotic state.

This, then, is my opportunity to describe how a young Army captain evolved into a combat commander and to explain the QRF's role and actions during those fateful months of July–December 1993 in Mogadishu, Somalia. While much is already known about TF Ranger, little is known about those who rescued them. This narrative seeks to fill existing historical gaps and record the metamorphosis of the quality fighting unit that will be forever linked to "Black Hawk Down."

CHAPTER 1

Home

Standing proudly and confidently outside the back door to Soldiers Gym at Fort Drum, New York, on a frosty, pristine December morning in 1993, I began thinking of the events that had brought me to that place in time. The feeling of being guided by something far larger than me was overwhelming. I felt grateful, lucky, and emotional. At the same time, I was at peace with myself for having accomplished in two dozen months what others could only imagine: surviving the making of history, helping my fellow man in the turmoil of human tragedy, and accomplishing every goal I had set forth for my infantry career. I had lived the epic life of the infantryman, fought the outnumbered battles, been on the rescue missions, and helped to rebuild when called upon to do more than just destroy. I had achieved the American fighting man's deepest-held hope by performing as expected when called upon. Standing there awaiting my family's arrival, I felt fully alive.

Home: one of the defining aspects of being human. When people ask, "Where do you come from?" or "Where is your home?" they're seeking a reference point from which the grandest of generalizations are made. You are treated differently because of your home, whether this city or that, the North, South, East, or West. You could be from an entirely different

1

country. Sometimes I feel lucky that I have no real fixed-point home, at least not in a geographical sense. My home is made up of flesh and blood and emotions, profoundly human. For me, home is two parents, one wife, three sons, and three daughters. For all of the adventures and exotic places I have experienced, I wouldn't trade the feeling of the return home.

This homecoming was going to be different. Our company was returning heroes—not conquerors, just heroes. We had rescued the best our country had to offer, Delta Force and the Rangers, from annihilation, and a welcome greater than we could have ever imagined awaited us in the cavernous Soldiers Gym.

Our homecoming began earlier that day far across the planet being chased by the new day's sun. Redeployment from Somalia was a relentless blur of emotion, commotion, routine, and anxiety. No one wanted to be the unluckiest of all, the one killed or wounded in the last few days or hours, after all we had been through. Our final day came as a welcome relief from the tensions of waiting to be sent home. As we finally departed our home away from home, the University of Mogadishu, for the final time, I had the feeling that all my soldiers and I had graduated with far more knowledge than could ever be learned from all the books that must have once been there. We left as we had come, in HMMWVs (the so-called "Humvee") and 5-ton trucks, single file, but war-wizened, searching for signs of the enemy: a sniper, an ambush or, most horrific of all, the command-detonated mine. We felt absolutely naked with the customary one magazine apiece for all redeploying soldiers riding to the Mogadishu airport. We knew how much ammunition it took to sustain a firefight, and one magazine is certainly not enough.

The convoy slithered quickly out the muddy gate, locked and loaded, our Tunisian protectors waving a final farewell. We turned left with my now-familiar HMMWV in the lead, my soldiers following, and drove down Main Supply Route (MSR) Tiger for the last time. In a swirling throng of brightly dressed Somalis, we passed the huge logistical center called Sword Base on our right and turned quickly left again at the first Pakistani checkpoint. Passing the infamous "camel market" on our right, we swerved and bounced under the watchful eyes of the .50-caliber gunners of Hunter Base and the usual mob of Somalis waiting for a handout or work from the soldiers of the logistics outpost. With the fine dust swirling around us, we waved at "Porky the Elder's" many wives and seemingly dozens of children as he looked on, somber and well-meaning as usual, arms folded over his massive, protruding belly.

Checkpoint 1, on the outskirts of the city, which we had constructed, was now occupied by members of the 2nd Battalion, 22nd Infantry, our replacements. This structure reminded me of so many pictures I had seen in books and war movies: thousands of sandbags, placed high and low, surrounded by concertina, protecting soldiers in overwatching positions as they guarded their fellow soldiers. Two of those soldiers had the mundane duty of checking every person, vehicle, and donkey cart that passed through this obstruction to free travel and commerce, searching for the one idiot who didn't want to walk around the checkpoint with his AK, RPG, or explosives. The image of offloading forty to fifty Somalis from a dilapidated Datsun pickup truck, running the "magic wand" metal detector over them, and then watching them all get new and unusual handholds as they remounted the Datsun brought a smile to my face. These delay-causing hassles caused many Somalis to find other routes into the city besides MSR Tiger.

Continuing along, we passed Checkpoint 2 at the top of the first big hill, which was occupied by members of the Indian Army standing guard in their white United Nations (UN) T72 tanks and BMP3 Armored Personnel Carriers (APCs). Winding left, the road offers a great view of the Somali "bush" country and your first awesome view of the Indian Ocean. More bunkers, more wire, more men in uniform standing guard on a piece of terrain on a distant shore.

Along the route we picked up our helicopter escort for the trip into the city. Every precaution was taken to ensure we arrived at the airport without incident. As the AH-1 Cobra gunships and OH-58 Kiowa observation helicopters danced around our formation, we waved and felt a true comradeship with soldiers of the sky. If it hadn't been for their daring and extreme bravery on many occasions, none of us would be here today. Looking to the left, I saw my old bush command post, my own personal mini-firebase among the thorn trees, camels, goats, and sun-beaten landscape. The soldiers in my headquarters and mortar section had labored hard to build the huge bunkers and mortar pits, lay concertina wire, and camouflage the entire area, making it barely visible, except to those who knew its location. It was now occupied by three bright white APCs and a myriad of other white Indian vehicles that, in their usual fashion, seemed to boast, "Come screw with us; we're waiting."

Jostling along, sucking in the fresh sea breeze, and watching the helicopters dance, I realized that these would probably be my greatest and most memorable moments in life: the unforgettable ones when you grab your grandchildren, place them on your knee, and rattle on and on about the exotic land, its people, and the service you performed for the good of all mankind. As the road approached the coast, the huge refinery tower, 350 feet tall and occupied by an Indian observation crew, came into view. I remembered climbing that monster with my platoon leaders and had to smile again. What a view—50 miles in any direction. It overlooked the city, the countryside, the dunes, and the Indian Ocean way over the horizon.

Approaching the refinery and Checkpoint 3, I checked along the roadside and into the hills, searching for a special friend, a little nine-year-old girl who had befriended our command element while we stayed in the bush. She had been the first person in the country I can remember who had smiled and welcomed our presence, never once asking for a handout. My command post (CP) team had a few good times searching the dunes around the refinery looking for the bad guys with her and her brother and sister. At first, her siblings were terrified of us, but she never was. On our first visit, she had walked up, introduced herself in Somali, and just kept right on talking as if we could understand every word. The whole HMMWV was hooked. We started our first real bartering of water, MREs, and personal care items. She always got the better of us and we didn't mind. She was a great friend and made me believe that good can be found in even the worst of places. I pray often for her and her family's safety.

Checkpoint 3 was in the sand dunes and overwatched anyone or anything approaching from the Coast Road and the Refinery. The 3rd Platoon had done a magnificent job of setting up a blocking position, an overwatch position, and a roadblock and, using their initiative, of rigging a security rope system for the men stationed in that huge oil refinery observation tower. The 3rd Platoon also manned a lonely outpost that covered the

Coast Road leading into Mogadishu, with a magnificent view of the Indian Ocean and the multimillion-dollar, but lifeless, power plant. The plant could have serviced the entire country, but its tidal-, oil-, wind-, and coal-driven generators had been totally scavenged by a civil war-torn populace.

The mission of the outpost was to act as a warning center, observation post, and rest area for the roving patrols between the 3rd Platoon headquarters, the refinery, and the outpost, a total trek of 3,000 meters. HMMWVs also traveled the coast road and around the refinery and acted as a quick-reaction force if the outpost was attacked.

As our convoy passed the refinery, we waved to our left at the Indian headquarters element and the guard force in aboveground bunkers every 50 meters parallel to the coast road. The blue turbans and British-style uniforms reminded me of many movies I had watched growing up. The contrast of the old and new was striking.

At the outskirts of the city we were hit, as always, by the overpowering smell. So overwhelming, the stench brought visions of death, disease, pollution, and degradation and blotted the wonderful salty ocean breeze from our minds. At the huge trash dump, nearly lifeless wraiths of humanity scrounging out a horrible existence barely noticed us as we swirled up sand from the seashore, dust from the road, and mud from the wastewater of the Egyptian compound surrounding the Mogadishu International Airport.

We watched closely as we approached the U.N. entrance to the airport. We entered the throng of brightly clothed pedestrians, beggars, and the masses of children once again. The population of the city seemed to always be hanging around the airport waiting for something to happen. We saw "the look" many times that final afternoon and evening, the one that put daggers through your heart, that you tucked in the back of your soul while thanking God for Colt, Beretta, and K-Bar.

The Egyptian and American guards allowed us to pass through the heavily defended opening and we were once again angling left between the terminal and the large hangar where the Rangers and Delta stayed. As dusk settled over the land and the blazing 116-degree temperature started to plunge to its nightly 85, we quickly dismounted left and entered what I always had guessed to be some kind of underground parking area adjacent to the terminal. The last time I had been here it was pitch black and a brave and desperate band of men were fighting for their lives.

Cots had been arranged for us to sleep on this final night in-country, and the first sergeants arranged for the usual Meals-Ready-to-Eat (MREs) and water for all. Card games blossomed everywhere. Men tended to their equipment and some cleaned weapons; old habits die hard. Many of us turned inward and searched our memories for a time in our lives that meant more. Love, marriage, the birth of children, having made history: They encompass the same emotion, one that can never really be described, only felt.

The colonel and sergeant major called a commander/first sergeants meeting for the early evening and gave us the schedule for the following day. We would wake at dawn, fold and stow our cots, and report by company to the hangar where we would go through Customs. We would then board the 747 that would arrive in the morning. Also arriving would be a USAF C-5 Galaxy, which would bring our palletized and ISU-90 containerized equipment to Griffiss Air Force Base, near Rome, New York, from where it would be moved by ground transport to Fort Drum.

When the first sergeant and I returned to our CP, we disseminated the information to the platoon leaders and platoon sergeants. Then we all began unloading our magazines for the final time, placing 5.56mm M16A2 rounds in one pile and 9mm Beretta rounds in another. After collecting the ammunition, we all settled down to a restless night of listening to the wind blowing off the Indian Ocean and the Eyes Over Mogadishu—helicopter flights coming and going—all the while waiting for that final mortar or rifle-propelled grenade (RPG) attack that never came.

The next morning, almost as quiet as if we were in church, we folded our cots in the early morning darkness. Covered with dew and surrounded by the cleansing Indian Ocean breeze, our thoughts again turned inward. For the first time in my military career, I watched not only my men but the whole battalion gather their worldly possessions, pack, shave, and eat in silence. Some stared into small mirrors as if looking to see if this vivid experience had wrought some discernible change in themselves. Most saw what I saw: the hard, weathered faces and the steely, saddened eyes of the combat veteran.

When all was properly arranged in military fashion, we formed up and began movement to a large hangar farther down the flight line. It was the same hangar the Rangers had used as a barracks, the one that had been mortared nearly every day of their stay in-country.

Customs would be our next stop before the farewell speech by Maj. Gen. Thomas Montgomery, commander of U.S. Forces in Somalia. With all the troops lined up and undergoing inspections by the Customs agents, we saw our flights to freedom land, one beautiful white 747 followed closely by a dull gray-green C-5A of the U.S. Air Force. I was one of the lucky ones who passed through Customs unscathed, not even checked at all, as the agents were only doing a 10 percent full inspection of departing soldiers. I grounded my gear in the headquarters section next to the guidon and prepared for the grand formation, one final dog-and-pony show before our departure.

As it turned out, General Montgomery made us feel proud, telling us of our place in the military histories of both our country and the country we were still standing in. After the ceremony, we milled around shaking hands with those of other units we would leave behind, as we knew, in harm's way. When the word came to load, our well-disciplined but anxious unit quickly gathered its equipment and walked the last few hundred meters to the waiting planes. I climbed the ramp, took one last breath of Mogadishu, and entered the sterile, well-used, but comforting confines of modern civilization. I quickly found my seat and stowed the myriad carry-ons: weapons, night vision device, CVC bag, load-bearing equipment (LBE), and helmet.

Once seated in the upper cabin, I began surveying the world through the tiny porthole on the right side of the plane. I faced once again the city where I had met anarchy, fear, courage, devastation, comradeship, and the end of my youth. The white-walled compounds gleamed in the early morning sunlight and throngs of colorfully clad East Africans bobbed and weaved their way up the streets and around the airfield complex, just another day for them. Reality intervened and I began noticing the guard towers, razor wire, and the armed Egyptian soldiers, patrolling or keeping a watchful eye on the populace that was not to be trusted. We and our Egyptian defenders knew that, in the blink of an eye and the whoosh of an RPG, someone could be dead.

The now-familiar sights, burned into my brain, brought a sense of nostalgia to mind as I realized again that this was it, that in all likelihood I would never see this place again. I had learned to live with the sights, sounds, smells, feelings, and emotions that came with survival in a hostile foreign land and was preparing to depart that environment. I figured that my senses would never be so alive again.

With that thought in mind, I spiraled down to the main cabin and linked up with my men. We all wanted to go home. Life had meaning on this airplane, and we had learned that it was not to be squandered. The engines came to life and everyone moved to their assigned seats. The commanders, sergeant major, first sergeants, and primary staff officers occupied the first-class section and the remainder of the battalion occupied the main cabin.

I watched through my porthole as the monster plane began to taxi south, away from the terminal. The Plexiglas bubble shaded everything a light green. I watched the city for signs of trouble, some zealot trying to take a pot shot with a mortar, RPG, or rifle, but that didn't happen.

The lumbering turn at the end of the runway initiated an instant dust storm that momentarily shrouded my view. Now facing north, the pilot jammed the throttle forward, making the engines scream while he still applied the brakes. Then, with unseen forces pressing us into our seats, the aircraft lunged forward down the short runway and quickly pulled into the early afternoon sky. We angled up and out over the Indian Ocean, passing over the USS *Lincoln* Task Force with its Marine Corps Assault Carrier USS *Guadalcanal*, and various cruisers, destroyers, frigates, and support ships just over the horizon and just out of sight of the population of Mogadishu. The thought occurred to me that if I had stayed in the Marine Corps that could have been me down there on that float.

I watched the carrier task force for as long as I could before the 747 banked back left and once again we were over Somalia, heading northwest toward home. My seat gave me a perfect view of the east coast of Africa and Southwest Asia. As we followed the Red Sea on our way to Egypt, I realized I was flying over what many people consider the cradle of civilization and how very strange it was to be leaving the turmoil of anarchy.

For once I just could not sleep, but sat and watched the undulating, barren, and desolate landscape float by 20,000 feet below me. As we passed over the Sudan, I began to search the pastel shades of sand, maroon, and charcoal for the tributaries of the Nile. Watching the terrain, I wondered how anyone could survive such a hellish environment. Here and there you could see very small communities in the wasteland. Why didn't these people search for a better life? Why wouldn't they just start walking and never look back?

The sun was going down as we began our descent. It almost seemed like the shadow of the plane was chasing the darkness that quickly settled over the Egyptian desert landscape. Flying over the city of Cairo, it dawned on me that this was the first civilized city I had seen in nearly six months. Just to view lights twinkling, cars, hotels, streetlights all in a row, and upright buildings with intact walls and windows unmarked by holes from an explosive, artillery shell, or RPG was such a relief, and to see there was still order in the world and a place where the people had a purpose.

We landed at Cairo Airport and were immediately told we could not deplane, as it was only a fuel stop. I made my way to the ramp just to get a glimpse of the city, but was pushed back into the plane by a not very friendly armed guard. When the blackish-red sundown of the Saharan sky turned to pure nighttime ink in the blink of an eye, I was able to see the stars for the final time from the continent of Africa as we pulled away from the ramp and soared once again into the night, heading for Western civilization.

Our flight path took us across the Mediterranean Sea, shimmering in the moonlight, and over the continent of Europe, which, as usual, was mostly shrouded in clouds. When I could see a larger than usual set of lights, I tried to guess which city we were passing over.

We didn't stop at the U.S. Air Base in Ramstein, Germany, this time, as we had on our way over so many months before. Instead, we kept going across the English Channel, where I saw the cliffs of Dover, London, and probably Liverpool as our course took us to Shannon, Ireland. Landing in pitch-black darkness, we were amazed to see the airport all decked out in Christmas decorations, with a brightly lit sign atop the terminal wishing "Peace on Earth, Good Will Toward Men." AMEN to that.

English! I had just read English! Outside of our compound in Somalia, you couldn't read a thing. How sweet it was to just read your own language again. We were allowed to deplane into the Irish terminal and we all hustled into the airport, where we found a beautiful pub, a snack bar, and a gift shop, all modern and familiar. A reverse culture shock had us all full of life and raring to go, but, at 3:00 AM everything was closed.

Wait! Is that a phone, a whole bank of phones? As you can imagine, we were off to the races. Everyone made a quick call to say, yes, the plane did leave, we were only seven hours away, and yes, I'm okay and anxious as hell to get home.

Home. God, it was almost real. After months of being just memories that floated behind your eyes in the damnedest of places, we were now only one more plane ride and one more "Bernie's Busses" ride away.

When told to load back up on the plane, there weren't any laggards. Everyone was awake, because this was no dream. Even Fort Drum and northern New York in winter would be welcome sights.

Our spirits were very high when we took off to chase the darkness while the new day chased us. As the moon again glimmered on the North Atlantic, I thought of the people who had flown or sailed this route while making history in their own way. They had been starting a country or a new life, or both. This was much the case for us.

We were coming home far different people than we had been when we left. I thought of how great it was to be an American returning to the United States with all its beauty and wonder, its technology, and its mad rush to create a bigger and better life on this planet. Get away from the States and you truly become an American, with pride and a realization that we really are better off with our freedom, education, and, above all, dreams of a better tomorrow. God has blessed our country; I just really wish more people understood that.

We finally crossed into American airspace somewhere around Maine. It was truly a beautiful sight to see, with just a touch of sunrise on the rugged cliffs of the northeastern coast of North America. The frosty air seemed to make the crashing waves of the Atlantic stand still, frozen if but for a second, before churning onto the rocky outcroppings and then flowing back into the great liquid pool of the ocean itself. We were descending, passing through patches of clouds, just floating through cotton balls of mist with brief glimpses of a wonderland below. Snow and lights and trees, thousands and thousands of real pines, maples, birch, and every other assorted tree we have in America. Everything looked so fresh from above, clean and crystal clear, modern and working. No war, noise, or cries for help. No death.

At nearly 5:00 AM, we landed at Griffiss Air Force Base in Rome, New York, United States of America. With a screech from the landing gear and a huge cheer from us all, we were once again on U.S. soil. We taxied to a halt in front of Base Operations. It seemed like it became every man for himself as all the equipment that had been stowed neatly under seats, in overhead compartments, or in bins was now in a tangle; rifles and helmets wouldn't budge and load-bearing equipment was twisted in knots. The sound throughout the plane from nearly 500 soldiers getting their gear on again is unbelievable.

Then it hit us: winter. The cold air slammed through the open hatch and enveloped our world with a chill I will never forget. The 100-degree temperature change from 116 degrees when we left Somalia to the 16 degrees of New York following the twenty-seven-hour flight cut to the bone. So what? We were home!

Slipping on the ice was our next concern. That would really be funny, to make it through a war zone only to come home and bust your ass at the airfield. We were ushered down the ramp and into Hangar 1, all the while making sure everything and everybody was accounted for. "Bernie's Busses," the bright yellow junior high school busses with their too-small seating arrangements, awaited us. As the duffel bags and rucksacks were unloaded from the belly of the plane onto the S&Ps (open-bed tractor trailers with side racks), we started our organized shuffle back out into the more-than-crisp air and into the sweltering heat of the busses.

Bernie's Busses just reek of youth and everything that you leave behind when you grow up. How fitting to be reminded that you never really grow up. When you stowed your gear and tried to sit down, you had to draw up your knees and rest them on the seat back in front of you. I remembered these busses and hated them now as much as I did back then. No wonder Americans drive so many cars! You grow up just flat-out hating those busses, with their cramped little spaces and that smell.

It took a while to load the soldiers and all their combat equipment. Adults and their war toys and Bernie's Busses will never be a good match. Nevertheless, it is cost-effective transportation, and that's what we needed. They were exactly what we wanted at 5:00 AM on a freezing cold and desolate airfield in the middle of northern New York.

Everyone got situated as best they could for the two-and-a-half-hour trip. With twenty-five to thirty soldiers per bus, each in his own private hell—sitting on gear, sitting in gear, or with gear sitting on him—and the bus drivers, almost in unison, yelling, "Keep them gun barrels away from the winders; I don't want 'em smashed," in that great New York accent, we started the last leg of our trip home. Like a giant yellow snake, the busses, with military and civilian police escorts, lumbered into the breaking dawn of a new day with America's newest heroes in its belly. Everyone was tired, scrunched, uncomfortable, and absolutely elated to be heading north through snow and ice on the two-lane roads.

Most of us just succumbed to sleep in the rising heat of the jam-packed accommodations. To a man, internal clocks were set to awaken just short of Fort Drum. Everyone wanted to see what kind of welcome we would receive and to maybe, just maybe, catch a glimpse of a friend or loved one.

As we rolled on, I drifted in and out of a catnap, the drone and swaying of the van that the commanders rode in alternately putting me to sleep and jerking me awake. About an hour outside of Fort Drum, I woke up for good. The new day was dawning. Drivers were turning off their headlights as they headed off to work. McDonald's was already serving breakfast in Lowville. Our police escort cleared the way and blocked the ever-curious traffic at intersections so the yellow snake would have no fallbehinds. Around each turn the scenery became more and more familiar.

About fifteen minutes out, everyone started waking up and jostling their still-sleeping buddies. And so it was that we returned to Fort Drum on a crystal clear morning, turning onto Route 26, driving past Wheeler-Sack Army Airfield and climbing up what some of us called Agony Hill on 45th Division Road, and on up to Soldiers Gym, with gears grinding and elated soldiers whooping it up.

The busses pulled into the back parking lot between the baseball fields. A scene from hell erupted as soldiers all fought for leverage, getting untangled from equipment and one another. We dismounted the busses amidst the military police and our welcoming committee, members of the division and brigade staffs that had been assigned the mission to create the biggest dog-and-pony show imaginable. Handshakes, hugs, congratulations, "it's great to have you back," "awesome man," "great job." Colonels, majors, captains, lieutenants, sergeants, seniors, and peers of mine offering the kudos you get with your fifteen minutes of fame.

No handshakes or hugs from them, however, could compare to the ones I received from Specialist Pamer, Specialist Carroll, and especially Sgt. Chris Reid. These were my severely wounded soldiers who had been medically evacuated out of Somalia just a few weeks earlier. The last time I had seen Sergeant Reid, we were slamming him into a field ambulance on his way to a MEDEVAC helicopter, praying he would make it. Emotions were high when the company got to greet him, one at a time. As I watched over 100 men share a long moment with a true American hero, I remembered playing basketball with him on the night of 24 September 1993, a little less than twenty-four hours before his life would change forever.

I broke from the vision, shook my head, and walked down the main corridor to the back entryway. Just outside the door, I stood waiting for my family to arrive for the welcome back ceremony. The cool air kept me focused. For some reason I reached down to my cargo pocket and felt the Ziploc bag that still remained there. These were my most treasured items and my talismans, secret things that you just knew would keep you alive. I opened the plastic "safe" and searched through the pictures, letters, and favorite motivational sayings for my one truly prized possession: a Popsicle stick.

My middle child, Mikki Leigh, just five years old, had stayed up all night the day before we deployed, wrapping the flat stick with pink, white, and blue multicolored yarn, fat in some places, skinny in others, taped at both ends for security. As I was walking out the door of our quarters, she was last to say goodbye. I stood squarely in the door, draped in my field gear, and with tears in her eyes she reached up with her tiny hands clutching my gift and said the words that I will never forget: "Remember me." That Popsicle stick never left my uniform, never broke, and always reminded me that there was something to live for, and of the need to make it home.

Well, I was home, and after I slipped my precious gathering of wisdom and love back into my cargo pocket, I searched the parking lot and finally beheld my true home: my family and parents making their way up the sidewalk. They did not recognize me at first; I had changed, and looked like all the other soldiers returning from Somalia. Afterwards, they said I looked imposing, thumbs locked in my LBE, eyes forward, surveying my domain. We were all very confident, and being the leader of confident men gives you a feeling that is difficult to describe.

Wife, mother, and kids seemed to hit me at once. After the recognition hit them, it was sort of pell-mell, a great release of emotion and hugging, kissing, and "My God, look at you." My dad, taking pictures as any good journalist would, was still clicking away. I finally broke from the "Daddy, Daddies," and my dad and I stared at one another. I had "done good" and my dad was there to see it, to revel in his creation's glory. It felt great to know that the people in my life cared enough to always be there for me: high school graduation, Parris Island, Airborne School, graduation from the university and my commissioning, and Ranger School. It all paid off.

This was no school, but real life, and what better way to know that you have succeeded than to share these moments with those that you most care about. After a giant hug from my dad, we went into the gym and, amidst all the welcome home signs, flags, ribbon, and brightly colored banners, I found them seats in the bleachers. The band started up, our cue to head back outside. We were going to file in by company and then, with a little pomp and circumstance and after a motivational speech by 10th Mountain Division Commander Major General Meade, we would be cut loose to turn in our war gear and head back to a life we had only dreamed existed.

Being a company commander in a battalion formation is one of the true delights and terrors of every captain. The spotlight is on you; don't mess up a command or the whole company looks bad, but do it right and you are oh, so professional. And so it was that day, as everything went exactly right. The officers, NCOs, and enlisted soldiers performed flawlessly. Commands were crisp, movements snapped and popped, guidons were precisely parallel to the ground, and timing was perfect. And we have the movies to prove it!

It seemed a dream as we listened to General Meade tell us we were heroes and how proud we should be, and how proud those in the crowd should be of us. My skin just crawled as goosebumps and the feeling of rising heat flushed my body. I likened it to winning the Super Bowl—to have trained so hard and fought the hard fight, and won, then receive the gratitude of the fans and the tremendous feeling of self-worth that come with the championship.

Finally, the words, "2-14 Infantry, you are dismissed," a roar, and then being caught up in a camouflaged wave smashing into a multicolored one, trying to find my family, a boy in my arms, then a girl, little arms circling my legs, a kiss . . .

The rear detachment and the wives had a feast waiting for us. As we turned in our weapons to the arms room and opened up wall lockers, supply rooms, and the barracks, we munched on junk food and gloried in the feeling of being in our own digs. My office was bare but homey. My awards, still on the walls, traced my steady movement from private to company commander.

After loading all my gear into my wall locker, I sat in my commander's chair, looking at the training calendar and long-range schedule. Months of my previously scheduled "normal" life had disappeared amidst our involvement in real-world events and the making of history.

I happened to look down at my desktop and, to my amazement and surprise, realized I had left one of my field manuals (FMs) behind. A thick, white one: MOUT, Military Operations on Urban Terrain. The irony of that is just plain funny at this point. Lord, I was tired; what a roller coaster ride.

When all equipment was accounted for throughout the battalion, we were released from duty for the day by an order from Colonel Bill David, the battalion commander. We would get a half-day off, then be back by noon the following day to start shutting the battalion down for Christmas. Thank God for that.

The first sergeant and I made sure the troops knew what was going on and that all had rides home and a bed to sleep in. When the company area was finally deserted, 1st Sergeant Doody and I, with families in tow, bid farewell until the heat tab (as we called the sun) rose once more into the eastern sky.

I alternated between resting and playing with the kids. I danced with Michelle, Mikki, and Mimi; tossed a football with Michael; held little Mitchell, only a year old; finally watched some TV and listened to my stereo; then ate an awesome home-cooked meal: steak, potatoes, corn, mac and cheese from the little blue box, real iced tea—heaven-sent goodies after all the T-Rats and warm water.

With my belly full and after an afternoon and night of just being HOME, a stillness descended over my soul. With my eyes taking in everyone and everything, it dawned on me how oddly striking the sense of home had become. I didn't want to sleep, but knew I had to anyway. I went upstairs, took a hot, modern shower, and went to bed in a king-size-mattress-attached-pillows-provided wonderland of sleeping comfort. I fell fast asleep with visions still dancing in my head of the exotic other side of the world, and rested in complete comfort in the knowledge that I could sleep without fear of a mortar attack, the thwack of incoming automatic rifle fire, or the deafening, life-sucking roar of an exploding RPG.

Peace.

CHAPTER 2

Preparing for War

On 4 July 1993, I sat on the bank of the Saint Lawrence Seaway watching the awesome fireworks display over Boldt Castle in Alexandria Bay, New York. My wife and children enjoyed the show as the colorful rockets burst in all their glory. I inwardly wondered if the battalion was really ready for the life and death of Mogadishu, Somalia. The news had been bad over the last few weeks. A Pakistani patrol had been ambushed and literally destroyed, and warlord Mohamed Farah Aidid was supposedly consolidating power to force the United Nations effort out of Somalia.

AC-130 gunships and the initial UNOSOM II Quick Reaction Force (the 1st Battalion of the 22nd Infantry Regiment), with Cobra attack helicopter support, had been in action several times over the last few weeks. My unit, Company C, 2nd Battalion, 14th Infantry Regiment, had been training steadily since I took command on 29 January 1993. Now, as we prepared for a 28 July deployment to replace the 1-22 IN as the UNOSOM II QRF, I was confident in our state of training and readiness for the mission. We knew full well that we were being sent into the breach of the fight that was brewing. Many thought it inevitable that Combat Infantry-man's Badge qualification would result from this mission because, while we weren't going there looking for a fight, it was becoming increasingly clear that the fight was waiting for us.

The battalion train-up for Operation Continue Hope, the follow-on Somalia mission to the initial Operation Restore Hope, was an intense time for the battalion's officers, noncommissioned officers (NCOs), and enlisted soldiers. The pace of training escalated just one week after I took command, with a deployment to the Jungle Operations Training Center in Panama. At JOTC we learned a higher level of land navigation; waterborne operations, including landing craft, medium (LCM) procedures; and techniques for conducting both search-and-attack and cordon-and-search missions. We also conducted squad, platoon, and mortar section live-fire exercises as well as company and battalion tactical operations.

The company seemed to be coming together during our long, hard month in the jungle. A new commander needs to get a feel for his company and the troops need to find out what kind of leader he is. We trudged through the jungle enduring the same hardships together, searched out each other's strengths and weaknesses, and generally assessed one another. I gained a true respect for each and every man in that environment infested with black palms, howler monkeys, cutter ants, boa constrictors, and mosquitoes. At its conclusion, I rated the company's jungle school deployment—my first command performance—an overall success and was encouraged when the battalion commander, Lt. Col. William C. "Bill" David, gave it a B+. Colonel David always let you know where you stood, and I read his rating as an opportunity to take a good thing (B+ isn't bad) and make it better. But I was well aware that I was still the new guy in my soldiers' eyes, and that further proving and tempering would be needed to gain their respect.

Col. Bill David is a tall, impressive man. A soldier's soldier, you couldn't ask for a better commander or leadership style. When he spoke, you sensed both his strong and genuine kindness. A true professional, he cared deeply for his men and drove them hard to prepare for the rigors of combat. His training philosophy was simple: Train to reality. He didn't believe that you could fake a 25-mile road march, a maximum score on the Army Physical Fitness Test, or a night live-fire company deliberate assault of a trench line in snowy 20-degree temperatures. He wanted hard, professional soldiers who knew their business, warriors with pride in themselves and their unit. In the end, that is exactly what he got.

Following our early-March return to Fort Drum from Panama, we continued to train in the snow, even though we were going to be in the desert for our QRF mission. During an External Evaluation (EXEVAL) just two weeks after returning from the jungle, our company, C/2-14 IN, did a notable job creating a Russian Y defense in the below-zero environment of Fort Drum that stopped a battalion assault by 2-22 IN five days running.

After the frozen defense, we began preparation for platoon and company EXEVALs. Our tests would be search-and-attack for the platoon EXEVALs and a night deliberate assault of a trench line for the company EXEVAL. Both exercises would have blank-fire rehearsals culminating with live-fire finales using the entire platoon or company inventory of explosives and live ammunition.

The company proved its worth in a bitter-cold assault of the flooded trench line during a swirling snow squall at 0300 hours after two days of rehearsal. The mortars and overwatching machine-gun team opened up, tracers and explosions sending lances of red and blossoms of orange death into the bunkers and trench line. A Bangalore torpedo team crawled forward, the tracers just over their heads, to place their charge. Following the *bawoom* of the detonation, the assault team moved out, pelted by the debris and buffeted by the shock wave, charging through the breach and storming into the freezing, flooded trench to the first intersection.

The assault team quickly divided right and left, slogging through the trench, lobbing live grenades into the bunkers, and clearing with automatic weapons fire. Progress up the trench line was marked by chem lights (plastic chemical light wands) and flags. Forward of the flags, held above the trench lip on outstretched arms and wooden poles, the machine-gun team literally chewed up the bunkers and trench segments yet to be cleared. The mortar attack was churning up the enemy command bunker and the communications trench. Commands were coordinated to lift and shift fires and, on cue, with the rest of the company occupying the original trench line that was now cleared of enemy (silhouettes), the next assault team surged forward and destroyed the enemy command center.

A pair of green star-cluster flares launched into the sky signaled that all was cleared, mission accomplished. To a man, we were wet and frozen to the core after climbing out of the trench. We all walked back up the hill in silence to the waiting 5-ton trucks, knowing that we had done the hardest mission that can be assigned a light infantry company and done it almost picture-perfect.

Colonel David was pleased. The planning was thorough, the rehearsals had gone well, and the execution had come off without a hitch. I was maturing as a commander.

In between the two EXEVALs, I had time to apply my philosophy to train the company: "Stay alive"; "Use massive, concentrated firepower"; and "Let the troops feel and hear what a real battle will be like." My own training had taught me that you can't beat an enemy if you're dead (denoted in training by a blaring Multiple Integrated Laser Equipment System [MILES] harness or flashing Rotating Amber Warning Light System [RAWLS]). You have to think on your feet, flow with the situation, and at all costs remain "alive," whether in training or in country.

I had also learned that overwhelming an enemy allows you to fight again another day. By creating sequential fire coordination exercises (FCXs), first with squads on line, then platoons, and then the entire company, and by allowing soldiers to fire their basic loads during the exercises, soldiers have an opportunity to experience the sights and sounds of outgoing fire and come to understand that they are a force to be reckoned with. FCXs also provided an opportunity to teach the need to conserve ammunition, to lay down sustained fire (no lulls allowed), and to use battlefield sectors to move massed fires around the target area. When the FCXs were finished, every man in the company fully understood the how and why of laying down massed, accurate fire, and that, day or night, only heaven could help the poor SOB on the receiving end.

I had arranged to go first for the company EXEVAL to give the platoon leaders more time to practice the search-and-attack mission. Consequently, I knew that all three platoons were good when their EXEVALS started. When they finished, I was pleased to see that they were 100 percent. Each platoon went through the lane until they killed all opposing force (OPFOR) personnel during the blank-fire rehearsals portion of the lane and were completely synchronized on the assault during the live-fire portion of the sweep across the objective. When 2nd Platoon had to do the 2,500-meter lane three times, they were not happy, but they really knew the mission when it was over.

After the constant live-fire exercises and EXEVALs, Charlie Company was fully prepared for both offensive and defensive combat. I am convinced that the seemingly unlimited training resources, especially time and live ammunition, probably saved lives in the coming months.

The platoons were sore and ready for a break when May finally rolled around. The EXEVALS had consumed March and April. With spring in the air, the first 25-mile road march and the infamous Combat Olympics were on the short-range training schedule. No rest for the weary.

No matter how you train for a 25-miler, you will suffer when you do the march. Walk all day with a 45-pound rucksack on your back and your body adorned with all your other combat equipment (load-bearing harness, helmet, and rifle) and your body will pay a price. While walking, soldiers will eat munchies, drink water, chew gum, fantasize about being somewhere else, and do just about anything to keep from thinking about their feet, shoulders, and legs. When the pain breaks through the numbness, they'll often resort to so-called "Ranger Candy," (a couple of 800mg tablets of Motrin) and keep on marching to the next rest halt, and the next one, and the next, until the battalion headquarters finally comes into view and the hellish march is over.

The 25-miler was my first real physical hurdle, and once I had suffered through it with them, the men started to feel a lot better about their new commander. The headquarters section and platoons were coming together in their own right because the men had been tried and tested and had not broken. With shared misery comes camaraderie. The company was developing into a hard-core team, the warriors that the colonel wanted.

Charlie Company had one more gate to pass through before we could claim that we were the best company in the battalion: the Combat Olympics. Just as you might imagine, the goal of the Olympics is to perform a number of tests and competitions that prove your prowess in either a physical or military skill. The Olympics consisted of a 5-ton truck pull, a tug-of-war, a 10K run, a triathlon, marksmanship, a medical skills competition, a 5K litter carry with a climb up and rappel down the rappelling tower, an obstacle course, a canoe race, a softball game, a grenade throw competition, orienteering, and, last but not least, American Ball—not a game for the meek. Something like combat football, the game includes two goalies, two soccer balls, two twelve-man teams, and two rules: 1—to score, and 2—no weapons.

To make a long story short, we won the weeklong competition. I ran, rowed, and biked in the triathlon, then tried very hard to pound the Alpha company guidon bearer to a pulp in American Ball after he slammed me in the face with the ball. I made quite a spectacle of myself, but was well within the spirit of the game. Man, I was pissed. That episode brought my tenacity to the fore and, for many of the men in my company, made me the undisputed leader of the company from that day on. We were now a team.

During this initial six months of command, I tried to teach my lieutenants everything that I had ever learned during stints at the National Training Center, JOTC, and the Combat Maneuver Training Center, all fine places to learn the military trade. I had learned at the training centers that life is situational, meaning that no matter how detailed your plan is, the enemy may not follow it. Thus, you must always be prepared, think on your feet, and solve the immediate problem. I had also learned that perception is reality. If someone thinks you're better than sliced bread, then you are; on the other hand, if they think you're a soup sandwich, then you're that, too.

Our company had learned how to solve problems, do their very best on every mission assigned, and to look and act professional while doing it. I felt they were ready in all respects because they were physically fit, technically proficient, professionally sound, and mentally prepared. And above all, they were peaking at just the right time. All they needed was the ultimate test.

CHAPTER 3

Real-World Mission: the Big Show

July 28, 1993, was an absolutely beautiful day in northern New York. The bright blue sky held a sun that warmed our desert camouflage fatigues as we waited in the battalion quadrangle for the busses to arrive. Our destination was Griffiss Air Force Base. The commanders and a small advance party from each company would stage from Griffiss through Ramstein Air Base, Germany, and Cairo West Airport, Egypt, to Mogadishu, Somalia.

Loaded down with all of our combat equipment and carry-on bags, we each bid farewell to our loved ones and boarded the coach-style busses as our name was called from the manifest. We left in style for the first time since being at Fort Drum, as Bernie and his busses must not have been available.

Company C's advance party contingent included Staff Sergeant Tewes, a veteran of the 82nd Airborne Division and the invasion of Panama, who was a squad leader in the 1st Platoon; Specialist Prince, our supply clerk; and Specialist Randall, my primary radiotelephone operator (RTO). With the battalion and company executive officers and first sergeants bringing the main body later in the week, I wanted Tewes, a strong NCO, to help in positioning the company. Prince, of course, would set up the supply room and sign for any equipment the 1-22 IN wanted to leave behind. And Randall was just plain essential.

Like all good RTOs, Randall was simply the reliable right-hand man that all commanders need. It seemed that everything I didn't have time for, he did. He kept me informed about both the company's and the battalion's morale (he seemed to know everybody), collected the mail, handled radio watch, competed with me during PT and, being a good listener, patiently accepted my bitching when I couldn't bitch in the open. And, as the handler of all battalion radio traffic, Randall was one of my most critical—and valuable—command resources in any given situation.

The motor coaches dropped the advance party at Griffiss AFB's Hangar 1, where we hunkered down for some serious hurry-up-and-wait time, which passes slowly when you're waiting for transport birds. Some were briefed by the commander while others played cards, rested on cots lined up for contingency deployments, or caught up on what was happening in the other companies. And all ears listened for the landing roar of the enormous C-5 airplane.

Hearing the whining approach and then the screaming of the reversed engines, we gathered our individual equipment and got in line as names were called to load the aircraft. It's a long walk up the stairs in the belly of a C-5, a good 30 feet to the passenger cabin. The seats all face aft, so passengers feel as if they're flying backwards even though the aircraft is, of course, flying nose-first. After stowing their gear, all settled in for the eight-hour flight to Ramstein Air Base, and almost everyone slept.

Arriving in Ramstein to a new day, we were told—no big surprise here—that the plane was broken. It seems to be a disease with C-5s. If it lands in a really great destination, the crew often walks up and dejectedly tells you that the aircraft has malfunctioned. (Funny, but few C-5s experience breakdowns upon landing in, say, Iceland or Adak, Alaska. Must be something about the air in places like Germany, Thailand, or Colorado Springs.) We subsequently whiled away our time for two days in Germany, "waiting for a repair part." The Air Force put us up in barracks they were renovating, fed us in their great dining facility, and we had an impromptu beer fest the first night.

I called my son on his birthday, the 29th, and he was thrilled. He had thought he wasn't going to hear from me for six months.

Once the C-5 was repaired on the second day, we took off from Ramstein and headed for Cairo, Egypt. Cairo West Airport, about 20 miles outside of downtown Cairo, was the actual destination. More precisely, we ended up in a small, sand-blown, sand-colored, sand-blasted little American oasis of air-conditioned GP medium tents adjacent to the airport, yet seemingly in the middle of the Sahara Desert. Here, we got our first taste of the blast furnace heat we would be living in for the next few months when we deplaned for another wait, mandated, I believe, by crew rest rules.

With a little down time, Colonel David, Major Ellerbee, the S-3, Capt. Mark Suich, the Bravo Company commander, and I started a mean game of Hearts that lasted the entire six hours we were in Cairo West. (We later resumed the competition during the first few days in Mogadishu, as the other three were determined to snap my unbeaten streak.)

In complete darkness, the advance party boarded the C-5 for the final ride. The sun had gone down, turning the bright sky of day and the endless sea of soft sand dunes from a rose-washed, shadow-filled landscape to utter darkness. We ultimately arrived in Mogadishu sometime early the next morning.

My first view of Mogadishu, Somalia, came as we walked down the ramp and were herded into a covered parking garage area to wait for transportation. The airfield bustled with U.S. Army Cobra gunships and white Soviet-made U.N. helicopters coming and going, with a curious assortment of armored personnel carriers, some white, others camouflaged, all vying for a way onto the only road inside the airfield. The 1-22 IN had a welcoming party ready and gave us a quick brief on the route to the University Complex (where we would be staying), the SOP for live ammunition, and the Rules of Engagement. The advance party quickly traded one empty magazine for one filled with live ball ammunition. That simple transaction finally made it real.

At this point, anybody from the 1-22 IN was a veteran; they did everything right while we were the clumsy, unknowing new guys on the block. Horns blared momentarily and our rides arrived: 5-ton trucks, their beds lined three-deep in sandbags. We loaded up and copied the actions and posture of our hosts. The 1-22 IN soldiers manned the M-60 machine guns mounted above the cabs, and we held our weapons up and outboard over the rails of the truck beds. Our rucksacks, duffle bags, and the pallets from the C-5 would join us later. For now, the trucks rumbled to life and our adventure began.

Passing through the heavily guarded main gate of the airport, we locked and loaded our weapons, prepared to defend ourselves if need be from a supposedly hostile populace. At first, it was slow going through the gate. All around we could hear the sound of machine guns being loaded and the *crack-thunk* of the M-16 bolts ramming 5.56mm rounds home. The herky-jerky motion of the 5-ton monsters going through the gears slammed us momentarily into one another until we got our "sea legs." Careening out of the main gate with us hanging on for dear life, the trucks made a hard left, and then angled right as we entered the city.

Mogadishu was initially a smell, then a sight. The smell was a cross between burned and rotting meat, an oily stench you could feel. The city itself was built in the Italian tradition of walled compounds, block after block of whitewashed, terraced walls, the tops covered in broken glass. The peoples' clothing was amazingly colorful, yellows, purples, reds, blues, and greens, in every imaginable mixture.

As we roared down Jial Siad Street, a major east–west access route, we passed throngs of brightly clothed people. I had expected to see starving masses in the streets, like we had seen in the news, but no one seemed to be starving here. Splashing and swerving through countless potholes, the trucks raced to keep pace with the lead vehicle, not wanting to become separated and an easy target of opportunity for the guerilla fighters we knew inhabited the city.

We passed Pakistani checkpoints and a few jam-packed marketplaces. Although food seemed to be plentiful, there was no trash pickup, sewer system, electricity, or running water. And while the people were brightly clothed, you could tell that, for them, the future was far from bright. They needed help, and that's what we were here to do.

Brutal men had ravaged the common people of Somalia and ruined this once-beautiful seaside resort city. Those men still lurked in the shadows, not wanting peace, only absolute power. These thoughts raced through my head as I was propelled up a street in a completely alien environment and passed a people I had yet to learn anything about, except what I had read in CIA factbooks or outdated *National Geographic* issues. Looking past the people, I began to search the alleyways and side streets for signs of trouble. Finding none, I examined the faces of the people we were speeding past.

Most seemed as if they couldn't care less whether we were there or not, and our giant trucks racing by didn't seem to faze them. Still others, mostly middle-aged men with the demeanor of combat veterans, had "the look." They clearly hated us, our trucks, our country, and our God. Even if we tried, we would never convince the few who hated us so much that they believed we were not here to help, but merely invading their country. Meanwhile, the kids in the streets seemed to either love us or hate us. Some simply stared, but others threw rocks to show the world that they were not afraid of the mighty Americans.

We came to a T and turned right just outside the armed compound that was Hunter Base. Sandbagged guard towers bristled with .50-caliber machine guns, and concertina wire spiraled along the perimeter and atop the walls. Glancing around at the buildings of the logistical base, we could see fresh pockmarks and detonation holes, clear reminders that this city was not at all friendly to the U.N. effort. Straightening out, we headed toward the University/Embassy Complex, just northeast of Hunter Base. (The University/Embassy Complex was a large, walled area within which were located the University of Mogadishu Compound and the U.S. Embassy Compound. In turn, the Compounds were separated within the Complex by an internal wall.)

The camel market on our left was brimming with beasts, camels, goats, and donkeys, all there to be traded for necessary goods. Continuing on our right, we could see what used to be Embassy and "Rich Guys" Row (RGR), an area of once-spectacular mansions now just the gutted skeletons of formerly proud and beautiful homes. Squatters lived on every floor, their drying clothes hanging from the window ledges. As a makeshift form of protection, clusters of thorn bushes filled the empty windows.

Swirling dust enveloped the convoy, covering everyone and everything with a light film as we surged toward a Pakistani compound that constantly had an APC or truck positioned to guard the outpost. Day or night, that Paki outpost was our sign to make a hard right and, after wading the trucks through the seemingly perpetual standing, putrid water we would come to know was always directly in front of the compound, we realized we were just outside the Complex. We prepared to enter the gate under the watchful eyes of our soon-to-be guardians: the Tunisians.

Right across from the main gate of the University Complex was a refugee center. Hundreds of Somalis were always gathered in the street between the complex and the center. As always, the long line of trucks splashed the refugees, who looked just as pissed as you or I would be, as we slowly snaked our way into the Complex.

A command to "clear your weapons" rang throughout the convoy as we pulled into a turnaround for the trucks. Magazines were removed and bolts were yanked to the rear and locked back. The 1-22 guys knew the drill by heart, some even nonchalantly catching the ejected round in mid-air. We, on the other hand, needed a little more practice.

The call to dismount was given and everyone climbed over the rails onto the big dual-tandem tires or hopped off the rear end (not a good idea if you wanted to keep your knees). Six discharge barrels were placed around the perimeter of the dismount point and, one by one, we let our bolts slam forward and pulled our triggers as we aimed into the barrels— just in case. After we put our weapons on safe, we followed our hosts to our new home.

As I walked with the rest of the advance party, I sensed that the world didn't know how important this day was: the relief in place had begun. As we crested the hill on the way into our section of the compound, I looked with pride at the American flag flying over the battalion headquarters. Everything we did from now on would either disgrace or brighten the colors of the stars and stripes. Just before entering the 1-22 Battalion Tactical Operations Center (TOC), I vowed that my company would make a difference in this country. We wouldn't be "ugly Americans."

As I stepped in out of the sun with the rest of the commanders and staff, my eyes adjusted to what looked like any battalion headquarters in the Army. I faced down a long hallway with doorways on either inside and saw the American flag and 1-22 IN colors crossed just outside the battalion commander's quarters. Entering the battalion briefing area, with its maps, Somali clan organization charts, timeline, and operations orders (OPORD) briefing boards, we were welcomed by men who were obviously glad to see us—our counterparts. To a man, they were clearly ready to go home.

Although I knew that my company would be replacing C/1-22, I was pleasantly surprised to see their commander, Capt. Ed Rowe, a classmate from the Advanced Course. Now there we stood, shaking hands in a far-away land as we set about doing what we could not have imagined just one short year before.

A call to attention sounded as the 1-22 Commander prepared to brief us on the situation and upcoming missions. After being told to be seated, we settled onto the wooden benches that occupied the large room. We would become very familiar with those benches as we, in turn, would fill them every night for the next six months.

After introductions, the in-briefing began. We learned where the different Allied and American units were located within the Complex and were given an overview of the daily and weekly cycles of operational activities. This included an invitation to observe a scheduled cordon-and-search mission during the early morning hours of 1 August to see how these ops were done. We were also briefed on the "Enemy," with descriptions of his clans and where in the city he could be found. We were informed that the northern half of the city was pretty much Aidid's stomping grounds, including a particularly bad area in the middle called the "Black Sea."

The next portion of the briefing described key areas and access roads with which we would become very familiar. These included detailed discussions of the airport, Sword Base, and Hunter Base (which we had already seen); the Old and New Ports (just north of the airport, bordering "Indian Country"); and the K-4 Traffic Circle (where all major paved roads in Mogadishu lead). Units from Bangladesh and Pakistan guarded the area from two- and three-story buildings and a couple of ground-level guard posts. They also protected Via Lenin (the north road), Via Afgoya (the west road), the airport access to the south, and the eastern approaches to New Port. In the coming months, K-4 would become critical, as it demarcated operational areas as "bad" (everything north of it) and "seemingly friendly, or at least manageable" (everything south of it).

The briefing continued with detailed descriptions of area hospitals. Digfer Hospital sat between Sword Base to the north and the Complex to the south, and overlooked the so-called "Enclave" where the more affluent of Aidid's lieutenants lived. The tall hospital was surrounded by numerous 120mm mortar pits. Of course, you never saw any of the tubes unless local authorities wanted you to. The infamous "Technicals" were vehicle-mounted crew-served weapons (Toyota Land Cruisers with heavy mounted machine guns) that could also be seen there at times when they felt secure. Arms of every sort were stockpiled inside and guards roamed the building in full combat gear. Digfer was a nest just waiting to be stirred up—and also our number one target in the event we were allowed to conduct offensive operations.

Banadir Hospital, just east of the Complex, came in a close second to Digfer Hospital on our target list. Despite the naysayers who didn't believe the hospitals had any bad guys in them, it was at Banadir Hospital that we received our baptism by fire on 13 September 1993.

As the briefing continued we were told about the "Zoo," a site west of the city that was a good place to train. Additionally, its location on the outer approaches to the capital made it an ideal area for future ambush and roadblock ops designed to stem the tide of arms flowing into the city.

This early in the mission, we had no inkling of the size of the arms and troop buildup taking place under Aidid's command. Code-named Elvis, warlord Mohamed Farah Aidid played the most vital role in our existence in Somalia. The now-you-see-him-now-you-don't predicament he presented (of trying to find a lone individual in the sea of humanity that was Mogadishu) was not atypical under our mission parameters.

The briefing concluded with the announcement that we would view a videotape the following day of the QRF's assault on the Abdi house, their first ground offensive action against Aidid and his top aides. The nightly meeting then adjourned and we headed to our respective company or battalion areas to begin the process of individual, collective, and environmental assimilation.

My home for the next five months would be a long, white, Russian-built building on the University Compound, just down a hill from battalion headquarters. Charlie Company occupied two buildings. Mine, at the far western edge of the compound, housed the 1st Platoon and the Head-quarters section, while the 2nd and 3rd Platoons occupied the next build-ing to the east. The bleached white walls just screamed for some color, so I promised myself I'd do something about it. And, in an unusual stroke of luck, the battalion's chow hall, a markedly primitive dining facility, was right next door. (Primitive or not, it's always nice being near the food—and coffee.)

Captain Rowe guided my initial tour of the company area, while Staff Sergeant Tewes, Specialist Prince, and my RTO, Specialist Randall, began the hard work of preparing for the company's relief in place/transfer of authority, widely known today as RIP/TOA. Paperwork for the hand-off of radio frequencies, duty schedules, supply accountability, living quarters, site selection, and providing for the day-to-day logistical tasks that sustain the unit were all discussed and accomplished.

C/1-22 was leaving cots, water, and spares of everything just lying around, which was convenient, but there clearly weren't enough living spaces for the soldiers and officers to be comfortable. It was tight: too tight. I noticed, though, that esprit de corps among C/1-22's men was exceptionally high. They were, of course, happy to be going home and couldn't care less about the standard of living. Men sunbathed and played darts, volleyball, dominos, or one of the soldier's favorite card games: Hearts or Spades. You can catch soldiers anywhere in the world playing one or the other in their off time, with the typical wager being $1,000 a point, knowing it would never be paid.

During this initial tour of my company's area, I found out that C/1-22 had a TV, on which CNN and Armed Forces Network (AFN) were the only channels, and a VCR. Movies had been seen over and over and the news was constantly watched to keep everyone abreast of goings on in the real world, especially anything dealing with the Somalia mission and where we were headed politically.

After the tour of the company area, Captain Rowe showed me his/my quarters. He had one cot with mosquito netting, a table, a briefing board, folding chairs, and a footlocker: Spartan, but adequate. He had hung maps of the city and the countryside, and had collected all of his OPORDs from previous missions.

At this point I remember feeling almost overwhelmed. While not quite surreal, this was certainly well beyond my experience. Here I was in a foreign land on a real-world mission, facing imminent danger, the new guy on the block, discussing what it was like outside the wire with a veteran of the mission that now sat squarely on my shoulders. I had so many questions, and I wanted to know everything right now!

It also struck me then that life really mattered now: no games, no blank ammo, no engineer tape to fake a roadblock or a pretend minefield. No, this was life and death. And it also dawned on me that no simplistic rules governed the outcome, like if you knew the ropes you lived and if you ignored all you were taught or disregarded the rules, you died. Uh-uh. Here, mere Fate or just plain bad luck could alter the course of my life or those of my soldiers.

Ed Rowe helped me immeasurably. He sat me down and explained that I would learn. He said there would be bad times out there beyond the compound walls, but that not all the people were hateful and that the kids and the women seemed to like us. He told me to relax and to have good, solid standard operating procedures (SOPs) for the times when situations boiled over and firefights broke out.

After I soaked up all I could, he told me to change into my PTs for a run around the whole Complex. As I found out, this was a great way to relieve some of the stress while reconning our ever-changing home. Dressed in our gray Army PT clothes (gray shorts and a gray short-sleeved shirt with ARMY plastered in black letters across the chest), we donned our sunglasses and hats (mine a maroon and silver University of Alabama baseball cap) and headed down the blacktop and sand route.

On the run I saw the numerous Tunisian guard posts, every 50 feet, most placed high on buildings. The perimeter encompassed the Swedish hospital, the Combat Army Surgical Hospital (CASH) that would save so many lives, the 10th Aviation Brigade headquarters (our higher headquarters while in Somalia), and the U.S. Embassy Compound, which held all the foreign contingents to the U.N. and the U.S. Embassy itself.

The Tunisians on guard duty were a hard lot. They shot at everything that even touched the wire (i.e., dogs, goats, pigs, kids, cars, etc.) and took no crap from anyone. They were always congenial around the compound, but while on duty their demeanor was severe and professional.

The Swedish hospital was occupied by none other than Swedish nurses, and though their men tried to conceal them from us, every now and then you could catch a glimpse of the topless sunbathers on the hospital roof. This, of course, was a welcome distraction in a country where the women, as in most Muslim countries, were clothed from head to foot.

On the Embassy Compound, the assorted diplomats, advisers, doctors, and support staff of the other national contingents set up camp. Just around the corner of the Embassy was Landing Zone JAYBIRD, from which we caught mission-support flights on the various Black Hawks and Hueys of the U.S. and the white-painted Russian Hinds and Hips of the U.N. The running tour's halfway point was at the Embassy loop, the circle driveway directly in front of the Embassy, and from there we headed back around the sand track surrounding the CASH's tents at the far southern edge of the complex. If you took the longest path around the Complex, it measured 10K, a great stress-busting run.

Back at the company area, I was shown the facilities. These included long, 4-inch diameter PVC pipe "piss tubes" that reached 10 feet or so into the ground, with about 3 feet sticking up at a slant and a screen-covered opening. Three of these tubes were planted about 20 feet from my office window and yes, sometimes the splattering produced a stench that even the lime sprinkled around the area couldn't hide. The same stench marked the commode, or "throne" facility: a simple plywood shack with a door, a graffiti-covered interior, and a wooden plank seat with a hole cut in it that was placed over a cut-off 55-gallon drum. The drum could be (and sometimes was, on several embarrassing occasions) removed by the operators of the Somali "turd truck" even while we were doing our business. They'd just open the flat wooden covering at the back of the outhouse, remove the full drum, and replace it with an empty one. Nothing like having your ass in the breeze for all to see!

Captain Rowe and I changed into some dry PTs, donned our shoulder holsters, and prepared for dinner. As all good commanders do, we waited until all the men ate first. While standing in line, he described the chow as a mixture of T-rats, fresh fruit, Kool-Aid, coffee, iced tea, and condiments (mystery sauces). On good days, we might even have peanut butter, MRE bread, and some generic soft drinks or juice.

T-rats? Well, they come in cans of various mystery-meat stew concoctions (ostensibly turkey, ham, etc.), usually with potatoes and a wonderful, slimy, almost pure-fat sauce. Each meal was just good enough (if appropriately prepped with enough salt, pepper, hot sauce, and ketchup) to make you want to return for the next meal. Breakfast was a much-better egg/ham/sausage loaf that was easily digestible and, when washed down with hot coffee, wasn't all that bad.

All in all, the cooks did their damnedest every day to make a less-than-palatable gathering of food groups into the semblance of a home-cooked meal and sometimes, just sometimes, it was so good that if you closed your eyes, you couldn't tell the difference. They deserve a lot of credit for their efforts, especially at Thanksgiving.

After chow, around 1830 hours, I noticed that the whole company started becoming a bit agitated, everyone just seeming to be more alert. With the coming darkness, my senses were on edge. Then I heard my first large-scale exchange of fire at Hunter Base, about 3 miles away. I could easily see from our porch that Hunter had come under close direct fire from the high-rise buildings across the road. In the gray light of early evening, I watched the firefly dance of tracers, green (theirs) and red (ours) streaming back and forth between the wrecked buildings on one side of the road and the sandbagged and razor-wired compound on the other.

As my eyes watched the scene, my ears finally adjusted to the distant fight. Hunter Base gave more than it took as the .50-caliber machine guns on the perimeter *thunked* out a seemingly endless stream of tracers, some red ricochets arching far into the growing darkness. And every now and then a distant boom could be heard as an RPG was shot into Hunter Base.

And then it happened. KABOOM! A mortar round exploding inside *our* compound sent us scurrying like rats for helmets and flak jackets. KABOOM! Another mortar round landed! Lights were switched off and radios came alive with traffic. The fireflies danced again, only much closer and much louder, as the Tunisians' rifle fire lit up a vehicle driving the perimeter. Illumination flares began to brighten the skyline, streaming into the sky with a whoosh and a pop. Another KABOOM as the building rocked, dust fell, and the crack of the explosion and the momentary blast wave hit us.

Adrenaline rushed through my veins then, and I wanted to do something, anything. I hated sitting in the darkness waiting to be hit by something I couldn't see, let alone fight. In the movies, you typically heard the *thunk*, then the whining scream of a mortar round, with someone screaming "Incoming!" In reality, mortars are silent, indiscriminant death, unseen lightning. There is no whistle, no warning, just the explosion and flesh-tearing, molten-hot steel knifing through the air.

Silence. Deep breathing. Staring eyes, slightly bugged open. My first smell of shots fired in anger, the cordite, sulfur, and gunpowder burning my nostrils. Then the "all clear" sounded, and the lights started coming back on throughout the compound.

Each company did a quick head count and checked their respective company area, then reported their situation to the TOC. And nearly all of us headed outside to check out the blackened crater not 50 feet from the barracks, the silver fins of the mortar round just a few feet away.

I walked back up the hill from that still-smoking hole to start my first night of fitful, tossing, turning, and anxious sleep on a mosquito-netted cot. At 0400, loudspeakers blared the call to prayer from the minarets and, at 0530, our own wake-up call roused us to the cool, dewy morning of what would become a bright and beautiful day. Up and at 'em. Did last night really happen?

After morning PT and breakfast, Captain Rowe and I went to the TOC for the daily update. I learned that a soldier had been wounded in the mortar attack; the mortar and its crew still had not been located; the cordon-and-search back-brief would be held that afternoon; and that we would see the video of the assault on the Abdi house prior to the back-brief.

The rest of the day was filled with meetings, reconning (reconnoitering) our company and battalion facilities, and just getting to know the place, small as it might be. At around noon we ate an MRE and, from that day on, I vowed never to eat one again unless we were training downrange. It took a while but I started eating my care-package meals from home at lunch, whatever they were.

I soon realized that I needed my own space. Pride of ownership had started to kick in, and I wanted the 1-22 folks out of there before my company came. As bad as they wanted to leave, I wanted them to leave even more. Still, I knew I needed to go on the cordon-and-search mission to tap as much information as I could about this environment from these veterans before they departed. I also understood that I was beginning to change in ways that I wasn't really sure would be possible.

The conference room was quiet while we waited for the video equipment to be set up. Looking around the room into the faces and eyes of the 1-22 commanders, I saw a look I had only seen before in photographs of war: drawn faces, tired eyes. The A/1-22 commander was a bit smug as he had seen the only "real" combat. As we would find out from the video, he had led a platoon into the Abdi house after fifteen TOW missiles from Cobra gunships had slammed into it. All that remained of the meeting supposed to have taken place there were some choice body parts. The mission had not been a complete success because a few Somalis had gotten away out the back when the missiles started pounding the structure, but it was an awesome spectacle at the time. A one-sided firefight is sure something to see. At the time, though, the Abdi house raid was seen as a real mission, using real ordnance to deal with a real enemy. Looking at him in the conference room, I remember thinking, "Damn, I wonder what it feels like to be him." In retrospect, I have to chuckle at myself.

The cordon-and-search mission briefing came next. We were going out our so-called back gate, really just a hole in the far wall of the compound, to search a neighborhood very close to the university. Two companies would work abreast, with one in trail while support HMMWVs would provide a loose cordon. Personnel from the 2-14 would walk with their counterparts and be as inconspicuous as possible. All agreed that this was just a learning experience aimed at getting the 2-14 leadership's feet wet.

Many thoughts swirled in my head. My first real mission would be in the morning. While not an actual combat, only a hunt for weapons in people's houses, anything could happen and, I was told, usually did. Our main concern was snipers, but being ambushed in the dark, tight confines of a typical Somali dwelling ran a close second. Since most houses were within walled compounds, you always had to control the exit point, usually an iron gate, so that you could get out while keeping the bad guys in.

I was to join the C/1-22 company headquarters on the first mission to observe how Captain Rowe ran a real-world op. The commander has two RTOs, one for a company radio network (net) and one for the battalion net; a medical aid man; and a quick-reaction team (QRT) led by the executive officer (XO) and comprised of the mortar and antitank sections. For this sort of mission, the QRT was not used in their normal specialized gunnery roles. Instead, they carried extra water and ammunition and performed as a prisoner/detainee collection team following cleanup behind the rest of the company.

The three line platoons, each with about thirty men, would be the workhorses. They would conduct searches through block after block, all the while trying to remain in a cohesive line as they advanced through the communities. A cordon-and-search is a grueling and time-consuming operation that pits your nerves against an unknown and unseen enemy. If an enemy is found, it is generally on his terms. This typically requires the search team members to react to an ambush or sniper fire—not a favorite situation to be in.

The best thing that can happen in a cordon-and-search is that the enemy identifies himself by firing blindly at you and begins a mad dash for the perimeter. Since this rarely happens, the stress and tedium are usually broken only when weapons or ammunition are found. A primary goal of the operation is to get no one killed, neither us nor them, and certainly not some little kid in a too-dark back bedroom.

When the briefing concluded, Rowe went to give the company OPORD. He had the plan all worked out in his head and had many good SOPs already in place. The squad leaders had already started pre-combat check inspections to ensure everyone and everything needed was present and accounted for. My men had followed suit, and when I gave them their briefing, they seemed ready to just be pointed in the right direction. We were glad to be doing something, anything besides sitting around and waiting for C/1-22 to leave. We all cleaned our weapons and ammunition, ate chow, and then tried to rest through the usual 1900 hour probes at the

Tunisian perimeter defenses. I didn't sleep a wink that night, yet didn't feel the least bit tired when, at 0200, I was informed that it was time to "Get it on."

We formed in the darkness. The lights had to stay off in the buildings because the Somalis watched for activity within all of the compounds throughout Mogadishu. The swishing of uniforms and dull thuds and clanks of equipment were all that could be heard of a fully armed combat infantry company preparing for a mission. At 0300 on 1 August 1993, I set out on my first real-world operation.

The battalion's dismounted elements filed through the sweet, cool darkness of the Somali pre-dawn, slipping between the Swedish hospital and the 42nd Area Support Group perimeter, then through the Egyptian checkpoint, slithering silently like a black mamba to the opening in the Complex perimeter wall. The hole was a 5-by-5-foot opening usually sealed shut with packed dirt, concertina wire, and a metal plate, overwatched by two Tunisian guard posts. One at a time, we each passed through the hole and into a cactus patch just outside the wall. It seemed like being birthed as we went from the guarded confines of our mother (the University Compound) to the wide-open spaces of the real world in the city of Mogadishu.

Just as I made it through, I heard the HMMWVs of the cordon force start their engines in unison. Twenty or so vehicles roared to life and quickly moved out the Embassy gate to guard key locations and intersections around the battalion's perimeter. Because of our passing through the wall single file, we had to form up in the street and get into military order once again. Needless to say, we never went out that way again, as it presented too much opportunity for a disastrous ambush against us.

In minutes we were in position to begin the cordon-and-search. C/1-22 was the far right flank. Just as the veil of night was lifted, I was startled to hear over the loudspeakers orders from the Somali interpreters reporting that Americans were in the area looking for weapons. I knew the Somalis were pissed, but we were following orders and the people complied with the new soldiers in town.

The next sound in our area of operations (AO) was a massive soldier pounding on an iron gate, with a platoon interpreter yelling something in

Somali at the occupants. After all the training, all the years, all the sweat, classes, and training deployments, my first real-world operation had begun.

The knocking procedure was repeated over and over, hundreds of times. The companies kept abreast the best they could as the grunts searched hovels, huts, shacks, compounds, villas, and the predominant row houses. The streets, if you want to call them that, are dirt passages approximately one HMMWV wide. Pavement is rare and the going is slow.

My little entourage kept pace with Rowe's command element. He stayed abreast of the situation, concentrating on the radio traffic and reporting his progress to the battalion commander. The day wore on; the sun climbed higher, and still higher, until the temperature reached its usual daytime high of 116 degrees. We sweated and toiled. Soldiers asked people to come out of their houses and began the searches of dwellings and hiding places, including abandoned wells, where weapons could be secreted.

Men and women would segregate. Men, the dominants in the society, tended to oversee the activities while the women herded the incredible number of children from harm's way. When a weapon was found the man was questioned and told he was being relieved of his firearm or spear or knife. If the weapon was of minimal value as an instrument of war and the owner put up no resistance to its being confiscated, the search line would just pass right on through and continue its slow, sure advance to the end point. If, however, a weapon was fairly new, especially a crew-served weapon or RPG, the owner was usually detained for questioning at the Complex.

God help those who put up a fight, and there were a few that day. Infantry soldiers can be a lot like rogue cops when their lives are on the line. A Somali would be asked through an interpreter to remain calm and more or less accept his fate. Those who didn't were manhandled to the ground, had their wrists secured behind their backs with a plastic zip binding, and were whisked away to the Complex jail for questioning about their recent activities.

We had heard that the Bangladeshi interrogators were not the most pleasant individuals. Only hard-core troublemakers or men who needed to explain why they had twenty of these or fifty of those were detained. Typically, the questionable items consisted of small arms and ammunition.

As I kept pace with the ebb and flow of the operation, I went from being totally on edge to being completely calm about interacting with the populace as a foreign infantryman undoubtedly perceived as an intruder. The kids were especially wonderful, playfully mimicking your every move and trying to communicate to the best of their ability. Gestures, looks, and every other form of unspoken language could be seen throughout my sojourn into this first of many neighborhoods in Mogadishu.

Most of the people had seen so many soldiers, whether from clans or countries, that they simply went about the day as if soldiers were just another facet of normal existence. Others were quite put out by the intrusion and said so in heated, one-sided arguments, lashing out with their tongues and beating the air with their arms. In retrospect, these were the least dangerous encounters. The disturbing encounters were those when the occupants just stood there, seemingly aloof, silently inviting you to try your best to find something in their dark, smelly, often putrid abodes.

The usual combat house-clearing procedure consisted of tossed hand grenades, followed by three-round rifle bursts sprayed into each room and a violent assault through each door to secure the unknown. Cordon-and-search procedures involved a flashlight taped to the M16A2's muzzle with your finger just off the trigger as you probed and hunted in the darkness while waiting to be shot or bit or stabbed at a moment's notice. I greatly admired the way the men dealt with the unseen more than the seen.

Nightmares can lurk behind your eyes if you let your imagination get the best of you in situations like that. Consider that being decked out in approximately 70 pounds of combat gear—including a flak jacket, a helmet, a firearm, LBE with water and a basic ammunition load, a long-sleeved uniform, and combat boots—in 110+-degree temperatures while risking your life in the stifling confines of someone else's house is not the most glamorous of tasks. The men who deal with this kind of pressure deserve a lot more than just thanks.

It was a welcome relief when our first mission ended. We had taken nearly all day to cover a 30-by-30-block section of the city, right outside our southeastern perimeter wall. The sun had broiled us, soaking our uniforms with sweat that left telltale salt streaks trailing from our armpits and crotches, and our heads seemed to be melting under our helmets. When we finally consolidated our units for the road march back to the Complex, I felt a sense of accomplishment for getting through my first mission. I also gained confidence that I could handle operations like this when called upon to do so. Upon returning to the Complex, we cleaned our weapons, turned in our booty (the confiscated weapons), showered in the cold water of the shower trailer, and rested before evening chow.

On reflection, this mission provided priceless insights. First, breaking in the junior leaders by letting them get their feet wet as they worked alongside their soon-to-be-gone counterparts was invaluable. You just can't throw the whole unit into the breach right off. Further, the leaders look far more competent when they have already done a mission first without the majority of the troops present.

Next, this first mission put to rest the normal wild fantasies one experiences when facing the unknown. I learned that Somalis were not bogeymen; that little kids will be little kids; that boys will behave like boys and girls will behave like girls; that our men would do their damnedest to accomplish the mission even in the worst of circumstances; and that firefights were not going to break out all over the place just because we left the Complex.

I also learned that you shouldn't take away a man's personal firearm in a civil war that isn't properly concluded. Taking away a person's means of protection gives the opposing side free reign, especially at night. I later found out that the neighborhood we had searched on that first mission was, in fact, not hostile to our cause, and that we had made their lives a living hell by disarming them. This allowed Aidid's men to come down from the Black Sea at night to murder, rape, and pillage at will, because the people had no way to defend themselves. The clans in the city were, in fact, committing small-scale, localized genocide on one another, and we were unwittingly helping the wrong side.

The sense of accomplishment and confidence were building in me as the hours wore on. I had seen a great deal in such a short period of time. The anticipatory shock and fear of being on a mission where combat could have erupted at any moment without warning was bleeding off. I also felt that, for the first time, I had a jump on the rest of the company. The main body would arrive in just a few hours, and they would be the new guys. For the first time, I was there first. Although I was a veteran of just a single operation, most of them had yet to live through that experience. In those hours after the cordon-and-search, I realized that they would be looking for immediate answers from me. It also hit me like a sledgehammer that I was the leader, teacher, and mentor of 120 souls. And, because the parents, wives, brothers, sisters, and children of these men were all counting on me to bring their loved ones home safe and in one piece, I was also their guardian.

Sitting on the edge of my cot, before my men ever arrived in Somalia, I became their *commander*. When you finally shoulder the men and forget about yourself, that is exactly what you are: a commander. I changed, underwent a metamorphosis so outstanding that I search for the same feelings even today. That kind of responsibility is rarely given and, even more rarely, truly accepted.

One thing that had been bothering me was that, for whatever reason, after nearly six months of my command, our company was still just Charlie Company. We had no cool moniker, like "Chargin' Charlie" or "Charlie Rock." No, at that point in time we were nameless. As I walked to the TOC that night after chow, I realized that we needed a name. We would be choosing call signs at the upcoming meeting, and it looked like I was just going to be CHARLIE 6, a generic and rather lackluster handle. It dawned on me there was nothing mightier in the jungle than the tiger, and that we were in an urban jungle. And I recalled that my dad had always called me "Tiger" when I was a kid. In a flash of inspiration, I chose Tiger 6 as my call sign and decided that we would be Tiger Company from that point forward. And just like that, our new identity was born from out of the blue. I later realized that in the Chinese scheme of things, the dragon and the tiger are the two most powerful entities in the mystical world. And there I was in the Golden Dragon Regiment as Tiger 6. It suited the company and it suited me.

On 2 August 1993, the main body of the Golden Dragon Regiment arrived for its date with destiny. There was little fanfare; they were just another arriving unit as far as anyone else was concerned. The soldiers of 2-14 Infantry were tired, anxious, and full of emotion, just as I had been a few days before. They needed direction, and our little advance party set about the task of getting our friends and comrades-in-arms situated amidst the turmoil that was the departing C/1-22.

Although the bulk of the 1-22 veterans would soon be going to Hunter Base for redeployment, I learned that C/1-22 would be staying for one extra day until room could be made at Hunter. When space became available, C/1-22 would then bring up the rear for their battalion's redeployment. As you can imagine, the two companies, mine and Ed Rowe's, were packed like cordwood on top of one another for a while. We would be happy when they left.

I met the first sergeant and the XO, told them to get the company situated and, when that was accomplished, that I wanted to see all the leaders. In that first meeting, I told them who they were (Tiger Company), what they were (the best damned company in the country), and what we were going to do to make our stay in Somalia successful. It seemed a bit unsettling for them.

I wanted murals—giant, colored, colossal signs—that proclaimed our existence in this country and that we were taking on all comers. I also wanted orderliness and the best barracks this side of the Indian Ocean built for the troops. And I wanted a daily routine with fun built in to relieve the drudgery and tedium of our day-to-day existence.

I also gave them the rules we would live by. We would be perceived as the baddest folks in town, and I wanted it known that if you tangled with us, you had just grabbed a tiger by the tail, a mistake for which you would pay dearly. Tempering that attitude of ferocity would be a sincere effort to become known as a "good" company by helping where needed, doing what was right, and performing to the best of our ability, even if no one was watching.

I then told them our Rules of Engagement (ROE). If kids threw rocks, we'd throw rocks back. If our enemy fired a pistol, we'd fire our M16s. If our enemy fired a rifle, we'd fire machine guns. If they fired a machine gun, we'd fire AT-4 rockets. And if they are bold enough to fire an RPG in our direction, all bets were off and we'd launch consolidated fire their way. A commander's first duty is to protect his men and to let his men know that they can protect themselves; common sense would prevail.

When you are the little guy fighting for your life with a hundred rounds buzzing by your head and RPGs exploding around you, it's not exactly Operations Other Than War, it *is* war!

I finished by telling them that I would take their input on the routine and bounce it off the battalion duty day, and that we would begin our area beautification program as soon as the umbilical cord from 1-22 was cut. The ROE were accepted and the leadership began making plans that night for the renovation of the barracks, the latrine facilities, and company area defenses. Great ideas blossomed, and after a good night's sleep we would help C/1-22 leave and get started.

The good night's sleep didn't really come. The welcome-to-Mogadishu mortar attack happened right on schedule, followed by a full-blown skirmish at Hunter Base that kept us up most of the night watching the firefight rage and wondering if we would be called out to help. As it turned out, because the Somalis didn't know about the infantry battalion that had just moved to Hunter, they bit off more than they could chew. Hunter's defenses held and only a few minor casualties were taken.

As a result of diving under cots, throwing off the lights, and sitting in the pitch black waiting for the next mortar to fall, the platoon sergeants began in earnest to sandbag every nook and cranny of our barracks and develop SOPs for an attack. The gloves were off. Orders were taken to heart and executed to the letter. Lights would be extinguished, everyone would be physically accounted for, status reports would be sent over the landline to headquarters, and wearing flak jackets and Kevlars was strictly enforced. That first night solidified my reasoning with the leadership that this was a life-and-death place, and only the prepared would survive.

The next day started with PT (quick calisthenics and a short run), and then the send-off of C/1-22. I said goodbye to Captain Rowe as he and his company gladly departed the Complex for the last time. With their departure, the 1st Battalion of the 22nd Infantry Regiment finally disengaged from any TOC activities and the 2nd Battalion of the 14th Infantry Regiment officially assumed its duties in Mogadishu, Somalia.

Tiger Company welcomed the departure with absolute relief and began in earnest to carve out its niche at the Complex. The murals were started, wooden bunks and second floors were built to give us more room, briefing areas were fashioned, common areas were developed into fine works of art, and TV/VCR stands, water storage areas, and weight training areas were constructed. Over the ensuing weeks, everything came together, and the daily schedule kept the company on a pace that it could live with. I called it the Lifestyles of the Not So Rich and Famous.

Your hooch was your space; keep it neat and clean and—when asked to, for an inspection only—spotless and no one would mess with you. The following Battle Rhythm was established:

0500	First call
0530	Wake up
0545	Shave (every day)
0550	Brush teeth (every day)
0600	PT: run or lift
0645	Showers (mostly cold, occasionally hot; take one anyway, even if you have to gut it out)
0700	Breakfast (T-rations, Yum-Yum)
0800	Prayer or read from the Bible
0900	Check out the daily ops at the TOC
0930	Personal time (write home, read, clean weapons and ammo)
1100	Lunch (pogey bait, care packages, MREs)
1200	Squad training
1500	PT: run, volleyball, lift
1630	Dinner
1800	Battalion meeting
1900	Company meeting
1930	Tunisian firefight/mortar attack
2000	Mail call—the best part of the day, when we received care packages and hundreds of books from the Office of Naval Research, which had taken our company under their wing (my mom and dad worked there at the time)
2200	Lights out

And then we would do it all over again, barring any unexpected events or a planned mission.

Our battalion cycle was three days on battalion duty, three days on training out in the bush, and three days as the Quick Reaction Company (QRC) of the battalion's QRF. This schedule seemed ideal to keep the companies busy and rested, without one company ever getting too much action, duty, or training, and never getting bored.

Only time would tell.

CHAPTER 4

Escalation

On 8 August 1993, our semi-sheltered world was shattered by an event that forever changed how operations were conducted in and around Mogadishu. Shortly after their mid-afternoon arrival in country, four military policemen (MPs) from the 977th and 300th MP Companies were traveling along Jial Siad street, just west of the airport, when a command-detonated mine was exploded immediately under their armored HMMWV. The mine had been placed only a few hundred feet from a Pakistani checkpoint near the Medina marketplace. The devastating blast was heard and felt throughout the Complex a few miles away.

Bravo Company, the QRC, arrived at the site approximately thirty minutes after the detonation. They found a huge crater in the ground, 10-by-10-by-7 feet deep. The HMMWV was nothing more than a twisted frame and small, mostly unrecognizable parts, its Kevlar body completely ripped from the frame and shredded into a thousand pieces. The massive explosion, later believed to be approximately 100 pounds of TNT, instantly killed the MPs riding in the vehicle. They were Spc. Mark Gutting, twenty-five, from Grand Rapids, Michigan; Spc. Keith Pearson, twenty-five, from Tavares, Florida; and Sgt. Christopher Hilgert, twenty-seven, from Danville, Indiana, all members of the 977th MP Company,

Fort Riley, Kansas; and Staff Sgt. Ronald Richerson, twenty-four, from Portage, Indiana, of the 300th MP Company, Fort Leonard Wood, Missouri. Richerson's unit was one day away from rotating out of Somalia; he was conducting a relief-in-place orientation patrol for the three replacements when he was killed.

Bravo Company, sobered by what they saw, immediately initiated an ultimately fruitless cordon-and-search operation. Many of the soldiers became angry at the futility of searching for the perpetrators of such a cowardly act. When the somber soldiers returned to the Complex, they brought with them a new awareness of what could happen if you weren't 100 percent vigilant, 100 percent of the time, in this very hostile environment.

From that point on, the higher echelon U.N. and QRF commanders began planning a bypass route that could be controlled by friendly elements. Within a few days, engineers began work on a dirt road that headed south of the city a few miles, turned to the east toward the Indian Ocean, and then hit the Coast Road just south of the airport, to be designated Main Supply Route (MSR) Tiger. The big question was who would guard it and make it safe for the hundreds of supply and combat vehicles that would traverse it daily?

Life became very serious business after the MPs' deaths brought home the reality that it could be taken from you in the blink of an eye. This was clearly no training mission; it was, quite simply, us versus them, whoever "they" were. I determined that, no matter what, Charlie Company was going to be perceived as the most professional, most dangerous, most lethal entity in the city. To that end, our SOP established that whenever we left the Complex, my soldiers would be nothing but business: weapons out and ready, perfect spacing in the trucks, chin straps fastened, a grim and determined demeanor, and *none* of the usual grab-ass and kidding around. I remain convinced to this day that the discipline this instilled saved our butts on numerous occasions by letting the enemy know that we were always ready for them.

After two days off, the 2-14 Golden Dragons were ready to begin making their presence known. Colonel David decided the best thing to do was to dive right in, get the entire unit's feet wet, and then drive on. Any detected mistakes would be corrected before the next mission. A simple, comparatively easy mission was chosen: a cordon-and-search. Oh, joy!

After almost a week of nightly, sporadic mortar showers, we opted to search for likely enemy mortar positions in a fairly decent part of the city, just south of the K-4 traffic circle. To prevent biting off more than we could chew on this first mission, we restricted the search area to only a limited number of square blocks. The operation would also allow us to become familiar with the terrain we would be dealing with for the next few months. We were about to find out how we operated compared to the 1-22 and start on our way to becoming veterans.

As was to become the norm, our deliberate planning process on 10 August was aided tremendously by the superb work of the battalion's S-2 (Intelligence) officer, Captain Maisano, the Assistant S-2, 2nd Lieutenant Pettigrew, and the Assistant S-3 (Operations) officer, Captain Williams. In this and all future operations, these three consistently did magnificent work creating mock-ups of target areas out of cardboard and other scraps. Their efforts helped us all get a feel for the terrain and unique features of the neighborhoods in which we'd be operating. We were also provided with satellite photos which gave us the bird's-eye view of and around our objectives. The outstanding materials they supplied enabled us to efficiently conduct rehearsals and back-briefs to assure the leadership that all participants knew their respective roles and were aware of potential problems.

We rose from our cots early on 11 August, 0200 hours, got untangled from the mosquito netting in the dark, and donned our fighting wardrobe of Kevlar, LBE, weapons, flak jackets, and the miscellaneous equipment needed to conduct the operation. At 0300, the Tunisian guards opened the main vehicular entrance gates and a tentative 2nd Platoon, Tiger Company departed the Complex as the lead element, intending to take the first right turn and head east on Via Afgoya toward the city center. By the book, I stayed one platoon back and my command element listened on the radio for any signs of trouble, trusting the 2nd Platoon leader to navigate, control his platoon's speed and spacing, and be prepared to react to an ambush or sniper.

On this first mission, it proved to be too much, as the 2nd Platoon walked right by our first turn. When I realized our mistake, 2nd Platoon was near Banadir Hospital, a full block too far east. As I halted the column at the turn, I received a disturbing and ominous radio call from the battalion commander (BC). "That's strike one," I heard. "Wait there. Terminator element (Alpha Company) will pass through you." Looking back, I saw Alpha Company's lead element just starting down the road after exiting the Complex gate.

It had been an honor to be given the lead on the first battalion mission and I was damned if Alpha Company was going to just pass us by like we were errant schoolboys. I ordered 2nd Platoon to double-time (run like hell) back to me, reoriented them, and directed them to continue the mission, then radioed the BC that we had again taken the lead. To my great relief, he let us keep it.

Okay, lesson learned. I began leading from within the lead element, not from behind it. Over time, I realized that leading from the front means just that. The men see you, you are sharing the lead elements' dangerous position in the move, and you can make timely decisions concerning navigation and reactions to enemy contact. In the city, both on foot and mounted in vehicles, if your subordinates make a mistake and you are not there to quickly correct it, a whole operation can rapidly come apart.

We made the next checkpoint with no problems, had our spacing down to a science, were past the initial jitters, and 2nd Platoon was working like the well-oiled machine I had come to know back at Fort Drum. Then came another radio call from the BC: "Where are you?" I gave him the approximate grid coordinate and got a steely reply back: "No, exactly where you are. Give me a GPS reading."

The Global Positioning System (GPS) can give you a reading to within 1 meter of where you are standing if all the satellites are responding, so I called for the GPS. Well, guess what? "It's back at the company," was the reply I received from the XO. Knowing that bad news only gets worse with time, and with my command element watching me intently, I took the mike from Randall and responded to the commander, "I don't have a GPS with me."

In my head, I could see the other company commanders smiling at my predicament and the other RTOs mouthing "Oh, shits!" At that moment, the silence was so overwhelming that I thought it would shatter my eardrums, but I very clearly heard the next thing out of the radio. "Tiger 6," said the BC, "this is Dragon 6. That's strike two."

"Roger, over," was all I could manage as my perfect company very publicly got a taste of humble pie and relearned a lesson straight out of the Ranger Handbook: Don't forget nothin'.

We soberly continued the mission with a lot to prove if we were going to get any respect from then on. The linkup with the cordon element, Bravo (The Bastards), went well and on time, and the movement into position was perfect. We were just about to start banging on doors and rousting the occupants when I happened to look up and saw a United Nations flag. Calling an immediate halt to the impending debacle over the battalion radio net, I ran to the BC's location and informed him that we were about to semi-assault U.N. territory.

Upon further investigation, it turned out to be just that: the U.N. commander's complex. We had very narrowly avoided absolute embarrassment for the QRF. The look that I received from Colonel David told me that, at that instant, I was back in his good graces. Damn, was I relieved, and not just for me, but for the whole company.

Colonel David shifted us down and over from our intended start line and, at daybreak, the 2-14 began its first major operation in Somalia, the cordon-and-search of AO NEVADA. Soldiers were banging on doors and, with the help of platoon interpreters, began systematically searching everywhere for signs of weapons and the tools of war. We found AK-47s in wells, G3 machine guns on upper shelves in garage tool sheds and inside abandoned vehicles. Dozens of weapons were found in the closets of non-governmental organizations (NGOs), where they were supposedly being stored for the perimeter guards, but they didn't have any of the required weapons cards. These, of course, were immediately confiscated.

In reality, many of the NGOs were virtually held hostage within their own compounds. Aidid's men sold protection services for a price. Without payment, God only knew what might happen to them and their precious NGO compound. Because of the thugs, bullies, and organized criminals that roamed the city at will, it was tough just trying to help the average Somali.

During our search, we also came face-to-face with the horrors of this city of despair. The smell from the crap on our boots mingled with outdoor cooking odors, the smell of khat reefers smoked by the hundreds, and the stench of refuse just laying around in heaps where neighborhoods had tried to dispose of it in some orderly fashion.

For the first time, we finally saw the insides of a Somali mobiflex, the twig domes covered in green plastic where the utterly destitute lived. These were putrid dwellings in which skeletal mothers and babies sat in their own waste while flies eagerly fed upon the limp, saggy flesh of their bodies. Disease was everywhere, and you were glad for the gamma globulin shot you received before you came. These people were living our worst nightmares, yet continued to survive. After seeing them and calling medics to help where they could, we realized why we were in Somalia.

After a few short hours, we finished with the mission, consolidated on the objective end-line, and prepared for the tactical road march that would return us to the Complex. The mission was a success. No shots had been fired by either side, a hoard of weapons had been found, valuable intel was gathered, some men were detained for further questioning, and we had helped a few very desperate people who needed it. As usual, we also made friends with the local kids as wary parents looked scornfully in our direction. This was to be the trend whenever we conducted a cordon-and-search. Each mission finished with too few people helped and the eyes of the populace burning holes in us as we humped back, tired and sweat-soaked, to the shelter of the Complex during the heat of the day, finally to be mortared at night. Ahhh, the joys of real-world ops.

With our first mission accomplished, a few pats on the back for a job well done, and a steadily growing confidence, we began hearing rumors about the perpetrators of the 8 August murder of the four MPs. In a few short days, the rumors became reality. The commanders were sworn to secrecy to protect the knowledge that we even knew where the perps lived. It felt like we were being spoon-fed information at first, but then the orders came to report to Jaybird LZ for a recon of the objective area.

I arrived with Colonel David, the S-3, and the other commanders. As we approached the Black Hawk, two civilians, one male, the other female, were introduced to us. They were either CIA or Defense Intelligence

Agency (DIA) operatives, and the woman was bad to the bone. She was perfectly fit and beautiful, but in that assassin sort of way, somebody right out of James Bond, lethal and cold to a fault. She sat next to me by the open door and carried an MP5 submachine gun for protection. The guy had the gadgets and digital camera. We crammed into the Hawk, spun up, and lifted off Jaybird, accompanied by the usual sandstorm as we arched up into the bright blue sky and out of the stench.

We circled the city a few times so we didn't just make a beeline to the objective area and tip off the criminal element. Our attention was directed to a small white house with a green entry gate surrounding a courtyard. The house with the green door, as it would be called from now on, was nothing special, just another house in a sprawling packed neighborhood. Because it was located just northwest of the Airfield Complex, we immediately saw that we could easily slip out one of the Egyptian guard points and be almost in their backyard. Digital pictures were taken (a true phenomenon at that time), and timing and approach routes were discussed over the intercom. After the recon, we headed back for the formal planning of my first real raid, but with a twist: Nobody dies.

We planned it like a cordon-and-search. This one, however, would have a loose outer cordon to control traffic in the area at key selected ingress and egress points; a second, tighter inner cordon with men spaced within sight of each other whose orders were to let no one out; and a capture element. As we worked out the details, we all wondered who the element leaders would be.

Tiger Company was tapped to conduct the tricky portion of the mission: the capture. The Alpha Company Terminators would be the inner cordon and Bravo Company's Bastards would be the outer cordon. The Antitank (AT) Platoon of Headquarters and Headquarters Company (HHC), whose HMMWVs were equipped with Mark-19 40mm automatic grenade launchers and M-60 machine guns mounted in cupolas in the roof, would fill in at the intersections and control major traffic in and out of the area. They would also be an awesome firepower and maneuver force in the event the shit hit the fan.

That little house in an unassuming neighborhood halfway around the world became the battalion's focus and our life's work for the next few

days. The route in, actions at the objective, and exfiltration were repeatedly gone over in very close detail. By the night of 15 August, Tiger Company was thoroughly prepared to clear Objective Justice, the operational
name for the house and its occupants.

Planning and rehearsal had gone very smoothly. This was our first big
operation where things might go sour and result in the taking or inflicting
of casualties. Decisions during the planning process had to be thorough,
correct, just, and within the ROE.

As a company commander, I had been to the Advanced Course, where
tactics and decision-making are pounded into you for six months. On the
other hand, I was in this situation with some well-trained but very fresh
lieutenants with little time in the Army and far fewer experiences than me.
As a group of officers, we only had our training to fall back on. I realized
that we had theoretical knowledge but little practical experience. If I was
going to take care of my soldiers—and I mean really plan with their best
interests in mind—I would have to find a resource of experience to balance
the officers' knowledge.

That resource is the Noncommissioned Officer (NCO) Corps—an
Army-wide treasure. A great many of my senior NCOs already had combat
patches from Grenada, Panama, or Desert Storm. As a group, most of them
had been there, saw the sights and sounds, and knew what the men would
tend to do when lives were at stake.

My senior NCOs knew the rudimentary process of planning as officers
expected and many were skilled decision makers. The system preached that
the officers do the planning and the NCOs provide valuable input. In
truth, however, NCOs are often left out of the loop and rarely get to con-
tribute their valuable experience to the planning process itself. A company
commander and his lieutenants usually come up with the main plan, which
the NCOs must then implement at platoon and squad levels. The NCOs
sometimes feel that the plan has been jammed down their throats and must
be followed without voicing concerns. After all, who wants to change the
whole company plan, even if a major flaw is found in it?

The likelihood of the company just taking the officers' plan for
granted, right or wrong, is usually very high. The system works in the
training environment, where teaching lieutenants how to plan is the main

concern. On-the-job training that typically consists of learning by osmosis or from your mistakes that you try not to repeat is the training tool in the Officer Corps. But one mistake in Somalia could cost a life.

After some serious thought and balancing my need to train the officers with the lives of my men, I made a decision that really irked the lieutenants, new to the game as they were: I planned the Green Door operation (and, subsequently, all operations) with my platoon sergeants and the first sergeant. Initially, this caused quite a bit of animosity between my officers and me, but after just one mission they saw the wisdom of the decision and why the new process worked.

And why did it work? First, as previously mentioned, there was the experience issue. Second, the NCOs were amazed that I would trust them with the task. And third—and most importantly—when the plan was finished, I wasn't going to hear any growling in the ranks about the stupid plan that the officers had come up with. The NCOs had helped make the plan, agreed to it, knew it before they left my office, not second-hand from the lieutenants, and would back me 100 percent when I issued orders. They also had a vested interest in making it work. It was, after all, their plan!

It also gave me the opportunity to explain in a nearly one-on-one session with my platoon leaders how we (the NCOs and I) had come up with the plan and why certain decisions were made. In effect, it allowed me to pass on NCO wisdom without demeaning the lieutenants.

While the NCOs were briefing the squad and team leaders and preparing for inspections and rehearsals, I briefed the officers. OPORDs were still given by the lieutenants, but their focus was now on the execution portion (i.e., how they were going to make the plan work instead of just making the plan).

In 20/20 hindsight, I believe this was one of the best decisions I made in Mogadishu. Instead of the usual method of getting the NCOs' input (i.e., ask a question or two, then do what you were going to do anyway), I made it clear that I trusted the men who would actually conduct the mission on the ground. They were not only very serious about the planning process, but were also genuinely appreciative that I gave them the opportunity to use their experience and talent to the benefit of all.

Getting back to the task at hand, at 2000 hours we began moving to the Mogadishu airport, the HMMWVs and 5-tons proceeding along MSR Tiger, a route we would take so many times throughout our deployment. Being right in the middle of the city, and with its northern perimeter fence only a few hundred meters from the target house, the airport was the natural launching point for the Green Door operation. The battalion staggered company and sub-element movements by time so that we wouldn't raise suspicion in the city. Eyes-Over-Mogadishu birds (AH-1 Cobra gunships and OH-58 Kiowa scout helicopters) watched over us on our route, *whop-whop-whopping* their way in lazy circles through the darkening African sky with an awesome array of support on hand, if required. Also along the route, multiple Black Hawk helicopters carried the usual two snipers armed with Barrett .50-cal and M-24 7.62mm rifles to engage lawbreakers who decided to carry crew-served weapons in the open.

After a two-hour movement, a linkup under the airport terminal, and one last talk-through rehearsal, the battalion started out on foot, heading for an Egyptian guard post at the northern end of the airport. The HMMWVs would follow after the dismounted troops were in place, racing to their assigned locations to seal the perimeter from through traffic.

We began trudging along the inner perimeter road, heading north inside the airport compound, drifting in and out of the eerie shadows caused by the high-intensity lighting on the wall, coiled razor wire, and rolling terrain. One foot after the other while keeping your thoughts intact, going over the plan as you march. Remembering call signs, signals, code words, and navigation points. Breathing heavy, with the blood hammering in your head throughout the initial movement. Loaded down with flak jacket, LBE, helmet, NVGs, and weapons, moving at a brisk pace sped by adrenaline and the need to quickly get the operation underway.

Sweat trickled down the insides of our helmets. The refreshing salt air breeze blowing in from the Indian Ocean could not cool the anxious minds, tensed muscles, or the rising heat that is peculiar to soldiers who are about to engage in a life-and-death situation.

Many of us felt that we were on our way to avenge a loss that was totally uncalled for. We were right in going to rip these people from their house in the middle of the night. I'm sure that they felt they had gotten away with murder and no one would ever come for them. Their world and ours were about to collide in just about as startling and uncompromising a fashion as the one their command-detonated mine visited on the unfortunate MPs. If caught and sentenced, the murderers would be sent to a living hell, an island prison just north of Madagascar.

The lead element reached the Egyptian guard post at the northwest corner of the airport compound and, after a brief linkup with the sentries and our liaison officers, the giant metal gates were opened and the battalion task force slithered out into the city.

As we passed through the gate and into the bright, moonlit landscape, I felt naked. Crossing the no man's land just outside the perimeter wall brought visions of WWI and being machine-gunned in the open. Waiting for the burst that never came heightened my senses to a razor's edge. Finally reaching the comfort of the shadows and the sides of buildings, I was fine-tuned to the plan and its particular details.

Tiger Company and the rest of the battalion closed on the objective rapidly. Even at a stealthy pace, moving in and out of the shadows, we seemed to be moving incredibly fast.

According to the plan, we would turn off the main street and veer into the blackness of the tightly packed houses, knifing straight to the small walled compound with the green door that was our objective.

Having learned my lesson during our movement to AO NEVADA, I was very close to the front of the company formation, right behind the lead squad. As if to validate my being there, the lead squad missed an infrared chemlight that marked our turn and I spotted it, made a quick correction that didn't even slow the advance of the company, and guided the lead platoon in the right direction.

Traveling at night in an unfamiliar city, no lights, no street signs, and having to lead a whole battalion to its objective can be an enormous task for a young sergeant trying to see the enemy before he sees you. With a few grunts and hand signals we were back on track and heading straight for the objective house.

In my night vision goggles, the green and black phosphorescent shapes of each building gleamed before my eyes. Being with the lead squad, I saw the familiar shape of our target house. I immediately halted the company and, after lifting my NVGs for an eyes-on look, saw that we were very close to the objective.

The small streets of Mogadishu were more like cart paths. I had begun to count them as we entered the neighborhood, and they had ticked off very fast. Seeing that we were within hand-grenade range of our objective, I got everyone out of the street, then began signaling each platoon to deploy. Second Platoon went left and Third went right in overwatch, and First waited in the shadows behind Third as the capture team. In just under five minutes, the company was ready to take the perps out.

As the platoons moved into position, I called the BC and informed him that we were moving into position due to our close proximity. I made the call to move before being ordered to because if we were discovered just hunkered down in the street and out of position, we would lose the element of surprise and give the enemy the chance to escape.

Colonel David approved and quickly joined my company head-quarters, stealthily moving among the night shadows. He also set the rest of the plan into motion, calling the Terminators in to seal all the houses surrounding the target house and the Bastards to throw the cordon around the whole neighborhood. In less than fifteen minutes the target area was shut down. No one was allowed out of their houses or to even look out of their windows, soldiers occupied the streets, and HMMWVs held all intersections.

After the organized frenzy of just getting into position, the absolute silence of the night crept in again. Moonlight hugged the small East African neighborhood as we kept to the safety of the shadows. As if taking a deep breath, the battalion waited for what would happen next. The plan had been executed perfectly so far. Movement and setup were accom-plished, and the perpetrators of the four MP deaths lay snug in their beds with no knowledge of our presence. With a few words over his hand mic, Colonel David was about to change all that.

As we sweated in our squatting, kneeling, or hunkered-down posi-tions, making unbearable noises so imperceptible, except to the maker, we heard the approach of the psychological operations (PsyOps) aircraft, a loudspeaker-equipped UH-60 Black Hawk. The low thumping of its blades grew louder and the air began to stir around us.

In the time it took to depress an on switch, the night air came alive with the blaring sound of raspy Somali being screamed into the air from the loudspeakers, telling the people in the house to come out with their hands raised, that we would not harm them, and that they were totally surrounded and had no chance of escape.

To our horror, the downdraft of the rotor blades started picking up pieces of corrugated tin roofing from the houses and tossing them in all directions around our perimeter. As the neighborhood awoke, people tried to get a look out their windows or leave their houses altogether. Alpha Company made a superhuman effort to contain the neighborhood as the BC started shouting to get the chopper out of there. We couldn't hear a damn thing as the debris cloud caused by the helicopter swirled around us. Murphy had struck again.

In the once absolutely quiet neighborhood that was now near bedlam, it was our job to stay calm, get the perps out of the house, and arrest them without killing anyone. Acting quickly, I sent a team from 3rd Platoon to bang on the green gate to see if we could talk the people out of the house using the platoon interpreter. Everyone was extremely edgy, their fingers on triggers. I expected that, with our cover blown and the element of surprise gone, the perps would fight it out from inside the house and we would have to root them out, or that they would make a run for it. Instead, they did the unexpected by coming out into the courtyard between their house and the gate and surrendering.

We still had no idea how many people we were looking for, so when they came closer to the gate and unlocked it, we expected an ambush. My Third Platoon snipers, positioned in overwatch positions of the gate, were told to drop anyone reaching for a weapon, taking aim to immobilize, not kill.

The capture team was ready when the gate opened. Our interpreter told them to come out one at a time. Nearly in a panic, they all came at once. As the group came out, I realized that these were not all men, but women and children, too.

The capture team began gathering and segregating the captured household when one of the worst possible things happened. One of the women dropped her hands and reached deeply into her dress. For a brief instant,

I knew she was going to die. My head screamed NO so loud as I watched what she was doing that I can still hear myself today. The vision in my PVS-7s NVG was just not supposed to be there. The interpreter told her to freeze in Somali while about thirty American voices shouted the same phrase in English. Thankfully, the woman froze in her steps, although still grabbing for what we subsequently found out was a newborn baby she had placed in a wrapping around her mid-section. The interpreter and the common sense of my snipers saved her life.

The actual taking of the prisoners included securing them, which was done with white plastic zip strips; searching them for weapons or anything that might identify them or be of some use later in the investigation; segregating and safeguarding them; and speeding them to the rear in trucks that were waiting for each group. Although it seemed like hours to me, in actuality, just fifteen minutes had elapsed from the initial loudspeaker announcements to the removal of the house's occupants from the compound.

What came next, after all of the excitement of the surrender, was the clearing of the house with the green door. We did not have an accurate number or description of all of the perpetrators. We just knew that they were there, and that it was likely that weapons, documents, or other evidence that might later convict the terrorists in a fair trial were in the house. Thus, we had planned all along to clear the house no matter what happened.

But it was very important to us that we not be perceived as bullying, thuggish Americans just running around Mogadishu doing whatever we pleased. To this point we had done everything by the book and the mission to extract the occupants of the house was a success.

Not knowing if the house was really clear, I radioed 2nd Platoon and told 2nd Lieutenant Ryan to continue the mission. They were to blow an access hole in the back of the house, enter, and clear every inch of the structure. They had been shown how to turn a window into a door by modifying a standard engineer concertina picket, packing it with 4 pounds of Composition C-4 explosives, laying the device against the window, and lighting the fuse. A few seconds later, the ensuing destruction of the bottom of the window created a door.

When the rock, debris, and dust settled, the first squad fired CS riot control agent into the house and went in with protective masks on, the second squad following closely behind. I watched them disappear into the swirling gas cloud and said a silent prayer for the men and their skills as infantrymen. I heard the intermittent muffled shouts of "Clear, clear" as the men swept through the small structure.

Over my radio, I heard the final "All clear" and didn't have to remind them to begin gathering everything that would be of intelligence use. The systematic search of the house yielded a trunk and three suitcases worth of intel for the interpreters and S-2 types to sort through. We would get word as to the value of the contents at a later time.

By the time we were finished with the house with the green door, the sun was fully up in the sky. As the operation began to shut down, the little house on a dirt street in a city halfway around the world was now no more significant than any other house in the neighborhood.

From our standpoint, the mission was a success, even if the locals were pissed that we had blown a hole in the back of the house. My men's lives were far more important than some structure that could be rebuilt. Hell, we wouldn't even have been in this part of town if they hadn't killed our MPs.

As we began disengaging from the neighborhood, we made sure that the battalion kept control of the situation. Bravo Company held the outer cordon as first Alpha and then Charlie exfiltrated to Via Afgoya, the main artery leading back to the airfield. When we reached the open air of the city, the disciplined squads of each company spread out to present the smallest target while covering the most ground in the now sunlit terrain leading back to the shelter of the airfield perimeter. The moonscape of the night before was now just churned-up dirt and refuse thrown into the vacant area we traversed. The exfiltration was a little tense as we waited for retribution from an unseen enemy that never materialized.

We entered the Egyptian checkpoint exhilarated by our success. A dangerous mission that could have turned very bad at any point had been accomplished to perfection. The first actual battalion mission that dealt with life and death had come together as a plan, had been executed as planned, and had shown us that we could trust one another. It was a great rehearsal for what was still to come.

In my HMMWV on the way back to the Complex, in the swirling dust of the coastal road, I thought about the events that were shaping up.

The Tigers were becoming the go-to company. Slowly but surely, Colonel David was beginning to trust that my men and I could be trusted to make things happen. The sense of more to come was overwhelming. An escalation of hostile activity was very apparent to me, and I wondered if the others sensed it, too. And while I was absolutely jubilant about pulling off the mission, we still wanted to know if we had gotten all of the perpetrators, what would happen to them, and what treasures the contents of the suitcases and trunk held.

It would take the better portion of the day and the next to find out that we had captured two of the three actual detonators of the mine, one of them a militia brigade commander, and had seized enough intel to back up our claims in international court. Until their trial, the Somali men would be held in the jail on the University Compound just down from 42nd Support Group and be guarded by Bangladeshis who were, from what I had heard, rather inhospitable hosts.

The next day the battalion's euphoria was dampened severely when our short-lived success as a QRF in the offensive mode came to an abrupt halt. Almost like a slap in the face, the battalion's next order from our higher command was to guard MSR Tiger, the new main supply route that skirted the city to the south. In a three-day rotation, we would serve as the QRC, then as a support element, and then guard the MSR out in the African Bush. We went from quasi-Special Ops to the lowest of infantry missions in the blink of an eye. To make matters worse, rumors were surfacing that the Rangers or maybe even Delta were coming in to get Aidid. Although they were only rumors, they still bumped up against our professional pride. As we saw it, what on earth did we need them for anyway? Hadn't we just pulled off a totally successful raid?

The grumbling in the ranks necessitated a formation, at which I told the company that I didn't care what the mission was, we were going to be the best at it. The standard for the fighting positions would be high, and I wanted every bit of the NCOs' experience brought to bear.

I had to give the men a new focus and put a positive spin on the mission. This was actually a tougher task than it originally appeared, for while the entire MSR should have been covered by a battalion, it would only be occupied by a company with a mobile reserve. We had to figure out how to make that a reality.

Frankly, I wanted to get away from the Complex and its nightly fireworks just to break the monotony of the daily routine. I liked planning and executing missions, but thought that some time in the field would almost feel like R & R for the soul. I also wanted to check out the camels and goats and those that herded them. Still an anthropologist at heart—I had graduated with a cultural anthropology degree from the University of Alabama and was now getting to use my degree for the first time in my career—the idea of being out with the average Somali citizen sounded good to me. And besides, a little hard work never hurt anyone.

CHAPTER 5

Out in Africa

On 22 August 1993, the battalion formally began providing a secure route around the city. MSR Tiger started as a barren, undefended tract leading to and from the Coast Road. Eventually, it became the main route into and out of all of the U.S. compounds. From the Airport Checkpoint, guarded by the Egyptian Contingent, you turned immediately south and continued past a horrific refuse dump and the power plant, and then turned west at the refinery about 5 miles from the edge of the city. From there you worked your way through dune country and continued through about 10 miles of barren, thorn bush desert scrub before finally turning back north and going down a steep hill to enter the city's underbelly about a mile away, near Hunter Base.

Our new mission, to guard the MSR bypass around Mogadishu, was a shock to the system. We went from the relative luxury of the Complex to the hostile environment of the African bush, with its searing heat, blowing clouds of churned-up talcum powder-like vehicle dust, thorn trees and bushes, camels, goats, bugs, and Somali nomads.

Guard duty in the African bush was the farthest thing from our minds, even when we were driving toward the inevitable. We knew it would be hot, gritty, and physically demanding. Each platoon and the headquarters would have a position to create and defend. Interlocking fires and pre-planned artillery support would be nonexistent. Again, the book went out the window.

MSR Tiger itself was graded, hard-packed dirt that needed a battalion of about 600 men to be adequately secured. It would certainly be a challenge to do so with a 150-man company. When the Indians came later in October to become part of UNOSOM, they used a mechanized battalion with tank support. We were going to create, in essence, three small outposts and a mini-fire base, with a roving HMMWV reaction force to respond to any hostile action. Any one of the elements, whether ground or the roving QRF, would be hard-pressed by any concerted effort by an enemy force.

Each company of the battalion rotated through the same cycle of three days of guarding the MSR, three days of providing support, and three days of being the QRC. We were first in the barrel to guard. No company wanted to be the first, but I decided to set the example, even though we already hated the guard-duty mission.

On the first day, the company convoy broke out of the city just beyond Hunter Base and began dropping off each platoon and section that would guard a particular location. Each platoon leader had my command guidance, which was to build the best possible position to defend from any direction, develop a communication network, create a sleeping area, and be able to stop any traffic on the road that was not authorized by use of deadly force, if necessary. With that guidance, my lieutenants were given as much Class 4 supplies (building materials) as I could give them and were left to develop their areas of responsibility.

When the headquarters element turned off the MSR and headed into the bush for the first time, it was like landing on another planet. As the engines shut down and we stepped into our new environment, the heat sank in and sweat immediately began dripping. Insects, both crawling and flying, turned our way as if sensing new meat. Even the camels and goats were curious enough to mosey over to our new position.

The first order of business was to secure our turf. We began by running triple-strand concertina around the perimeter to keep the two- and four-legged creatures out. Individual fighting positions, mortar pits, and the command bunker were marked and measured—and then the fun began.

Command bunkers in the movies or on TV just always seem to be there. Although I had yet to see one in the field during infantry training, I had seen the massive, fixed concrete bunkers at Fort Benning. But no field bunkers. My two RTOs, the commo sergeant, and I would be moving dirt, filling sandbags, building overhead cover, creating concealment, and clearing fields of fire for almost the entire three days of our first rotation to the bush. When the fields of fire (lanes of interlocking death arranged to allow engagement of any approaching enemy) were marked and cleared, we stripped down to T-shirts, laid our LBE and weapons close by, and went to work churning the soil to load sandbags.

After hours of filling the bags, we still had to stack them to create firing positions, a commo platform, and a sleeping area, all with grenade sumps (holes at an angle in the floor of the bunker to hastily push grenades into in the event of attack). We wrapped it all up by placing the overhead cover and camouflage to conceal as much of the position as possible.

In retrospect, the African bush was not all hand-ripping, bone-jarring digging or back-breaking effort. In between bouts of hard labor, each element took turns reconning the area. The headquarters element had the luxury of our HMMWVs, and we began checking on the rest of the company. Each wilderness outpost started small, but quickly grew from nothing into a defendable fighting position/checkpoint. Of course, since we had the mobility, we began to search out possible enemy avenues of approach. It was on one of these scouting missions that we met our favorite little Somali girl and began our first real bartering sessions.

When bartering with a professional, like, say a small girl in an arid wasteland, keep your wits about you and find out what you can do to help. I learned from that little girl that the greatest gift you can give a child is a pen and some paper. Art, fantasy, writing, communication, expression, and pride can all be found in those two simple articles that we take for granted. Once I discovered this, I never went back without pen and paper to trade for shiny stones, flowers, or other little trinkets that meant something dear to her. Any possession being a treasure in the desert, I figured I was trading treasure for treasure with my African friend.

The first three days in the African bush consisted of hard physical work and adjusting to being in the field again. There was also a sense of urgency to create positions that would literally save our lives, if necessary. Adventure played little part in that first rotation and, when Alpha Company relieved us in place after our three days, it truly was a relief. We were tired, and the lukewarm, Mermited chow (named for the metal containers in which food was brought from the mess hall at the Complex that started out piping hot but typically arrived 1 degree or so above tepid) had taken its toll.

Six days later, when we returned for our next rotation at the head-quarters site, we were mentally prepared for the grueling conditions. What we were not prepared for, though, was finding that Bravo Company had left early without waiting for us to arrive, which allowed the Somali nomads to tear the positions apart to get the plywood, wire, sandbags, and anything else they could carry off.

We had to start over. With typical curse-filled infantry bitching, we called for more Class 4 and began again. Needless to say, it was not a pleasant first night back. Having to do the same work a second time takes resilience, and when you grit your teeth, succeed again, and meet the same high standard, a certain sense of accomplishment manifests itself within you.

After all the hard work, that night afforded me the opportunity to lay on my back and notice, for the first time since my arrival, the awesome view of every star formation known to mankind; to literally feel the silence, smell the breeze, and realize that I was living through something others could only imagine.

In the dark, as I looked closer at the sleeping forms of Randall and Als-brooks, my RTOs, and at Sergeant Sides, my commo NCO, on guard duty, I realized how much I cared for them. We had discussed hopes and dreams, shared jokes and laughter, and were comrades-in-arms. I knew in my heart that I had to get them home. I also felt the tug of the inevitable. Oh, how we wanted to make a difference, like a prizefighter waiting for the big fight. While we had proven ourselves on "The Raid," not a shot had been fired. For most of us, the event had been anticlimactic.

This was to be the hardest period for all of us, the waiting, knowing that something was going to happen, but having to sit and guard the MSR. During the next couple of rotations, Alpha seemed to be getting all the action, good and bad. They nailed a taxi that ran a roadblock, and somehow shot a Somali donkey pulling "contraband." Both Bravo and Charlie Companies felt bad for Alpha, all the while thanking God that it wasn't us out there making a mistake.

In all battalions, there is rivalry between companies. Some is healthy, as in our case; in others, it can be quite destructive. Imagine if a fellow company wouldn't stand and fight with you when you really need them because they didn't trust you. In the 2-14, we were intensely competitive, but we always had each other's backs.

After a couple of guard rotations, the battalion felt a little rusty and wanted some action again. We were tired of doing relatively nothing in the bush, firing the occasional mortar illumination mission and preparing for attacks that never came, while at the same time hating the fact that we just had to sit through the nightly mortar attacks and firefights when we were back for the QRC and support missions. The daily drudgery was starting to set in.

Colonel David sensed the battalion's unease and had us start planning missions. At our nightly meeting/briefing, when we were back from the bush, we constantly brainstormed contingencies that we began executing. Getting proactive raised morale and set us all on the right course.

We all knew that any real mission was based on the rotation cycle, the luck of the draw. It was really hard on Charlie Company, and particularly me, when we had to listen to Alpha Company one night as they did the first night raid into a Somali compound, searching for the mortar crews that were attacking us every night. We were all glued to the radio listening to the mission unfold. As it turned out, the mission went clean; no casualties, but no mortars, either. We all wanted to be there and it stung that we weren't. And we still had to finish our time on the MSR. Soon enough, though, it would be our turn as the QRC, and missions were in the hopper, ready for a GO.

A beautiful and remarkable thing happened the next night. Unexpectedly, the chaplain pulled into our little headquarters perimeter and asked if any of us wanted to take Communion. I was taken aback. YES, was the first thing out of my mouth; *how* was the first thing that entered my mind.

After sending one soldier into the night to rouse and ask everyone, I was surprised to find that in mere moments, all had joined us. In the black of night, under the glow of blue chemlights, I watched as the chaplain unrolled the precious sacraments from their velvet keeps, placed them on the hood of his HMMWV, and began the ceremony that would touch our hearts in a time of true need. I know there were tears and feelings of ultimate joy in the darkness that night, but best of all was the sense of being Christian soldiers in that faraway land, trying to do some good.

This became one of my dearest memories. I often wonder if all my men up and down the Coast Road took Communion that night, and if it made a difference in the weeks to come. All I know is that the chaplain had a huge effect on me that night, and, most important of all, I felt blessed.

CHAPTER 6

The Rangers Are Coming, the Rangers Are Coming

The rumors turned out to be true. A Ranger contingent, B/3-75; Special Ops Air Regiment (SOAR) Task Force 160; and a Delta Force team, the best of all the U.S. Military Services, arrived in Mogadishu on 26 August 1993.

From the outset, the Special Ops' arrival was tumultuous. You couldn't hide the arrival of so large a contingent, let alone when they came with the larger Special Ops MH-60 Black Hawks, AH-6, Little Birds, and black-clad, body-armored soldiers. The Somalis couldn't help but know the new arrivals were special when these "different" soldiers didn't come out to join the rest of the Americans, but instead stayed at the airport in the only large building available, The Hangar.

Our initial reaction was, honestly, professional jealousy. Why were they called in? Hadn't we done a good enough job during "The Raid"? Why weren't *we* allowed to get Aidid? We knew that was their mission. They were going to be allowed to steal our thunder, and possibly our Combat Infantryman Badges, which really matter to an infantryman. We hadn't come here to do guard duty.

The Special Ops Task Force was sent to capture Aidid, not kill him. Delta operatives are the experts at capturing, rescuing, and eliminating, if necessary, human and system targets. The Rangers were there as Delta Land Support, and TF160, The Night Stalkers, provided air support with the best in helicopter technology and aviators. We were outgunned, but certainly didn't feel outclassed.

Aidid, known as Elvis (his code name) to all of us, was the "Bad Guy," the warlord who was causing all of the problems in this destroyed, once proud and beautiful coastal city. Why he had to be captured was beyond all of us. It seemed absurd in the situation we were all living in that anyone cared what happened to one warlord or another. In our view, the city needed to be rid of him and his bloodthirsty, raping, pillaging, murdering thugs. And that meant going after the Enclave (the hornet's nest of the Bakara Market) and the hospitals (Digfer and Banadir) in force, not surgical strikes at individuals. Cleaning up the city, in our minds, meant taking down the warlord's infrastructure with overwhelming combined arms assaults.

With the arrival of the Special Operations team, the city was teeming with firepower and the institutional knowledge of combat. Aidid's forces, guerilla fighters hardened by years of experience in the Somali Civil War, were far more organized and numerous than we thought. A realistic estimate of more than 8,000 armed Somali "soldiers" awaited the combined U.N. forces in the city.

U.N. combat forces numbered around 15,000, including the QRF (our battalion of approximately 650 light infantrymen), Malaysians, Bangladeshis, Tunisians, Egyptians, and a Pakistani division. The Special Operations Forces, which were not under U.N. command, totaled fewer than 500 combatants and support personnel.

On both sides, the typical ground combatants carried a variety of personal small arms weapons and ammunition types. These included numerous variations of Russian-, European-, and U.S.-made assault rifles, machine guns, grenade launchers, pistols, and grenades. Aidid's forces carried anything that they could get their hands on, most often AK-47 assault rifles and RPG-7 RPGs. The QRF members, depending on leadership or squad position, carried a variety of standard M-16A2 rifles, M-249 squad automatic weapons (SAWs), M-60 machine guns ("The Pig"), M-203 grenade launchers, and M-9 Beretta pistols. Each man in my company typically carried three basic loads of ammo (630 rounds) for the M-16, grenades (antipersonnel, smoke, flash bangs, and CS), a Rambo knife, 4 quarts of water, a butt-pack full of personal items, and a first aid kit. Of course, they also carried extra bandoleers for the M-60s and SAWs, a PVS-7 night observation device (NOD), and, if they were a leader, a small PRC-26 radio. In addition to the above basic load, I also carried nine Berretta fifteen-round magazines that never left my side.

Delta and the Rangers have their choice of weapons and equipment from around the world, and some are pretty exotic. The Barrett .50-caliber sniper rifles, M-4 assault rifles, MP-3/4 submachine guns, Glocks, lasers, the finest NODs, ceramic-plate flak jackets, fast ropes—you name it, they've got it. Add to that the Little Birds equipped with the M-134 minigun that is synched to rockets, the miniguns in the doors of the Black Hawks, and the helicopters are being flown by the best pilots in Army Aviation, and you seemingly have an unbeatable team, literally David vs. Goliath.

A word about the minigun: This is a very serious weapon. The M-134 is a 7.62mm, 6-barreled machine gun with a high rate of fire (2,000 to 6,000 rounds per minute). Essentially, it's an electric Gatling gun. Just knowing they are in the area is a comfort, and woe to the bad guy foolish enough to irritate an M-134 gunner.

I would be remiss if I didn't mention the 10th Mountain Division's Aviation Brigade. They happened to not only be our higher headquarters; their AH-1 Cobras also pulled our butts out of the fire a couple of times during the deployment. The Aviation Brigade's Black Hawks also conducted the Eyes Over Mogadishu mission. This entailed flying over the city 24/7/365, enforcing the no crew-served weapons mandate that stated no one could legally carry a machine gun, rocket launcher, or mortar. The 10th Aviation helicopters carried two snipers, one armed with the Barrett and one with the M-24 sniper system that could acquire and blow the head off a target from well over 1,000 yards.

These missions were somewhat effective and kept the city under near-constant observation from the third dimension, truly death from above for anyone willing to break the U.N. rules. As we would learn, however, these missions were not immune to ground fire and were far from safe. As in all recent modern conflicts, many thanks also go out to the MEDEVAC pilots and their birds, not of prey but of care.

At the end of August and the beginning of September, the air simply crackled with the anticipation of a big fight brewing. The Somalis began to venture out nightly against each other's clans. Meetings and rumors of meetings caused everyone to conjure up the worst. Aidid was in hiding and was going to have to be rooted out. Delta and the Ranger contingent began to train in earnest just south of the city along the coast of the Indian Ocean. The SOAR Black Birds began to fly the full length of the city on long orientation and reconnaissance flights. The Special Ops ground contingent regularly prowled around the city, their long, heavily armed convoys snaking unmolested around the outskirts and along MSR Tiger.

No one in their right mind ventured into the Bakara Market area during the day, at least not in a wheeled convoy. The Rangers never really got on the ground and did a cordon-and-search operation in the city, as we had. We knew the people, knew the abundance of weapons, and knew the Somalis were a force to be reckoned with, far better organized and much larger than the intel reports described.

Everyone else in the city also knew of the Rangers' presence. It's definitely not a good thing when everyone knows you're there and can see when you come and go. Near-nightly mortar attacks aimed at the Special Ops hangar at the airport, targeted from day one, confirmed that fact.

The QRF, sequestered on the Complex and guarding MSR Tiger, was fit to be tied. We wanted a piece of the action. Everyone knew that the Rangers would soon stop training, acclimating, and orienting themselves. The Rangers had a mission, and we needed one.

So, when I was informed one night at a battalion meeting that the QRC would begin looking for the mortar crews that were launching into the Complex and the airport, we were fired up. We had been into the city; we knew our business; we hated the mortars; and now we were tasked to stop the nightly harassment. Man, were we ever ready!

Colonel David described his commander's intent. We would begin looking for suspected mortar firing sites and any residue of recent actions at these points. Any ammo crates, tubes, mortar plate impressions, or pieces of a mortar would be immediately suspect and individuals would be detained for questioning. Two circles were drawn on the planning map indicating the maximum ranges for both the 120mm and the 82mm mortars. These were the two most likely sizes and types of mortars being thrown our way. Dozens of fins from exploded mortars had been found and confirmed within the Complex. We would start in territory we already knew and work from the farthest point back to the Complex. Active patrolling would put the enemy mortar crews on the defensive for the first time and eventually they would make a mistake. All missions to find the mortars would be dismounted, putting us up close and personal with the populace.

First in the barrel was Alpha Company. Charlie was on the support mission in the Complex, ready to back up any contingency if Alpha couldn't conduct its normal QRF mission. Bravo would guard the MSR.

The first nine-day cycle after the Rangers arrived was peaceful enough. Each company conducted a patrol downtown, then back through area adjacent to the Complex, and ultimately out to the MSR.

Charlie's mission went well. We left just after noon and cordoned off a section of the downtown area that was filled with junked cars and had lots of nooks and crannies that were ideal for hiding a mortar. The dismounted trek through the city's side streets drew attention from our Somali neighbors. The Tigers left in broad daylight and snaked our way to the objective area. This was intentional, as we wanted our presence known. When the locals knew we were actively looking for something, they usually kept to themselves.

Leaving in the midday heat meant that sweat just poured off our bodies and drenched our uniforms. When the excitement of actually leaving the Complex in the open wore off and the search for whatever could kill us began, reality set in. I was amazed at how naked I felt, even with close to 100 pounds of gear, weapons, and ammunition draped on my body.

As the hard-core grunt work began, all the training and practice paid off. Alert as ever, the company made its way through the city, navigated to the correct location, spread the cordon out around the target compound, and, after a very brief "May we check your property," went in.

The command and support element remained at the compound gate, the only way in or out, and received reports from the interior of the search site. Although we had been in and around this junkyard before on an earlier cordon-and-search of Objective NEVADA, it was still an eerie feeling as I watched my men searching the labyrinth of crushed cars stacked four and five vehicles high.

Watching and listening as the squads advanced, their steady "Up," "Clear," and "Moving" calls kept the hand mike attached to my shoulder squawking reports of their success. The entire process reminded me of advancing through the military operations on urban terrain (MOUT) tire house, a replication of the lower floor of a building used for live-fire practice. Its high walls protected those outside and in, and its maze of tire walls filled with packed earth created the corridors and rooms of the "building." The benefits of the multiple day and night training iterations we had run through Fort Drum's tire house were evident as my soldiers smoothly executed this mission, validating the axiom that practice makes perfect.

A tap on my shoulder broke me from my reverie, and in a flash I stood face to face with a . . . news crew? What the hell? Surprised, and somewhat taken aback, I realized that I had been handed an opportunity. While most commanders would rather avoid having the news media along with them on a mission, living with a Navy journalist my whole life gave me a different perspective.

My father had taught me that a responsible reporter can give a truly unbiased account of events and create a historical record of your passing. The news media can also keep you honest and record the fact that you were doing everything right just as easily as it can record that you were doing everything wrong. The true dilemma in any combat situation is the fact that men and women will sometimes do the seemingly unthinkable to keep themselves and their buddies alive. And, of course, their actions can be caught on film for posterity, to either the amazement or detriment of those involved. As long as news crews are sensitive to the fact that war is hell for those fighting it, and that leaders must sometimes make life or death decisions in milliseconds, a truly symbiotic relationship between the media and servicemen can exist.

On the other hand, if the ugliness of combat is the only driving force for the story, a distrust of the media is fostered among those who *are* the story. Soldiers, sailors, airmen, and marines pay for the story with their blood, sweat, fear, courage, and often, in the years after, with the tears and pain of profound emotional difficulties. The news media records an event as history and a hot news item, but we soldiers live it, experience it, and are held responsible and accountable for it. If there is to be trust, it must be earned one case at a time.

In my case, the news crew from *Reuters* calmly and honestly asked if they could record the events of the day. After locking eyes with the reporter, we briefly discussed my rules, and I accepted his offer to record a portion of our lives. But my decision rested solely on the fact that I trusted my men more than I trusted him, and knew that my men would do things right whether a news crew was there or not.

An hour and twenty minutes later, Tiger Company had cleared the objective. The *Reuters* crew recorded us blowing the illegal ammunition we had found, including an old bazooka, some AK-47s, machine-gun rounds, and some explosives. Our search also produced a collection of AKs, RPGs, a G-3 variant, and some ancient weapons that, if used, would probably have been more of a hazard than a help.

When we questioned the owner of the garage, he told us that the weapons were for self-protection. Without delving too deeply into tactical nuances, I simply informed him that he was not allowed to have crew-served weapons. He accepted that and expressed happiness that we weren't going to arrest him, any members of his immediate family, or his workers.

During the mission, a crowd had gathered in the street, including a huge throng of kids. After the dark shadows and rust of the towering crushed-car maze, the street and its vibrant colors rushed us again. Our collective "Watch out, you could get killed" radar became active as the company began the march back up to the Complex.

It was late afternoon and the sun was beginning to go down. A cool breeze off the Indian Ocean pushed at our backs and stole the pungent smells away. With another mission accomplished, the company felt alive. Each step toward the Complex brought us closer to slaps on the back and "well dones" from our peers. We had found something, just not the mortar or its crew.

And, damn them, the nightly mortars still kept coming, not just into the Complex anymore, but also into the Ranger Hangar and other spots around the city. Even though the public didn't know it at the time, soldiers were being wounded almost nightly. Something had to be done. It wasn't just a mission anymore; it had turned into a vendetta.

A Q-36 counter-battery radar, capable of determining the gun location of incoming indirect fire, was brought in and placed at the airport. But it wasn't always there. One night we'd have a Q-36, and the next night we wouldn't. Obviously, we preferred having it, as its availability upped our odds of finding the mortar or mortars that were being fired and the QRC was ready.

The Q-36 works on the principal of a known point and the breaking of two planes, the outbound and inbound. Once you have the arch and the known points, you can triangulate and, with a little trigonometry, get an approximate location from which the rounds were fired. (Who said you'd never use math after high school or college?)

Jackpot! The next time rounds were fired, the QRC (Charlie Company) rolled out the front gate, heading for a grid location that put us somewhere on a line from the university to the K-4 Traffic Circle. To add a little flavor, it was dark and we happened to be experiencing the only rainstorm of our tour in Somalia. But what made this mission interesting was that we were proactively hunting using advanced technology and, for the first time, we had helicopters supporting the mission. The on-call birds were already in the air by the time we converged on the grid coordinate and found, of all things, an NGO compound. Damn!

To set the scene: The Rangers had been taking down compounds a lot like this one and, needless to say, getting into trouble because the compounds happened to be U.N. or Coalition facilities. I have to say that the intelligence they were going on was misleading and the buildings happened to all look the same in the dark. I also recalled avoiding similar embarrassment a few weeks earlier by noting a U.N. flag just prior to crossing the line of departure on a cordon-and-search operation.

Additionally, the press was absolutely hounding the Special Ops guys at the time, and it was a pretty touchy situation. There we were at the compound gate, with the Hawk hovering and the "sparkle" (a laser beam from the helicopter that could be seen in our NODs) pointing straight into the darkness behind the walls, with the aircraft's rotor wash whipping all around us. After the run from the trucks to the compound with our NODs on our heads, we all seemed to be surrounded by liquid green as the steam rose from us. (Night vision is a truly awesome advantage that helps us move quickly in the black of night.)

Urgency ate at us, and time was of the essence. But while we hated the bastards who were lobbing rounds at us, the fact that the target area was an NGO compound made me opt to forego standard infantry procedures and just knock. No tearing the gate off, no blowing a hole in the wall, no fast-rope insertion. I just knocked.

As it turned out, the terrified young Americans, a male and a female, who opened the door to let us in needed help. Their "Thank God, you're here" explanation described how the compound had been quickly commandeered for the attack and just as quickly vacated by the Somalis that launched the rounds. Our subsequent search did find a mortar baseplate imprint and the fresh markings of more than two men.

The occupants also explained that the NGO had paid Aidid's men front money for the "safety" of the compound. Taking advantage of the people who were there to help you is typical in the city's atmosphere of endemic corruption and no rules opportunism. Clearly, the warlords care nothing for their own people. Their only goal is taking care of themselves and the bands of thugs that ensure their power.

Still, the night wasn't a complete bust. We were getting closer and, in doing so, gained experience using the helicopter's sparkle capability. It's an invaluable aid when navigating the dark tunnels of a blacked-out city and would save lives just a short month later.

We also made allies of the NGOs and made points with Gen. Joseph P. Hoar, USMC, commanding general of U.S. Central Command (CENTCOM). General Hoar sent kudos for the good press we had gotten by simply knocking and visited us during our next MSR Tiger guard rotation. Quite a few of the company's soldiers received four-star coins during that visit, always a morale boost.

At the time, it seemed that U.S. Forces were making good progress. The Rangers and Delta had successfully raided Osman Ali Ato's garage, snatching up Aidid's moneyman up and carting him away with ease; our hunts for the mortar crews slowly but surely closing in; and the press was treating us pretty well. Militarily, the first week of September 1993 was looking up, even though the Tigers and I were heading out the next day for another oh-God-do-we-*have*-to? rotation guarding the MSR.

CHAPTER 7

Baptism by Firefight

The morning of 13 September 1993 began like any other pre-dawn mission, with the alarm going off to remind me it was all real, rolling the aching bones out of the cot, getting that damn mosquito net off of me, and dressing in the darkness. Oh-dark-hundred sure comes early. Socks, trousers, BDU coat, boots, LBE, helmet, weapons, radio check, and out the door to check on the progress of the company.

The collective "Get up and get it on" went smoothly and the company quietly prepared to conduct a simple cordon-and-search. Both Bravo (the QRC) and Charlie Companies would execute the mission. The target, designated Objective ODIN, was a mere 2,000 meters from the Complex in the vicinity of Banadir Hospital, a large, multiwinged structure about which we had very little information. Within ODIN were Bastard's objective (THOR), just across the street and southeast of the hospital, and Tiger's objective (LOKI), immediately south of the largest hospital wing. We noted that the Blood Bank was located in Objective LOKI, and that the building was not on the map.

From the darkness of their barracks, the battalion (minus Alpha Company on MSR guard duty) slowly moved onto the early morning roads just outside of each company area and began to get organized. Whispers of pre-combat checks for ammo, water, commo, and last-minute details passed up and down the assembled lines of combat soldiers.

Soon enough the colonel called for the companies to move. We quickly covered final details, then marched over to the Embassy, where the battalion formed up, made its final checks, and received UP reports from the company commanders once they were ready. The order to execute came and both companies, one after the other, stepped from the protection of the Complex.

Bravo crossed the LD at 0400 hours and led us into the cool, dark morning, passing through a 10-foot-high, double-sided iron gate. The brigade and battalion command groups followed and Charlie Company brought up the rear.

The long snake of soldiers slipped silently through the U.S. Embassy gate, turned right onto a dirt road that led into the adjacent neighborhood and, with casual glances at the huge, open field on our left, worked its way south. The armed and vigilant formation followed the Embassy wall, taking its time while keeping the requisite 10-meter interval between soldiers, and moved approximately 200 meters south to the next left turn, allowing our units to approach Objective ODIN from due west.

Turning the corner at the end of the field, our route became tight as we were bordered on the right by the walls of neighborhood compounds and the new Somali Police Academy, and on the left by the massive (8-foot-thick-by-10-foot-high) wall of the Blood Bank compound. Branches from tall, aged trees blocked the sky.

As the first tendrils of light began to streak into the morning gloom, the column broke into two lethal elements, each surrounding and slowly tightening around its objective. The plan called for the companies to conduct simultaneous cordon-and-search operations in their respective city block–sized areas. Intel sources and Q-36 shots indicated that the last mortar rounds fired into the Complex came from the area designated as Objective ODIN, in the general vicinity of Banadir Hospital.

By 0500 we were throwing the cordons around the blocks and preparing assault elements to sweep through the buildings and surrounding areas. I was setting up overwatch positions, high and low, that covered the massive hospital wing facing us, the company exfiltration routes, and the entrances to the buildings in our AO. The buildings included the Blood Bank and two smaller, flat-topped, grayish-brown outbuildings that were inside a massive compound. The enclosed compound was made somewhat eerie by the thick, high walls that cast an even darker shadow than the surrounding night. I also noted that there was only one way in and one way out, a double iron gate like those at the Complex.

I put one platoon low, one high, and tasked one to sweep the entire objective as the assault element. I sent the low platoon in first to throw up the cordon, then sorted out the tricky task of sending in the assault and high teams simultaneously.

To our amazement, our ingress and major chokepoint, the huge black iron gate, was unlocked. But, of course, it was so creaky that moving it sent horror-movie chills up your spine, probably woke the dead, and almost certainly alerted any mortar team in the vicinity.

My command team deployed with the assault force. Quickly crossing the courtyard, they scrambled up the ten wide entrance steps and braced against the wall on both sides of large, wooden double doors. Taking a cue from our mission to the K-4 traffic circle, we knocked. A very frightened Somali male answered the door and, through our interpreter, we told him we were coming in. The Somali was detained as a systematic room-to-room search began.

The first thing you noticed upon entering the Blood Bank was the inner courtyard, a square within a square that was open to the sky. Funny how certain things just kind of make you go "Hmmmm." Tensions were high as sections of the high team searched for access to the roof and the assault element was calling its "Clear," "Clear," "All clear" messages to the follow-on soldiers making their way up the right and left sides flanking the courtyard.

Then I heard a "Holy shit, we've got something here," and a shouted "GET YOUR ASS ON THE FLOOR!" Tearing ahead with my RTOs, I found that the assault team searchers had discovered the 120mm mortar and its terrified crew, clearly just rudely awakened.

My men were already zipping them up with long, plastic bindings, hands behind their backs, and preparing them to be moved. I was reporting the find to higher and exhorted the men to search for more perps, ammo, weapons, and contraband. I quickly realized that I also had women and children to deal with, as it seemed whole families were involved with this mortar crew.

Things started to move very fast, and keeping a clear head while maintaining control was critical. With RTOs Randall and Alsbrooks, I made my way back outside to check on the rest of the company and make arrangements for moving the mortar and ammo, the crew, and the assorted family members. Checking the two outbuildings, I found the overwatch element in place. Then, seeing nothing unusual, I scanned the hospital wing and headed for the company trains (our logistical element) at the iron gate.

While we were engaged within the confines of the Blood Bank compound, the sun had begun pouring its light into the neighborhood. Bright bands were visible on the higher buildings above the trees and, in the hazy gray of post-dawn, a crowd could be seen gathering north of us just outside of the hospital. I looked across the street and saw the brigade and battalion command groups (Colonel Dallas and Command Sergeant Major Brown; Colonel David and Command Sergeant Major Counts) watching Bravo Company troops work their way through the buildings in Objective THOR.

Turning, I saw a man tumble down the Blood Bank's steps and come to a stop in the dirt. One of my men, clearly pissed, was cursing at the man. The Somali had resisted and taken a beating for his efforts. While the perp was lifted to his feet, the rest of the mortar crew and their families were led single file out through the gate.

The RTOs and I walked back to the rear of the Blood Bank and were discussing the exfiltration with the Combined Arms Lessoned Learned (CALL) officer, a captain who was accompanying, when all hell broke loose.

An RPG came screaming down from the hospital, all sparks and whoosh, and with an ear-shattering explosion blew up against the back wall of the Blood Bank. The roar enveloped us but caused no casualties. Simultaneously, intermittent fire directed at the command groups and the left flank of Bravo Company erupted from the hospital wing facing us. Evidently, we were now officially invited to a firefight.

Ordering return fire over the radio while racing back to the Blood Bank, I took the steps in two big bounds and searched for a way to the roof. I needed to get where I could direct our fires, because at that point I was out of the fight.

Reaching the roof, I burst into an ongoing melee. Charlie Company was fully engaged across a 100-meter front between the three buildings and the immense hospital wing. Worse, from intel briefings we knew that the three-story wing, which stretched at least 300 meters, was a haven for the warlords and their gangs.

The stark reality of what that translated to in terms of how they'd respond when poked with a stick now smacked us dead in the face. The situation worsened steadily as the volume of fire from Banadir increased by the minute while we remained trapped in the enclosed compound. I had to do something, because we had to get out!

Before moving off the Blood Bank's roof, I alerted the AT-4 gunners to be prepared for volley fire on my order when we were ready to break contact, confident that the 84mm shoulder-fired rockets would effectively screen our movement. Racing back down the stairs and around to the rear of the building, I knew that we had to move southward through the 3-foot thick, 10-foot high wall. To breach it, I ordered the fabrication of a home-made Bangalore torpedo using a metal engineer picket and the 25 pounds of C-4 we had with us.

Contacting Colonel David, I informed him we would withdraw through an about-to-be-available hole in the back wall, then move along the same route we had used when we initially came into the area. That would allow us to provide cover as Bravo Company and the command groups disengaged southward on the other side of the road that bisected Objective ODIN, moving about two blocks in this direction before cutting back to the west. The problem they faced was the distance each platoon had to navigate while trying to disengage under enfilading fire from the hospital.

Bravo Commander Captain Suich and I both realized that we couldn't assault the hospital, as the risk of catastrophic collateral damage involving civilian patients was simply too great. Additionally, the steadily increasing volume of incoming fire clearly indicated that the size of the opposing force was growing as Somali reinforcements added to the numbers of fighters in our objective area. With no means of gauging just how large that force might grow to be, it would simply have been foolish to get locked into a slug-fest.

Miraculously, we were taking no casualties from the 100 or so Somali fighters that kept up a steady stream of fire into our perimeter. But as the clock ticked on, the Somalis began to swarm as fighters and curiously zealous civilians, men, women, and children, began filling the streets and pushing our way. A mob is an awesome form of human power, and I certainly didn't want my company forced into a situation that might require the use of lethal force against ordinary Somali citizens.

Think . . . think . . . think. I had to figure multiple problems out on the fly, and time started to slow down for me as I worked to organize my thoughts and make the right calls. While my men fought to hold our position—and preserve our lives—I mentally cycled through the critical tasks that faced us: Move everyone back from the explosion point; detonate the improvised Bangalore; secure the breach; exfiltrate the engineers and the first group; secure the far side of the wall; thin the lines; volley fire the AT-4s; move the platoons through the breach in an organized manner; get an accurate head count; leave no one behind; take the lead again; move down the street; cover our rear; cover the hole in the wall; cover Bravo's exfiltration; move, move, and keep moving; and report as required to Colonel David.

Sweat burned my eyes as I gave the order to blow the wall. I still remember that burning in my eyes as a huge shock wave rolled over me and knocked Randall to the ground. Obviously, we had used way too much C-4, but in the circumstance, too much was much better than too little. When the dust and debris settled, I checked on my RTOs and the CALL captain, then noticed a burning pain along the right side of my neck. I kept touching it and asking Randall if I was bleeding. Although he kept saying no, I continued to feel along that part of my neck until I looked at my hand and realized that there was no blood. Evidently, a piece of something moving at the speed of explosions had zipped across my neck and left just a faint trail of pain, nothing else. Lucky!

I moved with my command group to the hole in the wall and realized that we had blown a hole big enough to drive a sizeable car through. Rubble from the wall was strewn south in all directions. We would get out!

As the radio crackled by my ear, I began issuing orders to those of my men who were still on the roofs and fighting to our front. The squad leaders were beginning to thin the lines from top to bottom, and men were passing through the hole we'd blown in the wall, gathering on the other side, and searching for any enemy waiting to resume firing at us. While RPGs continued to scream overhead, I noted diminishing return fire from our positions as greater numbers of my troops made it through the hole.

Seeing that our withdrawal was organized and secure, I slowly made my way back to the roof of the Blood Bank, where I was bluntly asked "What the hell are you doing here, Sir?" by one of my sergeants. The chaos on the roof was all that you could imagine. Sweat-soaked men, my men, surrounded by the acrid smell of cordite, gunpowder, and smoke, fired and moved under fire to resupply ammo or give a friend some water, as pieces of what was left of the balustrade were chipped away by return fire. Death hung in the air, but was not on us. Morale was *high*, and more than a few "Come and get some, you bastards" and "Fuck you's" were tossed about.

The men had prepared the AT-4s, and we were ready to leave. No one was wounded and none of the warlords' thugs would dare close on our position from the direction of the hospital. The order for the AT-4 volley was given and neither we nor the Somalis really knew what was coming. With a simple command, "Fire," and a knowing smile from one of my rocketeers, twenty or more AT-4s were simultaneously shouldered, aimed, and fired at targets across the short expanse to Banadir Hospital.

The roar of the back-blasts engulfed us as our rockets streaked home. The sheer volume and weight of the explosions stopped everyone and everything in their tracks to look in the direction of the awe-inspiring spectacle. The hammered building shook as whole portions of the wing were blown away, and Somali fighters could be seen falling off the building.

The broadside worked. In the ensuing momentary lull in the fighting, our small band made it to and through the hole, albeit with ears seemingly stuffed with cotton. I couldn't hear much as the last of the company cleared the wall and headed west on the same street we had used to reach the AO just ninety minutes before. I remained at the hole in the wall until everyone was accounted for, made the report to Colonel David, and headed for the front of the single-file column to find out why it wasn't moving anymore.

I passed excited, tired, and reflective faces as I made my way up the company formation. The 2nd Platoon had led the way through the hole and should have been closing on the Embassy by now, followed by the 1st, then 3rd, and finally the Headquarters section, which was making its way forward with me through the growing mass of men.

Something was wrong. Reporting had stopped on the company net as I picked up the pace toward a large knot of soldiers standing at the edge of the wall that led to the open field we had skirted on our way into the objective.

Moving through a tunnel of trees to reach the opening, I arrived to find a new threat to my world. The 2nd Platoon and part of 1st Platoon were strung out all the way to the Embassy wall, around the corner and halfway down the other side of the field, and were pinned down by an enemy force that had shifted with us and was again growing in numbers. Returning only sporadic and ineffective fire, my men were isolated and held in check by an increasing volume of incoming fire. They were stuck, which meant the rest of the company was stuck.

Safety was just a few hundred meters down that road, but required movement in the open, around the corner, and into the Embassy compound. My men knew that, I knew that, and the enemy knew that. Firing at anything that moved, the enemy was capitalizing on my company's fear of being in the open.

I don't know why I thought of it at that moment but I recalled a story of great leadership that I had once read. At the Battle of Waterloo, the Duke of Wellington saw how terrified his men were of the vast army confronting them on the field of battle. The British soldiers, formed in tightly packed tactical squares to defend against a cavalry charge, were becoming frozen with fear. Although they had fought many campaigns together, the awesome sight of Napoleon's massed army simply immobilized the Brits.

Wellington's initial response was to remark, paraphrased here, that "men must every now and then be shamed into iron will." Then, in the most famous battle he ever fought, Lord Wellington mounted his horse for all to see. Watching their leader take up the most dangerous position of any man in the British lines, his men responded by fighting with super-human strength to protect him, overcoming insurmountable odds and repelling multiple massed cavalry charges and the French Imperial Guards.

My unit was not facing an enormous, fearsome, and well-trained army. But it was facing itself for the first time, and I was their leader. All eyes were on me as I stepped from the cover of the wall and began slowly walking through a hail of gunfire to the first man in a long line of prone soldiers. I was at ease with myself and knew what I had to do. I did not scream or yell or kick or slap when I reached my mortar section leader, Sergeant Sax. Knowing that I could show no fear, I merely reached down and calmly touched the large, powerful man. Seeing the light come back into his eyes, I told him to link up with the man about 10 feet farther down the road, form a buddy team, and begin a standard fire and movement maneuver to reach the Embassy compound.

Feeling eyes still on me, I looked up and saw three brightly clothed women in the field, caught in the crossfire and utterly terrified. The children with them had gone absolutely quiet and clung fearfully to their mothers. Loudly screaming for a ceasefire, I urged the yellow-, orange-, and purple-clad women across the road to safety. Passing me, one of the women grabbed my hand, squeezed it, and said "Thank you" in Somali. She is very welcome.

With surreal calm, I continued my walk as rounds, both incoming and outgoing, made the unique *crack*, *pop*, and *thwing* sounds that passing bullets make. And I was filled by the exhilaration of getting my men moving, the humanity of helping the women and children, the satisfaction of doing what needed to be done, and the utter pride of command.

The number of my buddy teams now firing and maneuvering continued to grow and, miraculously, no one was being hit in the open field. I continued to walk, feeling a sense of duty to the men that I have never relinquished. Through a simple act of what I am now told was courage, I had motivated my men to believe in themselves, to trust the skills they had acquired through long, arduous training, and to get the job done. And in those brief, desperate moments, the manner in which the men responded filled me with pride.

It is not at all unusual for a unit to experience a moment of uncertainty, a "What-do-we-do-now?" hesitance, an unexplainable questioning of their martial skills. Ours occurred strung out along that approach to the Embassy—and it would be the last such moment for my unit.

The mark of a great unit is its ability to shake off such paralysis to courageously stand and fight again. Before my eyes, my men did exactly that. With urgency, polished technique, and ferocity, they laid down fire, protected one another, and clawed their way to safety. Daring anyone to get in their way, they shed the green inexperience of the untested to emerge as skilled, sure, proven, and immensely confident veterans.

Seeing what I expected from them, the remainder of the company quickly moved from the cover of the wall to join the tactical maneuver of the men already under fire. They began moving so fast that I found myself bringing up the rear, where my RTO, Specialist Randall, caught up with me so that I could report back to Colonel David.

The BC was with Bravo Company and trying to get back into the Embassy by blowing a hole at the southeastern corner of the wall. Captain Suich had his hands full, having taken three casualties and being engaged in a difficult consolidation effort. Colonel David directed me to get back into the Complex as soon as possible, but to be prepared to cover their route back if they needed to come our way.

Then I heard Colonel Dallas, the 10th Aviation Brigade Commander, put this call out over the net: "I want every bird in Somalia in the air in five minutes." Clearly, his fun-meter was pegged. Colonel Dallas owned the AH-1 Cobra gunships that were now on their way to visit an absolute shit storm on the people shooting at us, and I couldn't help thinking how bad a day those Somalis were about to have.

As I made my way to an M-60 machine-gun-equipped HMMWV, a louder than normal *crack* signaled that Special Forces and Marine sniper teams were now engaging targets from on top of the Embassy wall. As they shot over our heads into the fray, the firefight seemed to turn on a person-ally grim event.

As I stood by the HMMWV, a Somali gunman ran into the field, dove under what was left of a demolished vehicle, and, for some reason, zeroed in on me. With both of us quickly exchanging a couple of maga-zines at each other, the battle had suddenly become intensely personal. I was actually just sort of shooting offhand, merely aiming, breathing, and squeezing off rounds as I had so often done in training over the years. But, somewhat embarrassingly, I seemed to have been abandoned by the expert marksmanship that I had consistently demonstrated on various ranges around the world. And, as my opponent's return fire kept coming at me,

I became increasingly frustrated. Hell, I damn sure ought to be able to hit a target at 200 meters!

Then the exchange got deadly, as the HMMWV I had been using for cover suddenly just . . . drove off! Watching it go, I found myself standing alone in the middle of that field, and felt my company take a collective deep breath.

Intense concentration focused my mind on just the target. Time slowed; sound faded; nothing existed but the duel. I methodically went through another magazine, aiming at the opening from which my opponent had repeatedly launched his rounds. He, meanwhile, calmly waited for me to expend both my magazine and my aggravation.

Momentarily out of ammo, I watched in dismay as the Somali rose from beneath his cover and fired a full magazine at ME! While quickly swapping magazines, I felt his bullets crackling the air all around me and spraying me with a shower of dirt and sand when they impacted low. I expected to be hit, but received not a scratch.

Pressing the bolt release, I aimed, squeezed—and killed my first human being. Dropping like a hammer had pounded his chest, the once dangerous Somali lay completely still.

I never saw him again, except in my dreams.

At that very moment, Cobras arrived on station and commenced firing, the Special Forces and Marine snipers fired, an M-60 machine gunner fired, and my entire company, all now safely out of the open field, fired. Everyone and everything fired at the same time. I just stood there and watched the earth churn as at least 150 weapons systems zeroed in on the dead man's location.

With helicopters hunting and firing, the AT platoon raced from the Complex to launch a shower of MK-19 grenades that pounded the compounds on the far side of the field. This finally kept the Somalis' heads down, allowing me to jog from the field in a couple of 100-yard dashes to the cheers of my men. My God, what a feeling! The memory still raises goose bumps.

After Bravo Company and the brigade and battalion command teams made it into the Complex through the south wall, Charlie Company headed in from the north through the same gate we had departed from only seven hours earlier. We returned unscathed and beyond ecstasy. Our march to the barracks was triumphant as we realized that our baptism by fire had been a success, that the mission had been successful, and that we had validated ourselves under fire.

What we didn't yet realize was that, although we had seen the dragon and survived on this day, that dragon breathes fire in both directions. And as Bravo Company had learned this day, we would come to know that the honor and privilege of serving in the profession of arms can exact a terrible price.

The battalion's success on 13 September 1993 yielded some benefits. The Golden Dragons were pulled from MSR guard duty, the task falling to a Military Police unit. We were thus freed to train for whatever was to come, as tensions were obviously escalating. And we also seemed to have earned some respect from the Delta and Ranger Special Ops folks, as evidenced by their sending us a liaison team.

In retrospect, our tough, realistic tactical training, push-the-limits fitness program, and gung ho (work together) collective attitude had worked in our favor. So, too, did the fact that we had expended a helluva lot of ammunition! Needing to resupply, I directed the XO, 1st Lt. Andrew McDonald, to order 10 percent more ammo than we had fired, not then realizing that this seemingly innocuous SOP change would keep us alive in the very near future.

CHAPTER 8

Black Eye over Mogadishu

In the days following our baptism by fire, we slowly resumed the normalcy of routine. Once our swelled heads finally began to deflate, we started to consider viable offensive missions again. In particular, the battalion started focusing on the Black Sea area, Digfer Hospital (a known Aidid stronghold), and the Bakara Market area, confidently predicting that, sooner or later, something was going to go down at one of those sites.

We felt very much a part of the American team in Mogadishu and tried hard to prove that we were every bit as good as our Ranger counterparts. (Just having the Rangers and Delta in the AO raises the standard for everybody.)

In the training cycle, the Tigers opted for "The Beach," a beautiful haven on the shore of the Indian Ocean where we could train in peace and relative luxury. Located about 20 miles south along the Coast Road, the secluded beach area was wrapped in the natural sounds of wind and the waves that washed the white sand or crashed into the volcanic cliffs flanking the azure blue cove and its ever-flowing surf.

It was here that we set up three ranges (one each for machine guns, small arms, and grenades and AT-4 rockets) and fired our weapons out into the sea or south into the white dunes. Since we were in the bush, we did not have the normal range support that would have been available on a stateside installation. A typical U.S. live-fire range is characterized by known-distance target lanes and pop-up targets, and everything is constrained by very restrictive safety regulations. In Somalia, no one was going to build a range for us, and resources other than the land, the sea, and our own imaginations were severely limited. Consequently, we had to be a bit creative.

Almost anywhere you go in the world you can find 550-cord (strong nylon cord used as parachute suspension line), 100-mile-an-hour tape (sort of like civilian duct tape on steroids), 2x4s, 4x4s, and 55-gallon drums. These basic items will enable you to make fine ranges capable of challenging the marksmanship of even the best squads and would-be snipers. The items can be arranged so that any soldier can practice his own proficiency and become a lethal component of a skilled combat marksmanship team.

The goal of every combat shooter is one shot, one kill. But the reality is that the confused, chaotic, and fluid nature of your typical firefight tends to make soldiers duck, flinch, jump, roll, hop, scoot, and struggle against involuntary waste release, often all at the same time, while simultaneously trying to meet that lofty one shot, one kill standard. (We combat shooters are especially comforted by the knowledge that this reality equally affects the enemy's combat shooters!)

In essence, much of the time is actually spent firing into an area known or suspected to be occupied by enemy shooters. Focus is the real goal. It is achieved by concentrating on the target area, reacting to the moment, being situationally aware, anticipating the shot's effectiveness, and lining up the sights to the area where you want the round to strike. In a firefight, opportunities to cleanly aim and squeeze off a shot, and then watch the bullet into the target, occur less frequently than a Cubs World Series game. But blind fire just lets your adversary know where you are, and wild fire just wastes ammunition.

A study by S.L.A. Marshall found that relatively few members of any fighting organization actually do the killing (i.e., finding a target human being, lining up the sights, breathing, and then squeezing the trigger to drop the target). Marshall also found that some men never fired their weapon during battles in which they participated. This indicates that a great many soldiers simply do the obvious by firing toward (rather than at) the enemy, and usually only when it becomes personal (i.e., me or them).

In combat, the sense of being alone with your own thoughts is intense. To get everyone working as a team, firing as a team, takes effort and practice. Moving coordinated fires around the battlefield so that the platoons and companies are lethal and effective takes training time and ammunition.

English archers were skilled marksmen in their own right, but when formed together their massed assaults on an enemy were devastating. Likewise, men who fought in the Napoleonic, American Revolutionary, and American Civil Wars learned to volley fire—massed lead blazing toward the enemy from resolute and incredibly brave men who stood their ground. Massed fires (e.g., the ambush that annihilates the enemy in a matter of seconds; preplanned artillery barrages; or well-sighted final protective fires meant to stop an aggressive assault) are devastatingly effective. The timeless tactical principles can be taught using Civil War–type ranges and targetry and can quite effectively be used by a modern-era light infantry company to gain a profound expertise when it comes to manipulating the arms in the company's inventory. Combining the arms with well-practiced skills exponentially adds to their effects.

I first viewed Civil War ranges at Fort Shenandoah, a small compound used by the North/South Skirmish Association, just outside Winchester, Virginia. The NSSA is an historical and competitive organization that seeks to maintain knowledge of Civil War–era arms. They do not reenact battles, but rather efficiently slaughter wooden stakes and clay pigeons at distances of 50 and 100 yards, firing both singly and in squads. The average man can load and fire a two- or three-banded Enfield (the rifle de jour of the Confederate soldier) three times in a minute; the marksman of the 17th Virginia, my father's outfit, could do it five or six times. The idea is to break nine clay pigeons or separate a hanging stake by blasting it in two in ten minutes or less, best time wins.

Speed has just been mentioned, but what about accuracy? Many times I watched the men of the 17th go clean on targets 100 yards away—that's a football field. The magic was created by working together, massing fires, and pouring it on fast and accurate. I greatly respect the men who stood toe-to-toe and gave as well as they got; what courage!

In Somalia, I copied the range style of Fort Shenandoah. Soldiers were placed on line to face a vertical 4x4 or a hanging 2x4, or a pyramid of 55-gallon drums placed 200, 250, and 300 meters out in the sand. To add spice at night, I used chemlights in water bottles bouncing on the waves of the Indian Ocean to hone low-visibility skills.

The 4x4s were for massed machine-gun fire. Two lines were placed in the middle of the upright "stake," spaced about 6 inches apart. This stake was placed about 25 meters in front of my squad automatic weapons and M60 "pig" machine gunners. At first, they all laughed and thought it would be really easy. Well, twenty minutes after the initial bursts the stake remained standing, smiling back at the exhausted gunners. The drill showed them just how far they needed to go to become accurate machine gunners. In the end, I could put a stake up and the accurate, massed fire turned the 4x4 into slivers in just a couple of minutes.

The same style drill was built for each of my squads. I hung a 4-foot length of 2x4 parallel to the ground using 550 parachute cord on each end and another pair of 6-foot-tall "pillars" that served to keep the target swinging. The movement caused the concentration and anticipation I was looking for and, as each 5.56 round slammed through the target space in the middle of the board, the anticipation by the squad mounted to the breaking point, literally.

This training was not only effective but a great deal of fun. Thousands of rounds were used to hone their skills, while the fun of the ranges made each trip out to The Beach a personal and group challenge. Friendly side wagers and small tournaments arose and a good time was had by all. Night and day, rounds pounded wood, sand, and surf as the soldiers enjoyed perfecting their craft.

The time wasn't all spent firing from the offhand or prone position; much of it was used to learn about each other and to unwind. Some patrolled together, some swam, some "hunted," and some just lay around and talked of home and loved ones. Friendships and camaraderie were solidified.

The Beach turned out to be a boon. The peace to be had, listening to the surf and wind, helped cleanse the soul, as did the night quiet, the fresh air, and the vast star-filled sky. But the greatest benefit of The Beach was the acquisition of a sense that we could trust our weapons, our skills, the skills of our friends, and the skills of the squad and platoon on our flanks. The company became lethal on that beautiful beach, a true irony of life.

The night of Friday, 24 September 1993, found Tiger Company back at the University Compound. The company was rested, accomplished, and used to the routine. I played basketball with Randall and Sgt. Chris Reid from 3rd Platoon. The shoot-around lasted until dusk, when I had to withdraw to attend our nightly meeting. After the meeting, many of us took notice of and watched a firefight that was touched off near Hunter Base. The rolling *chug-chug-chug* of .50-caliber machine-gun fire from Hunter and the familiar sound of the enemy's mass-fired AKs sounded normal. Many of us watched the tracers for a few minutes before the usualness of it sent us to the security of our bunks.

I hit the rack to the sounds of that firefight. After a deep breath and a flip of the mosquito net, I leaned back, sighed contentedly, closed my eyes, felt the breeze from my fan, and actually felt calmness in my soul.

Around 0200 the CQ tore at the flap to my room, hollered my name, and told me to get to the Battalion TOC ASAP. I awoke instantly, totally clear-headed, and with a feeling this time the call for the QRC was no exercise. I directed the CQ to wake the company leadership and be ready to move at a moment's notice. To the sounds of "Get it on," I sprinted up the steps to the battalion command post in full combat gear. When I entered the TOC, Colonel David was there with Major Ellerbe to brief me on an emergency mission: A Black Hawk was down somewhere near the New Port. An Eyes Over Mogadishu mission bird had been hit by an RPG and subsequently crashed, and was being circled by other helicopters that would remain on station until we arrived.

Colonel David took me outside when the first HMMWV arrived. Throwing a map on the hood of the vehicle, he said, "Mike, the bird is down somewhere in this area here," circling with his finger an area just northwest of the New Port. "The wreckage is burning. Go find the glow." He also gave me the frequency and call sign of an OH-58 pilot orbiting the site and told me to link up with him to be guided in.

In an instant, as my men ran to the waiting 5-ton trucks, I realized that all the years of learning how to plan, all the 124-page operations orders with annexes, all the training days at NTC, CMTC, and JOTC had now all come down to "Go find the glow."

We swept into the night, like a long, metal snake whipping through the Tunisian gate, hurtling toward a tragedy with no known Enemy and Friendly Situation (no paragraph 3, Operations, with all of its myriad details and directions); no detailed Service and Support Plan for logistics or MEDEVAC; no detailed review of Command and Signal. Everything was on us to make it up as we went along, hoping that higher headquarters and support elements would follow our lead.

Thank the Lord we had established, practiced, and proven SOPs to guide us. From the time my men rolled out of the rack, we were following our SOPs. The men trusted their training and used it from the outset. They didn't need to go to an arms room to draw their weapons or ammunition; they had three basic loads for all their weapons right beside their bunks. Only the crew-served weapons ammo and the AT-4 rockets needed to be gathered from the presorted-by-platoon ammunition supply point.

The men climbed over the tires to load the trucks (much faster than waiting at the tailgate) and sat with the buddies they knew would be on their right and left in any ensuing combat action. Accountability is crucial when it comes to loading and reloading. How do you know if anyone is missing? Simple: Who is supposed to be on your right and left? Is that who is there? If not, where is the one who is supposed to be there and why is this guy there instead?

The road movement itself even employed an SOP. We maintained sub-unit integrity by loading in order—1st Platoon, 2nd Platoon, 3rd Platoon—and if we got into a fight, the order shifted from first to last, so it would rotate through 2/3/1, then 3/1/2, and so on, ensuring that no one had to take point every time.

The ride to the airport was filled with radio checks and nervous soldier talk, bravado, and other pre-combat checks. The plan was quickly disseminated among all the troops in the back of the noisy, gear-changing trucks whose tires churned dust that covered the company in a talcum powder-like film that stuck to the dew- and sweat-covered soldiers. The night air filled our lungs to the brim with cool ocean air and our nerves churned the adrenaline in our guts.

As the kilometers passed, we all became more thoughtful. I once again thought of the million things that rush through a commander's mind on the way to combat, for this time we knew we would be in contact. Would there be an ambush on the way to the airport? If so, would we blow through or stop to fight? Where would we really meet the helicopter? What if we don't link up with the helicopter? What is the best route? Where will we stop the trucks? After we off-load, should the trucks stay put or move to a safe area? What if there are casualties? How do we MEDEVAC: air, ground, both? What's the order of march? What's the best dismounted route to the objective? When we get to the objective, who goes where? If there is an ambush, should we fire and maneuver or just suppress and hold the ground? How do we go about the search? What if we're under fire? How do we get the wounded crew out? How do we recover remains? What do we take from the crash site? Do we destroy the bird? What if we're surrounded? What happens if we lose commo with an element? What if the trucks are attacked, destroyed, or just leave? What will be the dismounted route out? What will be the mounted route out?

All of this raced through my mind as we headed to our rendezvous.

When the questions were filtered and the problem-solving process (i.e., recognizing and defining the problem; gathering facts and making assumptions; developing possible solutions; analyzing and comparing the possible solutions; and selecting the best solution) was complete, I made mental notes of each item. This would make up the final briefing around the trucks before the dismounted trek into the heart of the city.

Life is situational. My men and I knew that, and we were going to have to pull this one off without help from the rest of the battalion. But I had faith in my men and at this point I think they had faith in me. This was going to be our first real test, we could feel it. It was like having studied for a midterm exam, and it was now exam day.

The unique sound of blades beating the air into submission over the airport broke into my thoughts and I reached for my radio's hand mike. As an OH-58D Kiowa helicopter orbited above our convoy, I made contact with the pilot. He was aware of the situation, knew where the Black Hawk was down, and assured me that he would get us to the objective in the most expeditious manner possible. He flew; we drove. Into the night, lights off, we rushed to beat back the enemy and save our fallen comrades.

Our trucks stopped just north of the New Port. With our PVS-7s ready, we dismounted, made last-minute pre-combat checks, and got into ground movement march order: 1st, HQs, 2nd, and 3rd Platoons. I gave the last-minute instructions I had thought of on the way in and then positioned myself within the lead platoon.

With the battalion in a follow-on mode, I didn't know if I could make radio contact with higher or not, but knew that I should report our progress. No answer. With that, and the urgency of the task at hand, I waved the company forward. Follow me!

Stepping away from our trucks and the ready escape they represented, we entered a gloomy tunnel of black shadows and gray, moonlit walls. Turning on the PVS-7s, our world instantly changed to green and black. Nothing moved but us.

The city was still. Dirt and broken plaster crunched under our boots. Internalized once more, the eerie silence was broken only by the sounds of every step, hop, or leap of our movement through the war-torn streets.

Debris from rampaging technicals and civil warriors, and just the messiness of daily life, littered the beleaguered neighborhood. With no street signs to follow and no real knowledge of the downed Black Hawk site, we moved as quickly as possible, anticipating ambush at any moment.

Guided by the sparkle of the OH-58s laser, we made good time down the wide streets of northeastern Mogadishu. In fact, we weren't much farther to the north of our Green Door raid objective. We advanced steadily west, block by block, following the sparkle as we searched for the glow, all the while knowing that something was about to happen, as foretold by sporadic pops in the distance. No enemy would shoot down a bird and then not have a look. An age-old guerrilla tactic is to wound something and then wait for the rescuers in a baited ambush. We were living that scenario right then.

The walls held their gloom tight and the progress up the street was punctuated by the crackle of my PRC-126 radio. Huffing and puffing, sweating, yet feeling the chill of the night air, I pounded along with the 1st Platoon, always scanning for the bright beam of the sparkle in the hazy green of the night optics.

Then we saw it: the glow. Filling our PVS-7s with a smear of almost white light, the wreckage of the helicopter seemed to grow from a building on the right side of the street up ahead, its main compartment smashed into the flat side corner of a multilevel structure. The section where the pilots used to sit was either sheared or crushed beyond recognition. How could anyone survive that? I thought to myself.

Then all hell broke loose as rifle and machine-gun fire tore into our advancing formation, tracers streaking toward us in the Somalis' typical fire-a-magazine-and-haul-ass mode. Thank God the initial fire was high and inaccurate. Before we could get pinned down, I called for the AT Platoon that was under the command of 1st Lt. Furman Ray. One left, one right, and one dead center, his HMMWVs, with MK-19s attached to their roofs, immediately raced up the street by the downed bird and began to chunk out the nasty 40mm grenades from their grenade-launcher machine guns.

The MK-19s characteristic *chunk-chunk-chunk-chunk* sound was followed by a brief, anticipated silence in the AK-47 and M-16 fire, and then the *wa-woom, wa-woom, wa-woom, wa-woom* of four detonated grenades. The mixed high-explosive and antiarmor rounds began impacting in the enemy area of resistance, which was morphing from an L shape to a U shape on the west, north, and south sides of our position. We countered by adopting a T formation on the highest ground and ensuring coverage of a just-in-case retrograde route.

A steady firefight broke out, with Tiger Company holding the helicopter crash site. Tracers came and went from the street to our front and along the route of egress. The 1st Platoon moved one squad to the left and put two squads in and around the crash site, forming the first arm of the

T. The 2nd Platoon went right to form the other arm of the T, and the 3rd Platoon deployed along our egress route to prevent being cut off from our transportation.

With the UH-60 Black Hawk glowing from the fire still ravaging its main cabin, I directed the men to improve positions and take the high ground, which happened to be a three-story building in 1st Platoon's AO. From that vantage point, we could see the neighborhood and develop the situation, including detection of any encirclement or flanking maneuver by the Somalis.

After the adrenaline-surging rush to the crash site, the shock of the initial view of the dead bird, and the accompanying "Oh my Gods," the unit quickly coalesced and set about doing its job. Riflemen, machine gunners, and MK-19 gunners suppressed enemy fire and allowed us to achieve a level of site security. I called for fire extinguishers, which the XO, 1st Lieutenant MacDonald, brought forward by HMMWVs, and we set about combating the flames. It took five extinguishers to snuff out the fire in the cabin, but then we realized that we still had to handle the molten stew in the crew compartment.

Holding our own in downtown Mogadishu, I took a deep breath and gave the word to start searching for survivors. No one had rushed to us as we approached the crash site. Personally, I was disheartened by the lack of aircrew in the immediate area; there should have been at least four crewmembers: pilot, copilot, and the crew chiefs. We had no idea what happened to them and could only assume they died on impact or were taken away by the Somalis.

As the company returned fire, the higher echelon leadership of the company began a more detailed search-and-recovery operation. First Sergeant Doody began to resupply the company with ammunition and water, exposing himself to intermittent fire from the surrounding buildings while running from position to position.

As we sifted through the wreckage of the helicopter, I realized that it would be extremely difficult to find anything until it became lighter outside. Everything was black or olive drab and in deep shadows. Dawn was approaching in the east and the time was nearly 0500.

My command HMMWV, parked at the junction of the T made by the platoons, gave enough cover from sniper fire that I put the RTOs and myself behind it and tried to make a commo link to the rear. All the HMMWVs made easier targets for the Somalis, but each carried more powerful commo gear than we were carrying on our backs. This enabled me to contact Colonel David at the airfield and tell him our situation. We were holding and would need to make a better search. He told me to stay the course and recover what we could.

Just after I made initial radio contact, I looked to my rear and saw a small figure making his way up the street of our egress. He would stop every few feet and ask a soldier a question. The soldiers all pointed at me. As bullets twanged off the walls above our heads and plaster showered us, the aged and courageous elder made his way to me. Crouching behind our truck awaiting his approach, I directed platoon fire and that of the MK-19s.

When the distinguished man approached, he looked down upon us, tapped me on the shoulder, and, as if nothing was going on in his neighborhood, pointed and calmly asked me in a solemn tone for permission to use his mosque. Allah, be praised, and Lord, help me. "Yes, of course," I said, "but please be careful out here." I know he understood me, but his look said, "They are shooting at you, not at me." He then slowly and deliberately made his way around the corner and into the courtyard of the mosque. Never once did he flinch or appear nervous.

As the sky lightened, you could look down the street of our approach and watch the shadows being eaten by the progression of sunlight up the street. As if on cue, the Somalis began to gather in force. We watched them running to this building or that as our anticipation of a real fight grew steadily. Technicals, the Somali crew-served weapons jeeps (usually Toyota Land Cruisers with 12.7mm heavy machine guns mounted in the rear), began probing up the streets and into the loose perimeter. Tiger Company reacted by holding its ground and placing a withering, concentrated fire in the directions of the probes. There was no penetration of the perimeter but we were steadily becoming surrounded.

As the sun flipped the lights back on at 0530ish, we could see into the wreckage of the helicopter and the tail boom clearly lying in the street nearly a 100 feet away, where it had fallen from the sky. It was then that the gruesome part of the job had to be taken care of, as there were certain to be remains in the downed aircraft.

Because the fire had increased, only five or six of us resumed the search of the crew compartment. We immediately found blood under and around the smashed flight compartment. The crew compartment was ash, smoldering, spitting with small electrical discharges, and very, very hot. The roaring flames were gone, but you certainly couldn't grab anything with a bare hand.

Sifting through the ash, we eventually located the remains of Sgt. Ferdinand Richardson of HHC/2-25 Aviation. We knew this because I had raked the barrel of my M-16 through the ash, and the front sight post had snagged his gleaming silver dog tags. We retrieved all that we were able to find.

Finding one set of remains drove us harder to locate the rest of the crew. But reality quickly sank in and spread in our small group: There simply wasn't much to find. We didn't talk for a while, just looked at one another. Desperate to find anything else, we began to throw and push pieces of superheated wreckage into the street, hoping to find anything for the families. No one needed to say anything more. I could also sense a hatred building in the small group of searchers. We were getting mad while dismembering the aircraft to gather sensitive items, commo gear, unexploded ammunition, and weapons.

Enemy fire began to ping more often in the wreckage and the sound of battle started to build as increased sunlight allowed both sides to better see and engage targets. Tracers dimmed and soldiers pointed to their front to direct their buddies' fire into known enemy locations in the buildings. With the situation going from bad to worse as daylight increased and the number of Somalis rose, I called for and received rotational sets of Scout Weapons Teams (SWTs), each with two Cobra gunships and a Kiowa from 10th Aviation.

We held the tallest building in the neighborhood and used the height advantage to keep the enemy from closing with us. Several enemy casualties could already be seen in the no man's land between our buildings and theirs. Death stalked us all in the early dawn.

Bandit 6, black death under rotor blades, arrived with his SWTs. After contacting me and a simple target-marking exercise, the gun runs began. Shell casings from the Cobras rained down hot and hard, the tinkling crash and bounce of brass hitting the deck making you look up until you got used to it.

As enemy fire increased and more and more Somali gunmen approached our perimeter, I asked over the radio if we could fire TOWs from the helicopters. Bandit 6 told us we would need to get permission from higher. Unknown to us, Major General Montgomery, the U.S. Forces Commander in Mogadishu, had been listening to our frequency, the predicament and the escalating firefight, and he gave the go-ahead. After confirming the higher 6 call sign, Bandit 6 and I began to get organized to smash our enemy with overwhelming firepower.

After identifying and marking targets, and ensuring they were the right targets, TOW missiles whooshed from their pods and screamed toward known enemy-occupied buildings. As wires draped over our buildings, into the street, and even over our bodies, the *karumps* and *kablams* of the missiles' impacts on the buildings began.

As the increased sunshine of the new day began to superheat the morning, a full-blown firefight, with engagements on north, west, and south sides, began in earnest. Magazines were emptied, brass links from machine-gun ammunition tinked in between the roar of the SAWs and "pigs" (M249 and M-60 machine guns), men yelled, and MK-19s hammered at the surrounding buildings. Platoon leaders chose targets. Squad leaders directed fire and distributed ammo and water. First Sergeant Doody seemed to be everywhere. Bandit 6 flew and pulled the trigger as I focused on the targeting, direction, approach, and egress for the SWTs. Slowly but surely I became adept at simultaneously running three SWTs: one on target, one on station, and one back at the airfield's forward rearm and refuel point (FARP).

Outnumbered, nearly surrounded, running out of ammunition, but positioned well and, most importantly, covered from the third dimension, we were holding our own. Then we took our first casualty.

A soldier from the 1-87 Infantry, attached to bolster the numbers of our Antiarmor Platoon, took a round in the neck while firing his M60 from the cupola of his HMMWV. Doody, on the scene immediately, helped him out of the vehicle and began stabilizing the paralyzed soldier under fire. Another 1-87 soldier took the place of his fallen comrade and began to pour fire in the direction of the enemy. In almost the same breath, a seriously skilled Somali marksman, who had the distance and elevation, sent his next round straight through the windshield of the same 1-87 HMMWV and into the thigh of the machine gunner. Doody had his hands full and requested support from other fighting positions. As soldiers raced his way, I called for medics and a field ambulance to extract the wounded. The standby Mortar and Dragon Sections, minus their crew-served weapons, acting as medical personnel proved to be the best SOP we had established. Working with either the physician's assistant or the battalion surgeon, these men saved numerous lives.

Under constant small-arms fire and with wounded who needed extraction, I called for and received death from above over and over. The TOWs whooshed into the buildings in a seemingly never-ending process, even bringing some structures to the ground with direct hits.

Somalis were dying and my men were being wounded. Roiling black clouds, interspersed with explosions and red and green tracers, filled the tiny neighborhood. Shacks were flattened, chunks were torn from the masonry, and fresh bullet holes pocked almost every building in the area. The smell of cordite, gunpowder, and the ever-present odors of Mogadishu itself crept into my nostrils and burned their way to my brain. My senses were alive; I was alive; but for how long?

Reality set in. To this point, the whole deployment had been almost surreal. It hadn't seemed like life and death; nothing had personally happened to anyone in our company. Now it was becoming personal, as soldiers were being hit, blood was spilled, and pain was evident. I felt screws tighten as, in an instant, I became a very serious, intensely focused man, warrior, and commander.

From behind the HMMWV where my small command element hunkered against the rapidly escalating firefight, I viewed the microcosm of that time and space. As if in slow motion, I viewed my men. All sound had become a single, swelling orchestration of killing machines and the exertions of resolute young soldiers fighting for their lives and the lives of their buddies. I started on the left, viewing each and every man in turn, some firing in unwavering defiance of the threat, some working for the men firing, finding ammo or water, some running or crawling for a better position. In that moment, I solemnly and completely realized with a harshness that broke my boyhood imaginings that combat was harsh, real, painful, and desperate—and that it came at a price.

Broken from my reverie, I watched the wounded soldiers loaded for evacuation and saw Doody, now really pissed, jump up into the cupola of the 1-87th HMMWV and just rip into any enemy weapons flashes he could find. His actions this day would earn him a Silver Star and near reverence from all of us who witnessed his competent ferocity.

I continued directing the SWTs and began visualizing our exfiltration from this little patch of hell. Distributing the downed helicopter's sensitive items and ammunition to the platoon leaders and keeping the remains of Sergeant Richardson with me, I began to inform the platoon leaders of my egress plans. When the order came to withdraw from the downed Black Hawk site, 2nd Platoon would disengage first along the egress route held by 3rd Platoon.

Because we were almost surrounded, 2nd Platoon would be the spearhead after we cleared the portion of the egress route held by 3rd Platoon. Next, 1st Platoon would clear as we then rolled up and away from the crash site and headed for the trucks together. All vehicles under the command of 1st Lieutenant Ray would cover the company's disengagement and follow on to the truck linkup site.

Via radio, the trucks were told to be turned around and positioned to make for either the New Port or the airfield, depending on our overall condition. We didn't yet know whether we would fight out of the pocket we were in and then have unchallenged movement to the trucks, or if we were going to have to fight all the way back to the trucks. In the second instance, the truckers and anyone with them would have to prepare a hasty fighting perimeter that we could get back to.

By 0630, the area was swarming with SNA militia fighters and even some overtly defiant Technicals constantly firing their 12.7mm heavy machine guns. The enemy vehicles began darting in and out of cover to fire at us and hide from the Cobras, which were dancing all over the sky to keep the wolves at bay. If it wasn't for the aviators, we probably would have been overrun in at least one sector, and our very survival would have been in serious doubt.

After two hours of an ever-expanding firefight, Colonel David finally gave us the order to disengage and return to base with the remains and sensitive items we'd recovered. As planned, I pulled 2nd Platoon from the northern sector. With a massive volley from the MK-19s and machine guns of the platoon, the 2nd's men fell back while the Somalis hunkered under the withering fire. The T built early in the darkness began to collapse on itself as 2nd Platoon moved through the 1st Platoon sector toward the wreckage, turned the corner, and headed east through the 3rd Platoon.

While 2nd moved through, 1st Platoon began consolidating for the move, firing at ground level but getting all the soldiers down from the occupied high ground of the parking structure and back to more defensible positions around the mosque at the center of the T. Meanwhile, 3rd Platoon kept up a steady cat-and-mouse game with the SNA militia that had penetrated the flanks of our main position.

All went well until I received a frantic call from 2nd Lieutenant Ryan, 2nd Platoon's patrol leader: "We're surrounded." The connotations of that statement caromed through the minds of all listening on the net. In the calmest voice I could muster, I told Ryan to stay calm and fight his way out. "Roger; WILCO," was his answer, and in a very deliberate manner, 2nd Platoon fought and killed the opposition and opened our route out.

Withdrawal under fire is one of the most precarious and hazardous maneuvers an infantryman can make. Exposed to fire while moving, usually with wounded, typically after a long, hard fight, and weakened by lack of food, water, sleep, and ammunition, the infantry company must fight like a wounded animal in a no-holds-barred frenzy that exemplifies the very nature of the U.S. Infantry's "Close with and destroy the enemy" approach to combat. You must kill and the enemy must reel from your assault, scared for their lives by your ferocity and determination. In the city, you must be oriented 360 degrees, even when you are channeled by the linear reality of your surroundings, all the while looking to the front and rear, up and down, seeking to keep anyone from shooting down the street you are on and to provide covering fire in the brief instances when you must cross side streets. Bounding forward by leap-frogging en mass sustains the momentum.

Snipers and freak circumstances must be handled in the "life is situational" context of fluid combat, and you must always be mentally prepared for the inevitability of Murphyisms. No matter how well conceived or executed your plan, the enemy will sometimes slam his fist into your guts, and you have to take the blow and keep on moving.

With a sniper, you take cover, identify his position, take the building, and kill the SOB. Alternatively, you deal with him using superior firepower, in our case AT-4s and Cobra gunships.

Freak circumstances can be blamed on God, bad karma, or Murphy. My worst nightmare came at around 0645 on the morning of 25 September 1993. Tiger Company had successfully broken contact and was slowly but surely punching our way by fire and maneuver up the main egress route. With just ten blocks to go and the MK-19 HMMWVs to my immediate rear firing and moving to keep the Somalis engaged, I made my way back up the street with the last men of 3rd Platoon. Knowing that I had everyone accounted for and my rear covered by the AT juggernaut, I focused on the immediate problem of getting safely back to the trucks on foot.

As I turned to absentmindedly run across the first gap in the buildings and the street to my immediate front, I heard a commanding shout that stopped me in my tracks. That shout saved my life. Sergeant Reid from 3rd Platoon, the man I had just been playing basketball with the evening before, was in front of me across the street. As his shout died in my ears, 12.7mm rounds from a Technical up the side street started pounding into the walls, buildings, and the intersection I almost headed into.

Reid fired at the Technical, putting down covering fire that got me across the street while the Somalis briefly stopped firing to take cover. When I got to the position Reid had just occupied, he had already turned and begun moving up the street. As I stopped to provide covering fire for the Headquarters Section, I heard a huge explosion. Turning, I saw a ball of flame and felt the blast wave of an exploded RPG. Damn it! We only had three more blocks to go . . .

In a "no good deed goes unpunished" quirk of life, Reid was down. Forgetting everything, buddies from 3rd Platoon and I ran to his aid.

Without aiming, a Somali had just rested his RPG on the lip of a compound wall and pulled the trigger. The result was that one of my best men lay in the street, blind, deaf, right leg nearly severed (later amputated), and left arm blown off. This strong man neither yelled nor cried out; all he said was "Help me." And we did, working like madmen to get tourniquets on both his arm and his leg to keep him from bleeding out. We then hefted him into a HMMWV that hauled ass to the waiting trucks. We ran, fired, ran, fired, and, drenched with sweat, finally reached the location of the trucks. A quick count, an "All up" from each element, and we began moving back to the airport.

The HMMWV Reid rode in rushed before us to a waiting MED-EVAC helicopter at the airport. We wouldn't see him again for quite a while, as he began a journey of pain and immense courage that would ultimately, and still does, inspire all who know him.

We had arrived at the linkup point with our hair on fire after attending to Reid, but the company's leadership remained calm, directing fire where necessary as the men loaded the vehicles. Urgency was the order of the day, not panic. From the back of the trucks we could still hear and see fire from the Cobras dancing up and down the street, the ships' rotary cannons efficiently sounding Somali death knells. Brass still fell around us, and every now and then we were buffeted by downdraft. The chaotic noise began to calm to a dull roar, and our individual personal danger quotient dropped a notch as the unit was moved by the trucks to the rest of the battalion awaiting our return.

Sitting in my HMMWV for the first time in hours, with the wash of fatigue creeping up my legs and back, I gave my report to Colonel David and the battalion command element positioned at the airport: 0 KIAs, 3 WIAs, all vehicles accounted for, remains and sensitive items accounted for, down to half a basic load, and in immediate need of a water resupply. He directed us to get back to the fold at the northern end of the airfield, where he would be waiting for us. The convoy passed the New Port on the left and built speed on Via Roma as we headed for the Egyptian guard point at the airport.

As the streets went by, our world phased down from total immersion in an adrenaline rush of tactical exhilaration, courage, fear, desperation, and the multitude of other emotions that come with combat, to a nearly serene start of—ho, hum—just another day in Mogadishu.

Calm rushed at us. Women quietly walked to the markets, unruffled men went to visit neighbors, and, as usual, children stared into our grime and grit as we passed by. The tranquil quality of the morning offended me. I had just been fighting for my life, killing, maiming, and smashing a neighborhood to dust and ruin, and these people thought nothing of it. Just another day for them, it had become one of bitter consequence for us, and a day that I will never forget.

I saw men just staring at one another, really looking, each glad to be alive, each wondering why he was. Once again, we had survived. But for the hand of God—and one of His greatest creations, Army Aviators—we would have been mauled.

There were no cheers this time, no whooping it up, no rowdiness, no cowboying. Instead, we were just veterans that clearly understood this was our true blooding, and it wasn't as much fun as just handing someone their ass. That someone had just hit back. Sobering.

The convoy made the airport in less than twenty minutes, just in time to see the MEDEVAC aircraft carrying Reid already in the air and heading for the Combat Hospital. Colonel David and Command Sergeant Major Counts watched the company enter the airfield and park dressed right, per SOP, and I saw them eyeing me and my men as we dismounted. My dismount ended in a bear hug from Colonel David that lifted me clear off the deck. Counts slapped me on the back, and both of them offered congratulations and well-dones.

I suppose I was still in shock and didn't really understand that we had accomplished as much as we did. We hadn't saved anyone; we took three casualties (one that just tore me up); and I frankly thought that I had merely done my job. Still, the accolades kept coming.

The men of Tiger Company were the heroes that day, not me. They had trained hard, they lived hard, and when the time came, they unhesitatingly executed their individual duties like the true professionals they are. I was so awed by their performance, and am so immensely proud of how well they did a tough, tough job! They are *all* good men, and it was my privilege to lead them.

The 25th of September 1993 should have sent a shiver through the entire Army. It didn't. The first Black Hawk Down in Somalia didn't occur on 3–4 October. It happened this day, when we least expected it, and seemingly as an ordinary event in the cycle of normal life. To me this action seemed inevitable. These Eyes Over Mogadishu birds had been flying and killing with such impunity that everyone thought they were untouchable. I honestly didn't think an RPG would be the weapon to down one of them, but I often wondered when we would be treated to the surprise of a Stinger or SA-7 missile. And just as the little Stinger system had changed the tide of the Russians' war in Afghanistan, a new and profoundly simple RPG tactic was changing the tide in Somalia.

Moving back to University Compound, thoughts of my second venture into combat swirled in my head. Mission accomplishment; task and purpose; SOPs; sparkle; the priceless Army Aviation; the absolute necessity of fully understanding and skillfully handling the Scout Weapons Team Cycle; combat lifesavers; casualties and their effects; worrying about the wounded; bravery; leadership; trust. A lot to think about.

Sergeant Reid would be stabilized and receive initial surgery in the 46th Field Hospital and begin recovery in intensive care. He'd be visited by as many friends as the physicians would allow, be honored with a ceremony for his bravery and steadfast duty, and then be loaded into a MEDEVAC bird and flown first to Landstuhl, Germany, then on to Walter Reed Army Medical Center. A great many of the critically wounded go through rehabilitation, counseling, and further education at Walter Reed to help them deal with being in a new category of American society: disabled veteran.

I recall thinking about the following commentary even then. The dead were mentioned that day, the horribly maimed given just a cursory nod. Three wounded just doesn't explain the anguish we all felt, or the lives each of the wounded would have to live.

It is strange how Americans deal with disabled veterans. The blind, the deaf, the crippled, the paralyzed, and any combination thereof—these are the least fortunate of all wars. The dead know peace and are memorialized. Today on the Web you can find dozens of sites about those who have fallen. The Wounded Warrior Foundation is trying but could never keep pace with the tens of thousands of lives transformed by war.

How wrong can we be as a nation? These are shattered lives, shattered dreams. Our nation needs to focus on the living, not just on the dead. Why can't we be allowed to see the men and women, know their stories, ease their pain with contributions, help them, share the pain, because of knowing? Why don't we have a Disabled Veterans Day when we focus not just on the sacrifices of the dead, but on the sacrifices of the living? Personally, I want to know about all of the casualties, and not just as numbers in a column on the evening news. As a nation we should not just ignore that it happened to them. Throughout history these soldiers have been ignored, why? I think we need to find the answer to that question, together.

A nagging question persisted: What had happened to the remaining crew of that bird? Hell, I knew they all had names, but at the time I only had one: Sergeant Richardson. I needed to find out . . .

I did. The aircraft crew that flew the ill-fated Eyes Over Mogadishu flight in the early morning hours of 25 September 1993 included pilot CW2 Dale Shrader, co-pilot CW2 Perry Alliman, Sgt. Eugene Williams, and Pfc. Mark E. Anderson, all of B/9/101st Air Assault Division; and Sgt. Ferdinand Richardson of HHC/2/25, 10th Mountain Division. After an uneventful first sortie, the crew had stopped at the airfield for fuel between 0110 and 0120 hours. As mortars began going off around them, the crew immediately reboarded to head for CP42 near the Pasta Factory.

CW2 Shrader flew a reconnaissance route designed to show the crew safe havens for downed aircrews. The flight included the soccer stadium where the Pakistanis housed units of their division. After that route was finished, he decided to take the crew to the Villa d'Italia, a notorious palace-like structure that was the suspected launch point for mortar rounds that targeted the airfield and the numerous U.N. compounds. After that, they would return to the port and then the airfield.

En route on the final leg, at about 100 knots and 130 feet off the deck, the aircraft took a direct hit from an RPG that severed the entire tail section. The explosive charge also sent a searing, overwhelming blast of heat into the cabin, whose side doors had been closed, with only the door gunner's hatch open. A jet of flame burst from the gunner's port as the UH-60 headed for the ground.

Shrader made five quick calls to base, then saw the lights of the New Port. With his collective control going to mush, he tried to establish a landing attitude, and then felt the crash. The flames were intense, and there were no signs of Williams, Anderson, or Richardson. I can imagine the momentary panic of trying to get out of the burning aircraft; releasing the harness and falling about 4 feet to the ground; flames everywhere; only the cabin remaining; the tail gone. At the front of the helicopter, CW2 Alliman was still alive, but injured with deep cuts above his eye. Quickly assessing the situation, Shrader pulled Alliman to safety up an alley about 50 feet from the downed bird. With rounds from the aircraft's ammunition igniting and Somalis closing on the crew's position, Shrader began calling for help on his survival radio. That's when militia grenades started to explode, the Somalis' preferred tactic for flushing an enemy.

After a brief firefight that expended the survivors' ammunition, Shrader and Alliman were in a desperate situation, down to a signal light and survival knives. Somali rifle fire and vulgarity sporadically peppered their area as bright flashlight beams searched for them.

Though fairly well hidden, things seemed hopeless. Then a friendly Somali came out and said, "American boy, American boy," and pointed to an armored vehicle. Shrader, taking the only option they had, decided they should go with him. The unlikely Somali led them to a United Arab Emirates vehicle that was part of the U.N. contingent, and it immediately evacuated them to safety at the New Port.

Don't tell me, Shrader, or Alliman that God doesn't work in mysterious ways.

I later learned that all of this was going on while Tiger Company was moving to the crash site. Living a warped mirror image of the same situation, we had literally passed like ships in the night; they found salvation.

We found the glow.

CHAPTER 9

Calm before the Storm

Three days later I found myself staring at the dawn of an Indian Ocean sunrise. Fresh, clean air passed over my bristly barracks-cut hair as I pondered why C/2-14 Infantry was so good.

The white noise of the breeze passing over my ears helped to isolate my thoughts. Two battles fought; a mindset linking death with life; facing the realities of casualties. Leadership is driven into the heart of the commander by the crucible of combat, the ferocity of action, and the choices made in the situation. Memories are seared into the deepest recesses of the brain and very little is forgotten. The calm I felt after living through it again was settling, maturing, and bringing forth thoughts of wisdom from my readings of past combat and fighters, the winners and the losers.

Charlie Company once again found itself at Range 10—The Beach—locked eternally in Colonel David's cycle. After three days of support duty, we wanted to train. You would think that soldiers would find training mundane or anticlimactic after combat, but the reverse was actually true. Professional soldiers want to hone their skills to perfection, knowing that perfection enhances survival odds. Thus, my officers and NCOs calmly led the men in a training round-robin of marksmanship, combat lifesaving, actions on contact, fire and movement, reconnaissance, leadership role-playing to the lowest man, and weapons cross training, enjoying, along with the men, the toils of the infantryman.

You never can tell when a private will have to become a squad leader or a platoon leader will have to assume company command. Over and over for three whole days we prepared for the next confrontation with the enemy and decompressed in our own thoughts.

As I watched my men, I thought of how much we had gone through since the change of command on a blue-matted gym floor on that cold January day. Around me I saw professional warriors practicing their trade. The sense that we were a team was profound. I trusted each man to do his job and each trusted me to do mine. While bearing the burden of hardship, these men knew that I would never let them die or be maimed in vain. I don't know if you can call it love but I longed to protect my men and to keep them safe, not from harm but from waste.

In a strong unit, a bond develops that is so precious men are willing to die for it. When that bond forms, it is the key to success. Forever strive for it; never toy with it; never doubt its existence. The bond between a commander and his unit, the one that makes them work effortlessly together, accomplishing the seemingly impossible, making the right calls, not complaining, and working through every obstacle as a team, is the dream and crowning achievement of every commander's career.

Like a good marriage, forging a strong unit takes time, understanding, flexibility, latitude, and patience. You must be allowed to make mistakes and grow your way to success, and you must allow your subordinates opportunities to strive, to fail, and to eventually succeed. The soldiers, sailors, airmen, or marines in your care must know that you care for them more than for yourself, and the commanders above you must know that you are fiercely loyal to both them and to your men at the same time.

Loyalty is rooted in respect. Respect is earned in both directions and never an entitlement. Those who demand loyalty are lost; those who demand respect are blind. Subordinates will follow you into hell if you care for them, if the mission is necessary, and if they trust that you have their—and the unit's—well-being fully in perspective. Truly great units are easily identified. They just seem to work better than the others. Their teamwork and devotion to one another is evident, from the commander to private soldier.

In every profession, enough practice, diligence, and plain hard work achieve a level of knowledge, competence, insight, and keen intuition that describes an artist. Delta, Special Operators, and Rangers constantly train to such high standards that they achieve the artistry of their profession. Many units in the various services know that they have attained that artistry level as well, and are justifiably proud of the fact. At the end of September 1993, I viewed my Tigers as Rembrandts, maybe even da Vincis.

As I moved around the training perimeter, I thought of the 10th Mountain Division's history as hard-nosed warfighters. Starting in World War II with training in the Rockies, hard men, volunteers all, who believed at the core of their being that they were elite worked hard to make the impossible happen. They subsequently proved their ability to do so on Riva Ridge and all over Italy. Not in the limelight, always seemingly overshadowed by the likes of the 82nd or 101st, the 10th Mountain men proved time and again that they could perform beyond the normal light infantry unit. That was our bedrock, and my men knew the history and trained for that excellence.

Leadership cannot be overstated. The Second Brigade commander, Col. William E. "Kip" Ward, was compassionate, loved his soldiers, and was proud to lead them. His command style allowed you to be the best commander or staff officer you wanted to be. I keep with me his credo to "Bloom where you're planted," and strive to do just that. He wanted you to succeed, gave you your company with the knowledge that you would, fully expected initiative, broke the back of bureaucracy, got away from dogmatic process, and allowed you to learn your trade and "Train as you fight." It was never about making him look good. It was about your expectation of success and how to get you there. In essence, he created a family that trained together, played together, attended church together, and eventually fought together. He created success by believing in his men and his subordinate leaders, setting simple, well-conceived standards and nudging everyone until achievement.

Lt. Col. "Wild Bill" David drove us hard, but was always fair. Coming from the 101st and the 82nd, he knew elite units inside and out. Failure was not an option. He taught you to succeed by giving you an attainable goal (even though you may not have believed it possible) and allowing you to make it happen. By proving to you that you could accomplish any given mission, he built confidence. You had confidence in yourself, your unit, and the command and staff. As your subordinate leaders and men watched you grow and succeed, they gained confidence in you.

The company commander, me. What was my experience, and what did I bring to the fight? An only child's self-confidence; Boy Scouts; a National Rifle Association shooting background; the Paris Island Marine Corps boot camp experience; making corporal; completion of the Reserve Officer Training Corps program and achievement of a commission; subsequent completion of the Basic and Advanced Infantry Courses and the Airborne, Ranger, and Combined Arms Staff and Services Schools; repetitive rotations through the National Training Center, Graf/Hohenfels, and the Combined Maneuver Training Center; six years of mechanized infantry experience; and the pre-Somali deployment rotation at the Jungle Operations Training Center and true unit bonding experience formulated by Colonel David. I also cannot discount marriage and fatherhood, raising six children in the Army environment with the attendant moves, fears of loss, and the responsibility to something greater than myself.

All of that blended with Colonel David's straightforward plan to make us absolute experts at a few tasks: live-fire platoon movement to contact, clearing the objective, and night live-fire company assault of a trench line. I believe that foregoing pursuit of jack-of-all-trades qualification in favor of mastering the hardest, most complex missions made all the difference in Somalia.

I knew that my experience level was adequate, but by no means comprehensive. Successes in two lengthy firefights were now under my belt, during each of which I had made decisions that had saved face and saved lives. Infantrymen followed me.

As I meandered through those infantrymen at The Beach, I realized that they were the embodiment of American youth. They were from every walk of life and from all over the United States. We were a mini melting pot, men of different beliefs and origins who had forged a common goal to help where we could, but who retained the guarded viewpoint of the veteran. Hardened by the experience of tough training to 10th Mountain Division standards and hundreds of hours on myriad weapons and specialty ranges, these men were tough, experienced, and wise beyond their years. With brilliant and caring NCOs leading them at the squad and team levels, these men were prepared for whatever life would throw at them.

Amidst the smell of cordite and gunpowder, I completed my rounds through the ongoing training, shouting occasional "hooahs" as 2x4s and 4x4s were splintered and as 55-gallon drums were vaulted into the sky by direct AT-4 rocket hits. I felt privileged to be in the company of such men. I was humbled to be their leader.

Our final three totally uninterrupted days at The Beach went by quickly, and seemed to both purge the residue of the encounter with tragedy and to rejuvenate my Tigers. Searching the never-ceasing waves of the great Indian Ocean and the beauty of the vast blue sky above, I wondered: "What next?"

Colonel Dallas, Commander of the 10th Aviation Brigade to which we were attached in Somalia, was due to change command on 1 October. I thought that he might approve conduct of some bottom-up planned attacks into the heart of Aidid's playground before he departed. I also knew that Ato, Aidid's moneyman, had been nailed by Delta and that, since the Delta/Ranger Team was taking over the key missions, they likely didn't want us in the mix. Maybe the surgical strikes would pay off.

I didn't understand the wishy-washy nature of the U.N.'s approach to Aidid and Somalia as a whole. Why were we waiting for a surgical strike when we could destroy the warlords' hold on Mogadishu with a well-planned combined arms ground operation? Being too close to the problem and no longer politically naïve, I realized that my company and I were just little fish in a very big pond, and that no one was going to answer me. Our role, after all, was to execute national policy, not make it.

Slipping on my black gloves, putting on my shades, and donning my Kevlar, I made ready to travel back to where our fate awaited us. Calling over the first sergeant, I explained that it was time to pack up and get underway, back to the nightmare of the city, high tension, protesting mobs, NGO civilians being attacked, command-detonated mines, raised basic loads, and SOPs. Putting on our game face and donning our good paranoia, we headed for our in-country home, with only the Lord knowing what the future held for us.

Oh . . . and what made our unit so good?

WE did.

Grandstanding on my HMMWV.

The command team at the University Compound. From left: me; 2nd Battalion, 14th Infantry Regiment Commander Lt. Col. Bill David; HHC Commander Capt. John Rapsis; A Company Commander Capt. Drew Meyerowich; and B Company Commander Capt. Mark Suich.

Black Hawk recon of our routes into and out of the city.

The "Mog." Almost all of our compounds had the same look and feel.

Mural at the far western edge of our barracks.

2nd Platoon's "Fort Apache" mural.

"Welcome to the Tiger Dome" mural just outside my hooch. *Thunderdome*, the post-apocalyptic movie, was recent and on our minds.

Somalia coastline heading south out of Mogadishu.

Range training. Austere, but it honed our accuracy and ability to mass fires.

Night live-fire training at The Beach.

The commanding officer fights, too! Tiger 6 in action.

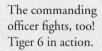

Staff Sergeant
Woolery and 2nd
Platoon members.

The bush "command
bunker."

The Rangers' first ground
recon, just south of
Hunter Base.

HQ Section
HMMWVs just
outside our barracks,
stripped down, not
up-armored.

Malaysian Condors.
We rode these into
combat the night of
3–4 October.

Remains of
Super 64 in the
"Labyrinth."

C Company's position at the Southern Objective on 3–4 October.

Somali children at Range 10.

The last day in Mogadishu— 19 December, 1993—ready to redeploy.

The command team with Maj. Gen. Thomas Montgomery at our farewell ceremony in the infamous Ranger hanger. From left: me, Capt. Drew Meyerowich, Lt. Col. Bill David, Montgomery, Capt. Mark Suich, and Capt. John Rapsis.

The arrival formation in Soldiers Gym on our return from Somalia—the first of the modern-era gym-style "Welcome Home" ceremonies we are all used to now.

Standing proud at The Beach range.

CHAPTER 10

Living History

October 3, 1993: a day like any other day in Mogadishu. The cool Indian Ocean breeze fluttered through my mosquito net, the cot dug into my shoulders, and the fan-driven, persistent city stench swirled in my nostrils, driving me on the way to consciousness. Along with me, the Tigers began to stir; another day in the "Mog."

Upon awakening on any given day, you generally don't think you are going to die that day, or dwell on potentially life-threatening situations that might find you, or that you will make history. Those just aren't normal thoughts. You stretch, roll out of the rack, blow through the aches and pains, get ready for PT, and brush your teeth expecting just another lackluster day.

I tried to begin each day not with loathing or expected doom, but with the deep American sense of adventure. I tried to live each day to the best of my ability, all the while believing that I would live forever. I had disassociated from self-protection and fully believed that if I took care of the soldiers, they would take care of me.

So, what was to become the most harrowing, life-threatening, and, some say, heroic day of my life began with casual ordinariness. It was a Sunday, that 3rd of October, a morning for lifting, a T-rat breakfast, Bible study, and prayers.

After finishing my personal routine, I headed for the battalion TOC, where I met with the staff and enjoyed the camaraderie while wondering if anything was in the wind. Oddly enough, on this day Colonel David corralled me to introduce the new Ranger LNO, Major Nixon, a tall and robustly built man with a firm grip and a friendly demeanor. My gut told me something was up. Nixon and his RTO were there for a reason.

Walking down the corridor of the battalion headquarters, Colonel David half-jokingly remarked that, since Tiger Company and I were QRC, something was bound to happen. I took the omen seriously; the others laughed. I believe you make your own luck, but I also believe in the unseen nature of things and the unexplainable. "I'd better get prepared," I thought. Striding past the battalion colors—history in cloth and symbolism—I passed through the old tan metal door with its ancient creak and out into the crisp African morning.

While walking down the sunbaked concrete steps that I had descended innumerable times, I sorted through my thoughts. "If we're called, where will it be? The Black Sea?" We had been given the Rangers' most likely action locations just weeks before. An educated guess, then, said it would be the Black Sea, the Bakara Market, National Street, and the hell that existed there.

Further questions washed through my brain. "Were the Rangers going to finally get Aidid? Are we on the verge of going home? What is it really like in that hellhole in the northern part of the city?" Signs, such as the hush-hush atmosphere in the TOC and the frequent fleeting glances between the Ranger LNOs and Colonel David, indicated that Aidid was indeed zeroed in and that a mission was actually going down today!

As much as I wanted to be a part of the mission, wondering, in fact, why we were not in the OPORD briefing, my gut said that we were an afterthought to Delta and the Rangers, and that they would get the mission done without us. They had all the toys, and professional jealousy ate at me. How many times had we been ready to conduct offensive operations but never carried them out? To a man, we were ready as a unit. We knew the city, had accomplished missions, had been in firefights, and yet had never been invited to the party. Delta and the Rangers knew they could do the mission without us—were going to do the mission without us! "Well, damn it," I thought, "We're going to be ready, just in case. We will be ready."

There is no substitute for reconnaissance and rehearsal. By the time I'd made it back to the company command post, I had resolved to call the company leaders in and go over the current plan for actions in the Black Sea area. In my heart I knew the fun-meter was pegged and we needed some closure to the whole mission.

The Mog was becoming monotonous. We were like an idling engine, just getting hotter and hotter, ready for use, but with nobody to stomp on the pedal. Prepared or not, odds were we would be doing the same thing tomorrow. Delta and the Rangers were seeing all the action and were actually keeping us from playing a vital role. Thus, we were probably not in the need-to-know category for today's mission.

Well, more power to them. In all honesty, I wished them well as I hollered at the charge of quarters to get all the leaders together in my hooch in ten minutes, just in case.

The tension level was steady in my cramped office. I explained what I felt (only intuition), who I'd met in the battalion CP, and the gut feeling I had that we should go over the plan one more time. I explained the need to stay alert, and that I felt something was up that would make today the real beginning of the end to the Somalia mission. I guess I was hoping that if we got Aidid, peace and love would break out across the city. What a pipe dream!

The support plan into the Black Sea/Bakara Market area was fairly simple—on paper. Just take a right out of the University Compound, drive five minutes to the K-4 Traffic Circle, take a left, drive about two minutes north, take a right on National Street, go about two minutes east, take a left on any of the main streets headed north, and one minute later you were in the Bakara Market. Ten minutes, max, and you were in the heart of the Black Sea "Indian" country—and in the very heart of darkness of the human soul. From Fort Apache, 2nd Platoon's AO, to a place where a fire-fight *would* occur, the time from callout to in-site was just fifteen minutes.

The mission would be either to rescue, support by fire and maneuver, or police up the broken pieces. Not the best of mission choices, but choices that we knew how to do and had experienced in the reality of a life or

death situation. We went over the possibilities of driving into the fight, dismounting, and moving to contact. We reviewed the SOPs, the daily radio
frequencies and call signs, and command and control procedures. Those
were the things that separated us from the enemy: our ability to out-
maneuver enemy elements because we could fully communicate via radio
or hand and arm signals, then overwhelm his meager capabilities with
superior firepower.

We talked through various scenarios and went over the SOPs with an
attitude of professional reserve, suspecting that we probably weren't even
going to be involved. It was far more likely that we would sit on our
rooftops and watch the black gunships dart and dive, see the bright flashes
and hear the distant rumble of the firefight from afar, watch the smoke
curl into the bright blue afternoon sky, and just wait for the stink of
cordite to waft over us.

After the meeting with my leaders, I helped myself to a can of tuna,
my favorite, and sat in the quiet of my hooch, watching the fan track back
and forth, lazily pushing unseen air into and out of my mosquito net, the
dark green rectangle billowing, seeming to breathe on its own. With disciplined repetition, I diligently cleaned my M-16, my 9mm, and the magazines for each, reloaded and re-holstered, checked my canteens for fullness,
and ensured I had spare batteries for my PVS-7 and radios. Just in case.

The afternoon crawled, the temperature soared. Expectation and bore-
dom mingled in my brain, making me as anxious as a schoolboy waiting
for Santa on Christmas Eve. Because of the mission, afternoon PT and my
normal run around the University and Embassy compound was postponed.

At 1500 I could wait no longer. Returning to the TOC, I walked in on
an anxious staff already intent on the coming mission. It was explained to
me that just past 1400 the QRF had been notified by Task Force Ranger
that the Black Sea area was off limits to air and ground traffic.

At 1537 the QRC was placed on REDCON 1. Staring at the radio,
then at Colonel David, I went to notify the company; the raid was actually
going to go down. I made it back as fast as possible. At 1543 Lucy, the code
word for mission execution, was relayed and the aircraft took off. Everyone,
including me, began to stare at the radios; frequencies were aligned to give
up the ghostly sounds of combat; action was imminent, but we still had

to wait. The same helpless churning in my gut that I had felt that first night out in the African bush while listening to Alpha Company execute their raid as I sat on the sidelines began, and I realized that I wanted to be there. "Move to the sound of the guns, damn it," I thought.

In my mind's eye I could already see the victorious Delta and Ranger forces parading Aidid on CNN. Everyone knew they were good. They'd already pulled off six near-perfect missions in both the middle of the night and in broad daylight, and their action taking Ato, Aidid's financier, was already becoming legend.

But all of us knew that things weren't always perfect. We'd been taught that no plan survives the first contact with the enemy. I'd had it hammered into me at the National Training Center, the Combat Maneuver Training Center, and the Jungle Operations Training Center, and it had been confirmed by nearly every rotation downrange that I had ever had the privilege to lead soldiers on.

As the seconds ticked by, the crackle of adrenaline surged along my spine. I could just picture the swarm of helicopters, like black wraiths, swooping in from the ocean to inundate the Black Sea area with surprise, speed, shock, and, if necessary, overwhelming fire from the all-powerful mini-guns aboard nearly every bird. An untold number of Black Hawks, Little Birds, and assorted other helicopters were in the air, bearing down on the objective like a scene straight out of *Apocalypse Now*.

We would later learn that the initial force included members of Squadron C, 1st Special Forces Operational Detachment-Delta; a company command element and two platoons of Company B, 3rd Ranger Battalion, 75th Ranger Regiment; and specialized aviation support from the 160th Special Operations Aviation Regiment "Night Stalkers" that included eight MH60K SpecOps Black Hawk helicopters, a combat search and rescue team, the mission commanders' command and control aircraft, four MH-6J Little Bird attack helicopters (two with miniguns, two with miniguns and rockets), and four side bench-equipped MH-6 Little Birds carrying the Delta assault force. To those of us awaiting the outcome, the air support was professionally impressive because, at the time, the 160th was a very hush-hush organization. As of this writing, they remain the worldwide best in the combat aviation business.

Although unable to see the actual execution of the raid, we could still track events by the sounds over the radio. Every audio morsel, from radio silence to the overwhelming sounds of giant machinery hovering in midair, helped crystallize the mental picture. I recall thinking how smoothly it was going down as powerful voices fought the roar of the rotor blades and rotor wash, their words creating images of the mission's execution. "Fire; they're taking fire," I thought, as everyone listened intently. As time passed, we heard of a critical casualty when a Ranger fell from one of the helicopters, then a report of a U.S. 5-ton truck being destroyed. With fire increasing from every direction, SITREPS were pouring in.

Then it happened: "We got a Black Hawk going down."

All eyes in the TOC hit me at once. Needing no command, I sprinted for the door, made my CP in record time, and screamed "GET IT ON." Reactions were instantaneous, as everybody knew what that meant.

Because we were at REDCON 1, the trucks were staged and we were ready to go. The Tigers raced up the steps with their full combat loads and were ready and formed in less than fifteen minutes. Butt packs were full of ammo, water, MREs, extra batteries, and first aid kits. NVGs, extra grenades, star clusters, and bandoliers of ammunition were draped across bodies or tucked into every pocket or pouch. We needed to be loaded for bear, and we were.

Then, as the QRC quivered in the starting blocks, ready to react, ready to help, huffing, puffing, and raring to go now . . . we were told to stand by.

I returned to the TOC and asked what was going on. The response was that, reportedly, they didn't need us yet.

To this day I question that decision. Letting the Somali militia throughout the city get organized for the coming fight favored the militia, not us. The longer the Rangers held us at bay, the more time the militia had to arm, organize, and erect obstacles such as burning tires, stacked cars, and other assorted debris. We had seen this behavior before, when earlier engagements with militia forces were preceded by city-wide alarms being raised. Consequently, delay simply didn't seem tactically sound to me.

Deflation set in as the expected action didn't happen, and the longer we listened to the firefight, the more frustrated I became. From training and experience, men of arms tend to anticipate that the right calls will be made. But this call to wait was one that my gut said was wrong, and that men were going to die because of it.

Although things were already bad, they weren't overwhelming. In retrospect, I still feel that my company could have made it to either Cliff Wolcott's or Mike Durant's bird and gotten out before it got too crazy. But on that day, as time ticked by and the sun slowly began to set, the QRC continued to wait.

Georges Jacques Danton, a leading figure at the outset of the French Revolution, once said: "l'audace, encore de l'audace, et toujours de l'audace . . ." ("audacity, still more audacity, and audacity forever . . ."). We needed to be moving! I felt like a bullmastiff at the end of its leash. I hope the reader senses my frustration, because I still feel it as this is written.

This is the so-called fog of war, when reasonable men make the hard choices. To prevent our being ambushed on the way to the objective, the leadership kept us clear to see if the Rangers could self-rescue. In fact, we weren't allowed to pass Banadir Hospital on the way to K-4 because of just such a reasonable decision by Brig. Gen. Greg Gile, the 10th Mountain Division's Assistant Division Commander for Operations, and Colonel David. Their rationale was understandable: If we got hit and pinned down, the QRF and Task Force Ranger would suddenly have faced three simultaneous incidents in the city, a situation that would forfeit any initiative we might have established. Consequently, the Tigers and I were put on hold while the men down in the city were fighting for their lives and rushing headlong toward a tipping point.

Delta and the Rangers were still expecting to extricate themselves from the unfolding mess because in their hearts they believed they could. You don't make it into Delta or become a Ranger without getting into and out of impossible situations. Nevertheless, when the realities of the casualty count, the enemy's willingness to destroy you, and the imbalance of forces reaches a certain point, you can end up fighting and losing the heroic fight. (See Thermopylae.)

In my heart, I knew we would eventually be committed to the fight. The whole city wanted TF Ranger dead, and the Somalis had the means to achieve that goal. The Rangers and Delta were in a whirlwind, fighting for their lives . . . and they needed our help.

I repeatedly traced the route in my mind and counted streets from two entry points. National Street was the obvious entry, but in the event that it was blocked, I searched for the next logical point into the Black Sea/Bakara Market area. The Milk Factory, well north of K-4 and National Street, caught my eye as I scanned the map and noted the size of the road network there. If we were blocked from using National Street that would have to be the alternative, with the HMMWVs and 5-tons having to haul ass up there and snake their way down to the objective. Coming from the north might be the best way in, anyway, but I just wouldn't know until I had eyes on the target and developed the situation.

At 1629 we finally got the word to execute. Colonel David and his TAC (a slice of his operations center) would accompany us. We would use MSR Tiger—the long way. After working out some details with the commander, the Tigers were in the fight!

"Just in case" had arrived, and the 2-14 IN was once again headed into a historic fight. A minute after we left, Colonel David alerted the A/2-14 Terminators to get ready, surmising that this was going to be a long night.

Quiet and subdued, the first rush of adrenaline long since gone, we made the familiar exit from the Tunisian-guarded university main gate, the left at the Pakistani checkpoint, moved south toward the Camel Market and Hunter Base, and proceeded along MSR Tiger. Three minutes out of the gate, word was passed to Colonel David that a second bird was down (no coordinates provided), and that all hell had broken loose. Ominously, more and more dark smoke spirals fingered the bright blue sky to our north. We picked up the pace.

The sense of déjà vu was overwhelming. Just a little over a week ago, we were on our way to a bird brought down by RPG fire. I thought quickly of the casualties from that operation and fell into the same thoughtful solitude on this drive that all the guys in my HMMWV were lost in. The unusually long drive was odd, too. We were used to the "Quick" part of QRF and immediate movement to the objective, not this long, drawn-out approach. It made getting psyched up a bit harder to achieve and maintain.

After another trip around the southern part of the city and past the stinking Mogadishu trash dump, the company pulled into the main terminal at 1724, over an hour after Chief Wolcott's Super 61 was downed.

Colonel David proceeded directly to the Joint Operations Center (JOC), and I dismounted to give instructions to the company leadership to download one platoon and prepare for my return with orders. We would need the empty trucks for those that we rescued.

After the quick contingency plan, I headed for the JOC. Dusty from the long ride and sweating from the afternoon heat, I momentarily paused in mid-stride. Eying the golden horizon and oncoming darkness, I felt an almost overwhelming sense of urgency.

In full combat gear and fueled by adrenaline, I hit the JOC door, pulled my helmet off, and tried to get my bearings in the new surroundings. I immediately spotted Colonel David and Brigadier General Gile talking with a very tall and thin lieutenant colonel. The deference paid by my leaders to this man seemed odd at the time, but with my mind on the mission, and awaiting orders, I just didn't realize who he was, and no one told me.

The lieutenant colonel turned and guided me to a bank of television monitors and began briefing me on the situation. He stated that at this point the mission was accomplished, but two helicopters were down, and my Tigers and I were headed for the southernmost crash site. There was absolutely no panic in the air, just extreme urgency. The monitors showed real-time, black-and-white feeds from the Little Birds of a fight that didn't look too pretty, especially at the southern crash site. The images depicted chaos and desperate situations, and I realized that we were headed right into the thick of it.

Later, I learned that the calm and confident officer was, in fact, Maj. Gen. William Garrison, commander of Task Force Ranger. I recall how his manner and tone made me feel accepted and respected and that, for some reason, I immediately reciprocated. Some leaders are just like that.

During my brief time with Garrison, Gile and Colonel David had been discussing the possible use of armored personnel carriers (APCs). The thought occurred to me that this mission would have been a helluva lot easier if we had M2 Bradley fighting vehicles and M1 Abrams tanks on hand right then. Then I told both my leaders that if we could get APCs, we had plenty of cross-trained mechanized soldiers in the ranks—including me—and that "borrowing" the vehicles for the mission made a lot of sense with all the RPGs and small-arms fire flying around.

At this point the Rangers were hurt but holding. It was time to go, now! With grid coordinates marked on my map, I wheeled for the door and had reached for the handle when a voice from over by the bank of radios on the left said "Good luck." Turning toward the Ranger major who stood there, I blurted out "Take it back," in utter seriousness.

I had noticed in my life that when people wished me good luck I usually received something resembling the opposite. And, knowing full well that it would take a lot more than luck in the coming hours, I took his statement as an unwelcome omen.

That Ranger major saw that I was dead serious. Without annoyance or insult, and knowing that warriors have such quirks, he simply replied, "Then break a leg."

Both sentiments were well-intentioned; I knew that and so did he. We both also knew that I faced a daunting task.

Lives hung in the balance, and I was the chosen one. Whatever the coming hours had in store for me, he wanted me to succeed. With an exchange of smiles that meant farewell, I charged through the door and into history.

CHAPTER 11

Running the Gauntlet

The commotion at the Ranger Hangar and the JOC was building like a cyclone. Task creation was exponential as the minutes ticked by. The sense that things might go wrong was creeping into every aspect, but the hard line we all took was absolute: "They're in trouble and we *are* going to get them out!" When I left the JOC, I knew that the mission was far bigger than me, and that it would take everyone's maximum effort this afternoon and night to get the trapped men out. Failure was not an option.

The platoon leaders were waiting for me with a Ranger liaison officer (LNO), a hard-charging sergeant with a load of commo gear. So was Colonel David. He knew I had to brief the leadership on at least the grid coordinates and actions at the objective. Task, purpose, and commander's intent are what you need to give in the most urgent of situations. "Mount up," I said. With that, engines cranked and belched initial puffs of black smoke from the stacks; diesels whined as drivers did their universal pump-it-a-couple-times break-dance; sandbags were adjusted; and game faces were put on. With weapons at the ready, we lined up for a ride into hell.

Out the Egyptian gate we rode, with the antitank platoon leader, 1st Lt. Furman Ray, in the lead. My company command vehicle followed, driven by Sergeant Graham, with me and my RTOs, Randall and

Alsbrooks, aboard. The 2nd and 3rd Platoons fell in line, and the company trains, the 1st Platoon's empty vehicles, and Colonel David took the rear as we snaked out of the compound and headed for K-4 Traffic Circle. (We brought 1st Platoon's vehicles without their personnel because we needed the transport capability to bring back the Rangers.)

The plan, almost as we had rehearsed that morning, was to head north from K-4, turn right onto National Street, and then get directed into Site 2 by command and control elements in the birds circling above us. The crash site was in a huge city park that was nothing more than a labyrinthine tangle of ramshackle tin sheds in every conceivable arrangement. Once at the objective, 2nd Platoon would develop the situation, clear the route in, overrun the bird, and take up security positions while looking for Rangers and Delta operators. The 3rd Platoon would guard the ingress/egress route and the trucks for our departure. Numbers and names were not discussed at this point. Our bottom line was clear: Get in and save who we could.

The ride to K-4 took only five minutes. The still-bright sun was being filtered by the trees, low in the powder-blue sky, causing long shadows that dove deep into the alleyways. The air was filled with the smell of khat, cordite, and the foul sweat of a million people hell-bent on either tearing each other apart or watching from the sidelines as if this were some gladiatorial match.

As quickly as the small convoy was proceeding, with 5-ton trucks and HMMWVs straining at the gears, the world began to slow. The foul, coppery taste of adrenaline began to course through my system; I could feel my muscles ache for the release of pent-up energy. Colonel David's calm voice through the hand mike gave last minute instructions; at pace and with reverberating background noise, I understood him to say that we had to loop around K-4 once, picking up a couple of Ranger HMMWVs that were offering to help in the rescue mission into the Black Sea area and the southern crash site.

With the ancient roundabout fully in view, I picked up the Rangers in my field of vision, just off to my left. In an action that seemed more like a wind-up for a pitch, we swung around in front of the Ranger vehicles and opened a spot just behind my number two vehicle, then whipped around the circle in one fluid motion and headed for what looked like the waiting maw of a giant beast: Via Lenin, the main north–south route from K-4 to 21 October Road.

With high compound walls on either side of the road as far as the eye could see, Via Lenin looked invitingly cool in the shadows of the waning afternoon sun. Temperatures were beginning to drop, but we were again sweating at full capacity. For some reason, I told Sergeant Graham to "Stomp on it."

We shot ahead into a maelstrom. Immediately upon entering the opening to Via Lenin, the world erupted in a cacophony of violence. AMBUSH! RPGs and machine-gun and AK rounds sizzled in the air as green tracers and explosions ripped across, into, and between the vehicles of our rescue party.

In the horror of the instant, I thought only of the men and Colonel David. I jerked to look back, straining against the seat and my equipment. I saw flying debris and a light show of tracers, and heard the roar of engines and the explosions of RPGs against both the far and near walls.

The two platoons gave as good as they got, firing on the move at the flashes and rocket motor trails left by the inbound RPGs. Vehicles were hit; fire, blast glow, tracer burn, sparks off the vehicles, muzzle flashes everywhere.

"Get a SITREP," I told myself. God, it was loud. The noise of the ambush in the tight confines of the compound-walled enclosure was deafening. My voice choked with dust. I couldn't even hear myself scream into the hand mike; the voice in my head was all that I could hear. How we weren't hit in the lead vehicles, I will never know.

As we had traveled up Via Lenin, we had accelerated to create the gap the Ranger vehicles filled. The Somali ambushers probably thought we were going to slow down for the looping turn. Instead, we had taken off like a sprinter out of the blocks. That had to make us hard to track, but I heard later that the Ranger vehicles got hit directly in the kill zone behind us.

The intense firing at the opening to Via Lenin instantly separated Colonel David's party, which held position at K-4 while we kept moving to our assigned mission. The 5-tons swerved and followed me. I knew that men in a desperate situation were depending on us to get there, and that time was running out; you could feel it in your bones. With the sun going down, you had the feeling that hope was tied to the sunset. "Focus!" I thought to myself. "Think, damn it."

I counted streets as they zipped by in a seemingly endless walled compound–gate–small dirt street–walled compound–gate–small dirt street cycle. The flashes of vision at 55mph and above, speeding to get out of the hail of gunfire and certain death, were just blips in my consciousness. My brain had already started into its To-Do list: air cover—*now*; National Street, turn right; four major streets; fight while mounted as far as we can go; take a right, dismount, fight on foot; protect the wounded; guard the ingress; guard the egress; guard the trucks; get to the crash site, gather the wounded, collect the dead, destroy the sensitive items; withdraw under fire; mount up; get back to the airfield . . .

God help us . . .

The ambush was a real jolt. I could only imagine what was going on in the thick of it in the Black Sea area if we had just taken that much fire on an approach route. This was going to be no picnic.

Approaching National Street at a fast clip, we saw black plumes reaching for the sky and smelled the intense, acrid odor of burning rubber that overwhelmed the senses. It gave an oily feel to the air, clogged nostrils, and laid a cover of sooty slime on everything it touched. Burning tires, lit over an hour before, blazing in huge pyres, were interlaced with crushed and stacked cars and an earthen berm that ran from the northern compound wall to the southern compound walled entrance to National Street. The enemy was waiting for us and, due to their size, the 5-tons were effectively blocked from the only real way to get into the crash sites.

"Fuck!" I screamed, as once again we triggered another ambush. We returned fire, everyone straining for a glimpse of the enemy. Being trapped between these compound walls would leave us completely exposed—we had to keep them off of us! I yelled into the company command freq for everyone to keep going. Odds were that if we tried to bust through the obstacles at the intersections, the 5-ton trucks would never break through or clear the wreckage and molten rubber. In the event, we would be the next ones needing rescue.

On we roared, up Via Lenin, now looking for a new route, a new rescue plan, and new hope. I turned to our Ranger LNO and yelled, "Where the hell is our air cover?" We could see birds flying all over the city, but none were focusing on our situation. We needed the helicopters to blast a way through. The enemy was fighting for every block, which simply was not their normal behavior pattern. It finally dawned on me, somewhere north of National Street, that this was not the norm. The Rangers had stirred up a hornets' nest, and in about two minutes, my two platoons and I would be fighting for our lives.

As the Milk Factory came into view through the swirl of vehicle dust, I could see that the route to the north was blocked. Scanning our route, there was the ever-present compound wall to the west and urban buildings to the east. At the Milk Factory, another compound wall started on the eastern side again.

First Lieutenant Ray called and asked what I wanted him to do. Envisioning all eyes on me and knowing that this decision was critical, I gave the order to halt the convoy well before the roadblock. I was not going to drive into a "kill sack." We would get on the ground. At this point, the trucks were just giant targets and our mounted maneuver capabilities were limited by the wall to our left and the roadblock to our immediate front. We were heading into a dead end, hemmed in by the terrain and corralled by our enemy. Our options were to kill or be killed.

In *The Art of War*, Sun Tzu (c. 544–496 BCE) wrote, "In difficult ground, press on. In encircled ground, devise stratagems. In death ground, fight." Well past difficult or encircled, Via Lenin was now untenable death ground. We would fight our way out—hand-to-hand, if necessary.

With brakes squealing and engines still running, drivers brave as hell positioned their vehicles to allow us to dismount between them and the western compound walls. Slowly but surely, like ants drawn to a feast, the enemy began to react. You could hear constant slaps, *thwits*, and pings as rounds searching for soft flesh found metal, rubber, plaster, or concrete instead. But I knew, and my men knew, that RPGs would quickly be brought into play.

Enemy mortar rounds fired from Digfer Hospital to our southeast began falling as we dismounted. Somewhat disconcertingly, .50-cal fire began coming in from Sword Base, the U.S. logistics site west of us. As their unmistakable red tracers started tearing huge chunks out of the walls, we simultaneously welcomed the covering fire while silently urging their gunners to lift and shift so that their misses wouldn't come quite so close.

As the tracer light show began in earnest, RPGs began slamming into the walls, earth, and vehicles around us, some soaring high as enemy gunners reacted to the fire my Tigers poured into the enemy's hasty fighting positions. We were in a maelstrom. "Think, and make a decision," I told myself.

Radio contact with Colonel David was down. I had to make immediate decisions, or we were going to die in place. As plaster rained down, and with no air cover in sight, I couldn't help worrying that we would be snuffed out or have to be rescued ourselves, thus hindering the main mission of rescuing the Rangers. The best way to prevent that, I decided, was to clear the far side of the road, turn the vehicles 180 degrees, and run the gauntlet back to K-4.

After a quick discussion with the platoon leaders and the first sergeant, I directed the platoons to assault across the road while the vehicles got turned around from the front and hugged the near walls to protect the trucks as best we could. I gathered the support and HQ elements and the AT section and briefly explained the plan.

We opened up with everything we had, including MK-19s that launched round after round into every window, opening, and doorway across the road to our right and into the Milk Factory, which had become the base for plenty of armed targets. In a coordinated linear assault, 2nd and 3rd Platoons closed with the enemy, hauling ass in an assault wave across the open road to quickly clear buildings and force the Somalis to run or die. Most ran.

Directing the covering fire that provided the window for the assault, I could see our enemy break and run. The problem was that they receded like the tide and then slowly surged back when the pressure was relieved. This action was one of the bloodiest and heroic actions our company performed in Somalia.

Outstanding actions just north of K-4 include First Sergeant Doody's exceptionally brave sprint through a hail of gunfire to retrieve Pfc. Carroll, who had been shot in the shoulder and chest on his way back to the trucks. Machine gunner Pfc. Pamer's actions, too, went beyond the call of duty. His fearless sustained machine-gun fire while in the open protected his buddies and saved many lives. Although hit in a barrage of return fire, Pamer continued to pour hundreds of rounds downrange to buy time for the company to disengage under fire, even though he was wounded in the back and was "bleeding like a stuck pig," according to his platoon sergeant. Both Doody and Pamer would receive Silver Stars for their actions.

Our attack bought precious time to get the trucks turned around for the return trip through the gauntlet that was Via Lenin. Aggressive, brutal, and heroic, each man has his own story from that attack. As hard as the platoons fought in and out of houses, in the alleys, and in the courtyards, the action was intensely personal. Yet this fight validated our training and displayed the depth of the unit's cohesion. I was immensely proud of the single-minded effort that drove my men to perform, both as individuals and as a unified team, to accomplish the mission under severely adverse circumstances. Resilient, adaptive, brave, and aware, my Tigers were ready for the next ferocious step.

As Tiger Company began repositioning the vehicles, the Antiarmor Platoon's MK-19 gunners rained steel on any enemy who even thought about engaging our return convoy. Viewing the sights around me, my world narrowed. In the deepening dusk, blasts from mortars, MK-19s, and even .50-cal rounds sent showers of third-world brick and mortar in sprays of earth that filled my vision in every direction. We were churning the terrain as men ran to climb up the sides of the 5-tons, all focused on survival, even if hit.

Standing and reaching for my radio handset, I began an in-depth scrutiny of the combat action before me, one that would last a lifetime. Scanning from left to right, I became focused on—almost mesmerized by—the action. The heroism, tenacity, destruction, and white-hot determination I observed filled me with feelings of pride and wonder. The glory of it momentarily sucked me in and I began to lose my commander's focus. Consumed by the roar of engines, the crash and explosion of munitions, and the rushing of my own blood, the overwhelming actions filled my senses even as I kept telling myself to "Think, damn it, think."

This mantra finally broke through my momentary reverie and brought me back to the time and space I was in and to the mission at hand. Nearly deafened by incoming and outgoing fire, I jammed the receiver into my right ear, drove my gloved finger as far as I could into my left ear to shut out the racket, and depressed the rubber covering that surrounded the push-to-talk switch. "Dragon 6, this is Tiger 6, over . . . Dragon 6, this is Tiger 6, over . . . Dragon 6, this is Tiger 6, over . . ." My mind raced during the radio call: When will I get him? Will I get him? C'mon, c'mon; ANSWER! We've got to move, right now!

The greatest gift a commander can give his subordinates is the right to execute initiative—to do what is right and the time to get it done. Allowing a subordinate the luxury of initiative imbues confidence. I knew that as long as I tried to do the right thing at the time, the commander would approve. I just might have to move on my own, if for no other reasons than to protect my men and to preserve our combat capability.

Colonel David answered my third call. My SITREP gave the bare facts as I knew them: zero KIA; three WIA; situation in doubt if we remained on this course or tried to force our way off Via Lenin to the crash sites. I quickly explained the roadblocks and that we were turned around. "Return to K-4" was his reply. Unbeknownst to me, Major General Garrison was consolidating forces for a major, coordinated, and overwhelming push to the crash sites.

As I responded "WILCO," I was looking down Via Lenin with complete understanding that returning to K-4 would be easier said than done.

CHAPTER 12

Back through the Valley of Death

With my back literally against the wall and Randall and Alsbrooks by my side, I watched the AT Section taking fire from three directions at once. From the west, red .50-cal tracers from Sword Base churned the masonry wall into dust or carved deep gouges into the dry earth, creating a fine, talcum powder-like mist and releasing the fetid stench of mankind. Meanwhile, Somali rebels continued pouring rounds in from both north and east of our position.

For the moment, we were between courtyard walls, with the Milk Factory barricade and the neighborhood across the street to the east. The neighborhood itself was being shredded into rubble by flying lead, explosions, and shrapnel. Pock marks appeared in the walls, blood splattered or smeared as bodies came apart, and a deafening roar poured from the center of the neighborhood as it died along with the Somali fighters within.

Though frustrated by being fired at by both the enemy and our own forces, the men of the AT Section were focused on the mission and the task at hand. Their MK-19 gunners were chunking rounds as those armed with M16-A2s calmly placed sighted shots into the Milk Factory roadblock or across the road. There was no panic and no hiding from the enemy. Steady, skilled marksmen were simply going about the business of war. I was immensely proud of them.

"Mount up," I yelled to those around me. Although the 5-tons were all facing in the right direction, we still needed to get the HMMWVs turned around and headed south. To do that, we had to get everyone in the vehicles and race down the line of 5-tons.

Because climbing into the trucks had caused our massed outgoing fires to abate, surviving Somalis quickly started firing on our vehicles. Here, the point-and-blaze-away shooting technique typically used by the Somali National Alliance troops worked to our advantage, as time and again their rounds pinged off the trucks, shattered a mirror, or spidered a windshield. But the Somalis' inaccurate fire and the sandbags that shielded the men crowded into the backs of the 5-tons combined to allow few rounds to actually hit flesh.

My grim, determined, professional soldiers in the backs of those trucks, meanwhile, brought steady, aimed fire on targets at the edges of the urban landscape. Disciplined as always, they maintained suppressive fires as NCOs began counting to ensure that everyone was accounted for. I could hear them calling out names as I rolled past.

Adrenaline pumped through my veins as we watched the AT Section's M996 HMMWV (the mini-ambulance configuration) pull beside us, already pointing south. Eyeing everyone else in my stripped-down command vehicle, I gave myself a silent "All accounted for." I remember the Ranger LNO beginning to talk into his handset just as I keyed the mike on the company net to tell everyone that we were going back to K-4 as fast as possible and that they were to shoot anything that even looked like a threat. As the "Roger" and "WILCO" replies came back, we rolled forward and began picking up speed.

I stared into the faces of resolute, strong, and willing men, fighters eager to get back into the fight. We still had a mission to accomplish and these Somali bastards were keeping us from it. A sense of urgency clung to us. Although we had been turned back, there wasn't any quit in any of us. We were just going to have to find another way.

The K-4 Traffic Circle held the promise of temporary refuge but also reminded us of the vicious ambush and death we had passed through the last time we were there. And we were headed straight back through the ambush gauntlet we had come through not forty-five minutes before. The men leaned hard into the sandbags and rocked as the trucks lurched forward, belching diesel fumes into the darkening twilight.

Well-trained, the AT Section's M996 slowly accelerated to let the convoy's 5-tons catch up—15mph . . . 20mph . . . 30mph . . . and suddenly we were flying. Once in the open, a darkened expanse of broiling smoke appeared before my eyes. "Back down that road death waits," I thought.

"Fuck death; let's move!"

In near darkness now, everyone knew what was coming. The Tigers began a charge back down Via Lenin, heading south toward K-4 with an AT Section vehicle leading and my command vehicle following close behind. As we built up speed, dirt started boiling around us. Our thunder-run back through the gauntlet would either be a surprise or the Somalis would be waiting for us. Engines screamed again as drivers sought maximum speed, and the cold night air against my sweat-drenched uniform felt like air conditioning.

The darkening sky provided an eerie background for the rock concert-like light show of tracers and exploding RPGs. Only the mixture of city stench, cordite, and gunpowder kept us in the reality of the moment. I watched as both in- and outbound green and red tracers flashed through the smoke, with RPG rocket sparkle adding to the mix. Amid roaring engines and humming tires, men screamed insults at their enemies and their own fear as we drove on, hell-bent on reaching the uncertain safety of the K-4 Traffic Circle.

I began firing my weapon at the tracer origins, and action begets action; I fired, my men fired. We had driven into a very well-prepared trap, and by God, we were going to get out. Mad as hell, I fired in frustration and as a growing expression of pent-up rage. For the briefest of moments, I simply let go and abandoned thought to an exhilarating release of action. Fire poured across the hood of the command HMMWV from my M16A2. I aimed at nothing more than the initiation points of the green tracers or rocket plumes, determined to keep enemy heads down.

As I reached up to brush my face with a gloved hand, the almost simultaneous explosions of numerous RPG rounds impacted the wall to our right. A shower of masonry and searing hot slivers of shrapnel hit the sides of our vehicles as we flew by. I was sure one of those hot slivers hit the Ranger LNO, who was riding right behind me with his leg blocking the opening under the armpit in my flak jacket. If it hadn't gotten him, it likely would have hit me in the kidney. I could see him grimly tolerating the pain to continue the mission.

As the sounds rose to a crescendo, one last visual oddity appeared before my eyes. A large piece of metal had gotten caught in the under-carriage of the M996 in front of my vehicle. Jammed under the speeding HUMMV, the metal began showering the night with a giant rooster tail of sparks. The embers that flew into the swirling smoke created a display beyond the imagination of the most brilliant special effects artist.

With Sergeant Graham driving at full speed with the skill of a racecar driver and yelling as loud as he could at me, I came back from my berserker outrage. A calmness of spirit grounded me as, for some reason, I found myself at peace with myself and my role, not just in this fight, but in the universe. I saw that the barrel of my M16 was glowing red for the first time ever, felt the whipping wind, and noted that the light show continued, but I was back, and calm.

We were making progress, and I needed to know what awaited us at K-4. I reached for my hand mike and called, "Dragon 6, this is Tiger 6, over." Even though it felt as if our hair was still on fire, the colonel's answering call, "Tiger 6, this is Dragon 6; status, over" filled me with hope. We were just sixty short seconds from friendly faces and people who were not trying to kill us.

I reported the wounded, that our vehicles were pretty shot up, and that we would need ammo resupply before going out again. Then, as we approached the National Street turn, another ambush spewed its fire at us. In the swirling smoke from the burning tires at the rebel barricades, I caught glimpses of Somalis being knocked back by our fire and could hear and feel the impacts of incoming rounds.

Blasting south, the Tigers moved through the kill zone in record time and I searched for the opening in the walls along Via Lenin. With night finally closing in and the area shrouded with smoke from the earlier fight, I found what I was looking for and in seconds we burst into K-4. I kept the vehicles going deep into the circle so that everyone could clear Via Lenin. As truck brakes screeched, I dismounted to find friendly faces.

Although we expected more attacks, especially from snipers, for whatever reason, there weren't any. The trucks pulled into a defensive perimeter on the south side of the traffic circle. As the men began dismounting they suddenly found themselves faced with a mini crowd-control situation. Still, no one lost sight of the fact that the situation was serious, and that we still weren't even close to completing the mission.

As Colonel David told me what we were going to do next, I looked at my men and our vehicles. Everything looked shot to shit. Then the count came up one vehicle short.

With a knowing look at the colonel, I thought, "Christ, we've got to go get that truck. Nobody gets left behind—ever."

The backlight from the market and shops that surround K-4 made the road heading north up Via Lenin look like the maw of hell. Our vehicles had sucked the swirling mass of smoke from fires up the street toward the entrance to the roadway. Then, just when I started to shout "Mount up," a lone 5-ton truck, replete with spidered glass, flats all around and sandbags leaking over its side and onto the road, crept slowly into view. The faces over those sandbags looked even grimmer than ours had when we had started to roll. That 5-ton was shot to hell and back but, like the rest of us, was still soldiering on.

A spontaneous cheer went up to express our relief. When everything was sorted out, the linkup was accomplished. K-4 was full of Somali civilians, hundreds of them, and my company had become live-action news. Just to make a hole in the crowd to return back to the airport eventually took a couple of CS riot agent M203 grenade rounds to clear the path. As a result, we left K-4 wearing our protective masks. How odd; this experience was giving us a taste of everything. But we were only on course three of a five-course meal.

As my dad would say, we had "given as good as we got." We were wounded; so was the enemy, and more than a few Somalis fighters were dead. But our most pressing problem was that our mission was not yet accomplished. I thought, "We've still got men out there in the dark, bleeding, dying, and dreading a Custer's end."

For us, the night was still young . . .

CHAPTER 13

"Take a Deep Breath"

In boot camp, drill instructors commonly push recruits almost to their limits during physical training or when marching, all the while constantly monitoring their state of motivation. When the DIs could detect that the recruits were just about at "quit," they would stop the activity and bellow "Take a deep breath," pause a few seconds, then holler "Let it out." Then the intense activity would begin again. That momentary respite served to make even the most demanding events seem bearable.

The scene at K-4 in the nautical twilight of 3 October 1993 called for just such a "Take a deep breath" moment. The company hadn't been mauled, savaged, or decimated, but it had been sobered. As I looked from face to face, I saw that a cold reality, stark in its clarity, had pervaded the company. To its core, this living entity that was Tiger Company understood that what lay ahead of us was not going to be easy.

Our situation had become far more complex than when we had originally set out. We had wounded, our ammo was far too low, and some vehicles were pretty shot up. Water was being quickly consumed now, if not depleted. And the men of Delta and the Rangers were still out there in the growing darkness, fighting for their lives, bleeding and in pain. Those men were depending on us to link up and complete a rescue mission.

What just a few short minutes ago had seemed like a quick in-and-out mission was now going to take some planning. The enemy had said, "No." It was up to us to change their minds.

With a rapid final head count and vehicle assessment, we remounted, used CS to clear a path through the gawking civilians, and drove south toward the airport. After a short drive, we passed through the South Egyptian gate near the JOC and parked in a row alongside the terminal building with our bumpers to the retaining wall facing the ocean, north to south. We then proceeded to get a full accountability of the company situation.

Pamer and Carroll, seriously wounded, were unloaded from the back of the trucks, the blood from their wounds soaking the uniforms of both men to near black. Others in the company wrapped their less serious wounds with bandages and got prepared to move out again. Our Ranger LNO went for medical attention.

I watched the remaining men descend from the trucks, obviously concerned about their buddies and the "what next" of the mission. As the XO, 1st Lieutenant McDonald, got the seriously wounded to the next level of trauma care, I met with 1st Sergeant Doody and the platoon leaders to give them quick instructions. The priorities were to get as much ammo as possible from the Rangers (who looked like they were prepping for their own follow-on rescue convoy); to get water and ensure that everyone drank and filled their canteens; and to shore up the sandbags in the back of the trucks. While we knew that we were going back out as soon as we were ready, the when and the how were still undetermined. I would need to link up with Colonel David in the JOC.

We had gone through a lot during our push north out of—and our push back in to—K4. The frenzied activity that follows such an engagement is called consolidation and reorganization. Consolidation is the process of getting your shit back together; reorganization is the process of replacing your casualties and determining whose positions, responsibilities, and expertise would have to be filled, as well as the acquisition and distribution of the aforementioned ammo and water. And, of course, as adept practitioners of the art of multitasking, we all seized on the "Take a breath" opportunity.

As those tasks were being worked out by the XO, the first sergeant, and the platoon leaders, I turned and headed to the JOC. On the way, I felt the dampness of my sweat-soaked uniform, and took a moment to be grateful for the inbound soft sea air that blew away some of my own stink. I also felt the aftertaste of adrenaline on my tongue, an unpleasant copper-iron-salt mix best described as "yak."

And, as my hearing started to recover from the effects of the rifle fire and RPG explosions of the past hour, I slowly began to catch the far-off sounds of continued combat. The crackle of gunfire and flare of tracers reminded me of the last firecrackers and final fireworks of a typical Fourth of July night. For the briefest of surreal moments, I was back at Alex Bay with my family. Then the split-second image vanished, and I was back to reality.

On that walk to the JOC, and for the first time, I saw Rangers looking at me as if wondering why the mission was not accomplished. The looks seemed to echo my thoughts; why didn't we yet have their Ranger buddies back at the hangar and the mission completed? I could only stare back and grit my teeth. As I opened the door to the JOC, I thought, "They just don't know how bad it is out there." With a steely focus, I walked through that door and into the light.

The atmosphere in the JOC was not what I expected. There was no panic, just extreme concentration and professionalism. Information was being recorded and intense focus was being placed on every word coming out of the radio speakers. I strode past the operations officers on my right and made a beeline for Colonel David and Brigadier General Gile at the back of the room.

Just after 1900, I was briefed by my commanding officer. Colonel David began by explaining the overall situation and the damage that had been done. A running gun battle had taken place around the objective sites. Surrounded by hundreds, if not thousands of Somalis, mostly armed with AKs and RPGs, the northern crash site of Super 61 was still being defended in a loosely held perimeter around three main buildings near the downed bird. Ammo, water, and medical supplies were slowly being depleted.

Super 64's southern crash site had been overrun and everyone, including two Delta operators that had roped in, was presumed killed in action.

It was thought that one pilot might be alive. I realized then that someone was going to have to get to the site of Super 64 to retrieve the remains of the fallen and the sensitive items from the aircraft.

I also learned of a heroic effort by another helicopter crew. Super 68, flown by CW3 Dan Jollota and Maj. Herb Rodriguez, had been hit with an RPG and small-arms fire while it held a steady hover to offload combat search and rescue personnel at the northern crash site. Then, in a miraculous display of truly great airmanship after being severely damaged by continuous rifle and machine-gun fire and an RPG, this magnificent crew nursed the aircraft back and made a successful emergency landing at the airfield.

Colonel David continued, explaining that several other birds that had been hit either made it to the New Port or back to the airfield; that Company A's Terminators were on their way from the University; and that Company B's Bastards were coming in from their training site north of the city. Thus, we would soon have the entire battalion, another Ranger Ground Reaction Force, and all the helicopters that both TF Ranger and the QRF could get in the air to execute a rescue mission.

At the end of Colonel David's briefing, Gile also told me that the QRF and Ranger GRF would be linking up with the Pakistanis, who had tanks, and elements of a Malaysian mechanized battalion. With these added U.N. "volunteers," our firepower was growing exponentially. I was told to get my Tigers ready to head for the New Port as soon as all of our forces were consolidated at the airfield terminal. With an emphatic "Roger, Sir," I headed back out through the JOC door into near blackness.

The darkness that hit me just outside the door of the JOC caused me to take a minute to let my night vision kick in. It was then that I realized that I needed to slow down. As if God had wanted it that way, momentarily interrupting my vision made me adjust and reorient. It was like a necessary strategic pause. Sensing the intuitive message, I gathered myself and went back to my company, through the dark, but with my internal high-beams on.

As the effects of the previous adrenaline rush ebbed away, I felt the first signs of fatigue setting in. Back with the men, I calmly reloaded my magazines while talking with my officers and the first sergeant. Once they briefed what was going on with my casualties and our status on ammo, water, and medical supplies, I passed on what I'd been told by the commander. With the inertia of the burdened, we all went about our most personal and necessary tasks.

Life is situational. The Tigers would soon be in the situation of working with those we were never intended to work with while fighting from vehicles we were never intended to ride in to kill those we never came to kill.

At around 2015, Colonel Casper, the 10th Mountain QRF commander, arrived by helicopter from the QRF headquarters with an entourage of staff officers. Emerging from the aircraft, the colonel headed for the JOC while his staff officers linked up key players and primary battalion staff members under the northern edge of the terminal parking garage. While they began going over the initial plan on the hood of Colonel David's HMMWV, flashlight beams shone down to illuminate the maps and overlays.

Capt. Drew Meyerowich, Commander of Alpha Company, arrived at around 2025 with the remainder of the battalion staff. The combination of new arrivals and those of us already there made for crowded conditions as I linked up with Captain Meyerowich and we headed for the planners.

The scene around that HMMWV was bizarre. Captain Meyerowich and I found ourselves outside a ring of staff officers five or six deep around the hood, all trying to get a better view of the maps. Unable to see a thing—and in a rare mood—I loudly said, "It sure would be nice to see the plan, considering we have to execute it." With that, the group parted like the Red Sea and we were let into the inner circle of the brigade and battalion planning cells.

The comment earned me a lot of odd looks, but everyone knew I was right. Staff officers can sometimes be overzealous in their need to solve the immediate problem and ensure all the graphics are right so the boss is happy. But since Charlie and Alpha Companies were about to throw the next punches in this bare-knuckle brawl, the time for the usual staff process had come and gone.

Major General Garrison, Brigadier General Gile, Colonel Casper, Colonel David, and Colonel Gore all met in the JOC to discuss the concept of operations and the linkup procedures with the Rangers at the crash sites. After the senior leaders planning session, Casper, David, and Gore made their way to David's HMMWV under the terminal and directed that all the elements of TF 2-14 and the Ranger Ground Reaction Force were to link back up at the New Port. My Tigers would lead, with the Rangers and Terminators following.

As the orders churned in my head, I realized that the plan was going to take precious time that some of the wounded Rangers simply didn't have. Cut off with no hope of MEDEVAC dust-off, these men were going to die if ground forces didn't reach the tiny perimeter soon. This wicked problem confronted the leaders who, with heavy hearts, decided to save the unit with a deliberate plan that had a far better chance of success than continued piecemeal efforts to reach the battered individuals.

Everyone in the convoy to the New Port was tired but, to a man, ready to get the job done. Although surprised by the enemy's ferocity, Tiger Company was resolute in its determination to complete this mission. And, since none of us could imagine being left to the Somalis' tender mercies, we'd damned sure not leave our comrades to them!

The savagery displayed by the Somali fighters toward their own people tipped our feelings in favor of finishing the fight the hard way. As we loaded our vehicles for the short ride to the New Port, I honestly didn't expect any more surprises. The gloves were now off. This was no longer about humanitarian aid or MEDCAPs or civil/military relations. This was about brute force and bending the enemy to our will. We knew that the work would be gruesome but necessary to accomplishing the mission. We all also knew that we would win or we would die trying. "Come back with your shield, or on it." I now truly understood that ancient warrior's charge.

The men were eerily quiet as the long line of vehicles snaked through the dark to the New Port. No one spoke, as our thoughts turned inward. I thought of everything but the mission, reflecting instead on my wife, Pam; our kids, family, and friends; places I'd been; my childhood and the path I'd followed to this point in my life. As the HMMWV tires slowly rolled through the windblown mixture of sand dunes and dirt along the coastal road, I wondered, in the green and black glow of my NOD, whether this would be my last night on earth.

CHAPTER 14

Extraordinary Coalition

TF Ranger was in trouble at the crash sites, and time was of the essence. Still, it seemed to take forever to move the convoy just a couple of kilometers to the New Port. As we pulled into the huge parking lot next to the loading docks, everything was lit up in a mix of white and yellow lighting that created a false sundown effect. You could see, but not as clearly as you could in true daylight.

I found myself embroiled in a strange dichotomy that is not all that unusual in a combat environment. Ninety minutes before, I was engaged in an intense life-or-death struggle. Now, moving in convoy, the serenity of the moment struck me. Tranquil seas and shimmering lights atop undulating waves combined into a peaceful, pleasant, even reflective atmosphere that gave me a much-needed emotional breather.

As we pulled into the New Port, we could make out the bright white U.N. vehicles on our left. It had been a long time since my men and I had seen, let alone been inside an armored personnel carrier (APC). Considering what we had just gone through, and what we knew about what lay ahead, the solidity of the beasts was oddly comforting.

I dismounted and headed for a meeting with the battalion commander, his staff, and all those who would hold leadership positions in the

151

deadly night to come. Also walking toward the meeting were Delta operators. Ready for combat, these were serious men who were clearly ready to go—now!

Colonel David's plan was simple: Pakistani tanks would lead the convoy of Malaysian Battalion (MALBATT) German-built Condor APCs loaded with TF David soldiers. The route would be east around Via d'Italia, past Pakistani Strongpoint 207, then west on National Street to the release point. The fastest way in would have been the Via d'Italia route, but it supposedly ran through Aidid's stronghold and was reportedly heavily defended. Accordingly, TF David wasn't going "up the gut" right out of the New Port, but instead would go in on what we thought would be an avenue of approach that offered less resistance.

Alpha Company's Terminators would lead in movement and attack to break through to TF Ranger at the northern crash site, where one MH-60L Black Hawk, call sign Super 61, had crashed. Designated Combat Team (CT) Alpha, the Terminators would ride in APCs from the MALBATT's Company B.

The TF David Tactical Command Post, designated CT Bravo, with attachments from TF Ranger, would remain at Release Point Yankee approximately 1,200 meters past Pakistani Strongpoint 207 on National Street.

CT Charlie, my Charlie Company Tigers, would ride in MALBATT Company A vehicles. Third in the line of march, we would pass through CT Bravo and attack to break through to Black Hawk Super 64 at the southern crash site.

The entire rescue convoy was to remain mounted as long as possible. Each element would dismount only upon reaching its assigned objective.

The plan created a giant T with the base laid east–west along National Street and the cross bar on the west end of the base. CT Alpha would form the northern segment of the crossbar; CT Charlie would form the southern segment; and CT Bravo would hold the junction at the west end of the base. When actions at the objective were accomplished, we would collapse the T in order: CT Charlie would move first to reinforce Strongpoint 207; CT Alpha would move second to get the dead and wounded out, passing through CT Charlie to head straight to the soccer stadium;

and CT Bravo, Colonel David and the TF Rangers attachments, would be last off the field of battle. The end state was a linkup of all U.N. and U.S. personnel from all Task Forces and CTs at the soccer stadium.

The QRF LNOs, 1st Lt. Ben Mathews with the Pakistanis and 1st Lt. John Breen with the Malaysians, were personally briefed by Colonel David. His directions made clear what he expected of both elements in all phases of the operation. The colonel then asked, "Are there any questions?" Fully aware that the enemy still had a say in the matter, the assembled group okayed the plan.

It occurred to me then that I wasn't leading anymore and would not be linking up with what I had begun to think of as "live" Rangers. Instead, my Tigers and I would be going south to the doomed Super 64 that had been designated the secondary objective, the primary objective being the northern crash site of Super 61. I prayed that someone was alive on our objective, but honestly expected to be retrieving the remains of our countrymen who had given the last full measure trying to save one another. Amid flashes of our engagement on 25 September and the horrors we had encountered there, I steeled myself for this mission.

Heading back to disseminate the plan to my Tigers, it became clear that we weren't going to be leaving soon. My platoon leaders, XO, and first sergeant approached, accompanied by the newest members of our team, the commander of MALBATT Company A, Maj. Ab Aziz bin Ab Latiff, and an obvious Delta operator wearing the rank insignia of a sergeant first class.

Under the lights of the New Port, I could see that the Delta had a shock of nearly bright white hair and carried what looked like a football helmet under his arm. He told me to call him "Mace." This, I found out later, was in fact Master Sgt. John Macejunas—a legend in Delta and a man who had personally spent hours trying to get to his comrades at the downed aircraft sites.

At this point everyone wanted to influence the situation. Everyone needed to get information from me, give information to me, or hurry me up. Colonel David, meanwhile, just needed me to hold the works together. Our so-called "simple" plan was, in actuality, the controlled chaos in which myriad activities had to be accomplished to achieve mission success.

Major Aziz, a stout and forceful man in his own right, wanted me to see his vehicles. The Condors he was proudly providing were white. No, not that white—WHITE white. White like you ain't ever seen! Convinced that they would be easily visible from Philadelphia, I knew they were going to be prime targets for every enemy weapon system.

But these rolling targets were also lethal, each turret sprouting either twin 7.62mm parallel machine guns or 20mm cannons. Each also had spaced armor for protection, rode on four massive run-flat tires, and was driven by a competent, confident, and fiercely loyal Malaysian warrior.

Next, the XO filled me in about ammo and then asked what to do with the now spare vehicles. "Load the ammo into the Condors and get all the other vehicles with the trains," I told him, meaning the battalion support element.

Mace and his two RTOs, both also Delta operators, were fit to be tied. They had already been into the city, knew where to go, and even had a diamond-bladed saw to cut through obstacles on our way to the objective or anything that might hinder recoveries from Super 64. Mace and his RTOs did not hide their belief that if we would just get there, everything would work out.

I, meanwhile, knew that neither they nor I even knew how to get into or out of the Condor we were about to ride in. I also knew that what we were heading into wasn't going to be easy. Murphy's Law, the Fog of War, Luck, and the enemy would all have a say in how this night played out.

The emotion-driven urgency we all felt was real, and no one—not even Mace—wanted to go more than I did. Still, I had a mission to complete that, like Mace, I'd been turned away from, and that just didn't sit well with me or my Tigers. We just wanted to get to the sound of the guns and work it out when we got there.

But while we all felt that need to act, I couldn't let that need supersede responsible action. A combat truth is that ready-fire-aim isn't nearly as effective as ready-aim-fire, and is usually far less successful. I had a responsibility to channel that emotion while getting a viable plan distributed to the men of my company. It was to that task that I then turned.

With the time constraint, I called all my platoon leaders and NCOs to my HMMWV to disseminate the plan. I reviewed the situation, the route, the order of march, the battalion commander's intent, my own intent, and the tasks and purposes of each subordinate unit. Major Aziz introduced his platoon leaders and I introduced Mace and his RTOs. Language difficulties were immediately apparent. Without interpreters, just trying to communicate was going to be an interesting challenge. Thank God for "pidgin English!"

The plan called for TF David to exit the New Port as soon as all parties reported dissemination of the order. I realized by our position in the convoy that I would be in follow-the-leader mode, meaning I would keep an eye on the map to mark off prominent or key terrain as we went along and that I would be told when to head south into the objective area.

The hardest navigation responsibility would be conducted by the Pakistanis and the lead platoon of CT Alpha. Second Lt. Mark Hollis, Alpha's 2nd Platoon leader, was that lead man. He had gotten to Somalia only a few weeks earlier, having just graduated from Ranger School.

As a former mechanized platoon leader, I knew that being the lead platoon leader in a movement like this brought perils from the enemy as well as from your own element's followers. Because everyone relies on your navigation, they tend to follow where you lead, and they sometimes get a little slack in their own cross-checking to ensure you're going where you intended to go. As a result, things can go really bad, really fast.

It takes practice, forethought, and experience to make on-the-move speed and course-change decisions on a mounted march. Additionally, the pressure on the lead platoon leader is enormous when he knows that the entire battalion task force is counting on him. In addition to these daunting factors, 2nd Lieutenant Hollis was not only new to mechanized infantry mounted movement, he was also new to both the battalion and the Army. And his task was not just to move us from Point A to Point B— it was to lead the Task Force in a real-world combat maneuver!

Under the circumstance, I don't know that I would have put such an inexperienced officer in the lead of my unit when more experienced platoon leaders were available. Granted, he should have been fine, if only because the Pakistani tankers knew the area well, which meant that all he had to do was follow them to Release Point Yankee, then turn to the linkup with the Rangers and Delta just a few blocks north. Still . . .

Those of us in TF David saw ourselves as the last-chance rescue effort for our countrymen. At about 2230, the typically frenzied loading and final prep began in earnest as everyone did their last-minute commo, ammo, water, and medical checks. Maps were marked with the seemingly simple route. NVGs and spare batteries were checked, and we checked—and were checked by—our buddies as we sorted out our rides. We all knew this was it—TF David was coming out with TF Ranger, or wasn't coming out at all.

The Condors were different from anything in the U.S. inventory. Handles to open hatches were in odd places. Although view ports were available, we were not used to the limited view outside the vehicle that they offered. To me, they just created a sense of unease, since you could see so little in the orb-like visual area each port provided.

Just before moving out, I was called to the mechanized company command vehicle by Major Aziz. We were to ride with him. My RTOs, Specialists Randall and Alsbrooks, and both Mace and his RTOs joined us. I sat on the right side of the vehicle looking forward, with Randall and Alsbrooks behind me to my left. Mace was to my immediate left and his RTOs were forward of him. Major Aziz was in the track commander's hatch manning the 20mm cannon.

The side hatches were closed and a commo check went up and down the line. Engines roared to life, and unending noise soaked into the pores again. I oriented my map and began to listen intently. For this movement, course changes and corrections would be the most important measure of our progress.

As TF David adjusted in the New Port, the smell of diesel became overpowering. Being inside a track again brought back a whole host of memories. Instantly, I searched for the correct levers and popped out the back hatch to take in the view. I saw CT Alpha in front of me, and CT Bravo's TAC CP and Rangers getting ready to go all around us.

And up jumped Murphy! Confusing radio traffic finally boiled down to the Pakistanis not wanting to lead without night vision. They said they would have to use white light, and that doing so would make them even bigger targets than they already were. So Colonel David modified the plan. Then Murphy's brother-in-law showed up: The Pakis said that they would lead on the secure portion of the route, but the Malaysians would take the lead when we got to National Street at Strongpoint 69.

Lord, save us!

As best we could, this information was relayed in multiple languages along the command nets. In the end, though, there really was no way to know who knew the new plan and who didn't, and this confusion reigned on the net until 2310, when the order to cross the line of departure was given.

As warriors, every Malay was happy to be helping and fighting alongside us Americans, and there were a great many smiles and thumbs-up. Other than with Major Aziz and a couple others, we communicated in basic human ways. Eyes told all, hand signals were key, camaraderie bloomed quickly, and it didn't matter what country we were from. This was our collective moment, and we were throwing everything we had into it.

Mace and his RTOs were a reassuring element as they quietly monitored their own nets. Caught up in something they were not used to, they adapted like the professionals they clearly were, all the while knowing they could do little to influence the immediate circumstances. Still, they were like coiled springs, ready to act when necessary, acutely aware of their surroundings, and fully prepared to complete the mission. Having Delta in your midst is no small state of affairs.

Finally, after what seemed an eternity, the New Port gates opened and the Paki tanks moved out like smoke belching drunken elephants. Trailing behind like a herd of offspring, all in a nearly mile-long row, the remarkable coalition pressed forward into an uncertain future, from the light of the New Port into the dark of the Somali night.

CHAPTER 15

The Road to Hell

For the first time, I felt ensnared by the inexorable pull of events around me. Because I was not in charge of the overall event, I had to listen more than act. Thus removed from the usual center of decision making, I had to power down and simply follow. The effect brought on self-assessment, self-awareness, and a huge dose of fidget-itus. I realized that I was dog tired and a little hungry, and thirst hit me hard. As I drank from my canteen for the first time in well over an hour, I looked closely at my weapon, saw that it was dirty, and wiped it down. Then I clicked the push-to-talk button on my radio and actually listened for the click; cleaned my glasses and adjusted the Croakies strap around my ears; and felt for Mikki's Popsicle stick in my cargo pocket.

All in an only partly successful effort to keep from going nuts, each of us took a turn standing in the hatch at the rear of the Condor for a while to escape the cramped interior and the unavoidable banging into one another. When we first rolled out of the New Port, everyone was energetic, expectant, and ready for action. We slowly sobered as the vehicle crept down the darkened back streets of Mogadishu. Finally, one after the other, having seen these same sights over and over, we sat in the confines of the APC and endured the ride, resting as best we could for the fight to come.

During the planning, the route was thoroughly discussed among the leaders. At first, we intended to head straight toward the Villa d'Italia or, as I called it, "up the gut," because it was the fastest route along Tanzania Street to both crash sites. In my estimation, it was also the most likely expected route and, as we would find out, the most well defended. My suggestion to come in from a less likely direction—the east—was eventually accepted.

We were on that least likely route, heading east from the New Port, with me listening intently to the action. The full route moved along Via Roma to Via Londra, then turned north at Checkpoint 77 and continued on Via Jen Daaud through Pakistani Checkpoint 69, and finally turned on National Street and passed Pakistani Strongpoint 207. Without the aid of street signs, that was a lot to remember.

The Pakistani tankers in the lead were quite worried about the roadblocks they encountered and their lack of night vision equipment. About one kilometer from the New Port, when the Pakistanis encountered debris from a USMC HMMWV that had hit a mine in the morning, the Pakistani commander refused to go through, fearing the Somalis had mined it again. First Lieutenant Mathews, the 2-14 Infantry LNO, fired a magazine of 5.56mm from his M16 into the ersatz roadblock and rather forcefully told the tank commander to go through. The Pakistanis reluctantly complied.

The nearly 1-mile-long convoy continued east and north through CP 77 without any real incidents. At CP 69, the Pakistani brigade commander informed the battalion commander that the Paki forces could no longer lead the column. Unknowingly, then, 2nd Lieutenant Hollis of Alpha Company, riding in one of the Malaysian Condors, took the lead of the rescue column and set in motion a costly series of events.

The Pakistani tanks began to follow as the Malaysians ran over the roadblocks and flattened them. At first, it was just a noisy ride in the dark. But when the convoy finally turned left onto National Street and made some progress, all hell broke loose. The Somalis initiated a huge ambush once CT Alpha and the leading elements of CT Bravo were in the kill zone, a few moments past Strongpoint 207 on National Street.

It seemed like the lights had gone on and off on National Street, as if that was some sort of signal to execute the ambush, but it was actually just residual light flashes from all of the RPG and small-arms fires brought to bear on the convoy. CT Tiger had not yet turned the corner, but the tracer ricochets and overpowering noise of modern warfare traveled in waves over the neighborhood we were in. Then the fire found us, confined as we were between buildings, shacks, and all manner of dwellings, with the Somalis probing for weaknesses.

TF David, with its augmenting Ranger rescue team, fought back, moving forward as opportunities presented themselves. With the enormous amount of ammunition in the vehicles, everyone poured fire at every point of light coming from AKs or RPGs being fired on our flanks. We had more ammo than we had ever seen before, and our mission to get to the trapped Ranger and Delta forces became a force all its own. This time, we would not be denied. With a new comprehension of the term "overwhelming force," I also came to understand that, militarily, the ability to relentlessly fire without cessation builds an eerie and invigorating confidence.

Suddenly, the vehicles began lurching forward, only to stop abruptly. I looked around the interior of our Condor and at each of the men. Everyone had the same "What the fuck?" look that must have been on my face. But then we abruptly turned left, and a major shit-storm erupted as the 20mm cannon on our Condor began blasting away into the night. You could hear the expended brass falling with a streaming *tink* sound onto the cold metal floor. Incoming AK and machine-gun rounds slammed into the sides and roof of the Condor with distinctive *thut-thut-thut-tlack-tlack-tlack-tlack* sounds.

Then, out the right side portal, an RPG trail grew perpendicular to my sight line. We were in the middle of an intersection, with the 20mm cranking up the volume, when *whoomp, crump*, I was rocked by our vehicle being levered up from right to left by the force of the RPG impact and blast.

I clearly remember looking straight into Mace's eyes and seeing the same question there that he must have seen in mine—"Is this it?" We both knew that the RPG was burning through. It was a good hit. In that millisecond, Mace and I hung in an uncertain balance between life and death: Either the cabin would fill with a shower of molten metal and killing overpressure, or we would survive.

The vehicle settled and darted forward again. The hatch at my right leg became instantaneously and searingly hot—not glowing-red, visibly hot, but definitely hot enough to burn through my DCUs to blister the skin at my knee. Instinctively jerking away, I rocked with yet another thrust forward and realized then that I hated being inside this tin can just waiting to fry, burn, or get sucked out through a 2-inch hole. As much as I had previously reveled in the power of serving in mechanized infantry units, I now thought it would be far better to be on the street on foot where I could see the enemy. This was not fun, and a frenzied desire to get the hell out began to build.

With CT Tiger at the rear of the rescue column, keeping radio contact with my company and the overall mission was the priority. Tracking the actions of Terminator 6 and Dragon 6 were paramount because they would cut me loose to perform my mission at Crash Site 2. I listened intently as the Somalis fired huge quantities of small arms and RPGs at the convoy. The extremely heavy incoming RPG, mortar, and automatic weapons fire of the deliberate ambush, coupled with our cacophonous return fire, made the noise level inside the Condor deafening.

As if in a stupor, I swayed and lurched with the vehicle, one finger in my left ear and the handset plastered to my right ear. For what seemed like hours, we fought a running battle to our respective release points 1,200 meters west of Strongpoint 207. Somali fighters lay in the street and in alleys and courtyards all along the National Street route. Hell churned, blood flowed freely, and our souls were etched with the horror of war. The Rangers needed us and, behind an inexorable wave of steel and fire, we were coming. God help those in our way.

At Release Point Yankee, the north and south pivot to the two objective areas, the two lead Malaysian vehicles, with Hollis and his platoon of CT Alpha, began taking overwhelming fire from their front and right. Disastrously, the Malaysian drivers reacted by turning left instead of right, thus breaking contact with the main convoy. To make matters worse, radio traffic about the convoy break was obscured by radio traffic about the fight for Release Point Yankee. The enemy fire became so intense that Captain Meyerowich decided to dismount and clear the route to the northern crash site.

Hollis, trying to maintain control and continue navigating, was thrown all over his lurching vehicle and became increasingly disoriented. Each time he looked out a porthole, he was thrown in a different direction. Then, without warning, his vehicle abruptly picked up speed and began scaling curbs and any obstacle in its path. The Malaysian's platoon commander, Lt. Zunaidi bin Hassan, had ordered the two APCs through the kill zone of the Somali ambush. Unknowingly, Hollis and his second vehicle were leaving the main column far behind as they headed south toward Villa d'Italia, a known enemy strongpoint.

Meanwhile, the Pakistani tanks, which hadn't followed Hollis, had gone too far west in an effort to get away from the numerous RPG strikes they were taking. The outcome was that Hollis's two-vehicle force was turned into a "Lost Platoon." And while all this was happening, CT Alpha had dismounted to head north and into the tiny TF Ranger perimeter, CT Bravo occupied the pivot point at Release Point Yankee, and CT Tiger waited in growing anticipation for orders.

The main portion of the convoy, stretched nearly 5 kilometers along National Street, had to fight off repeated attacks from Somali hunter/killer teams intent on destroying the entire rescue effort. Hundreds of Somali militiamen were killed in the fighting around the release point.

I listened as CT Alpha began its fight to link up with the trapped Delta operators and Rangers. Hearing the order to dismount, I knew exactly how Captain Meyerowich felt, and desperately wanted out of the Condors as soon as humanly possible. Lined up along National Street like ducks in a shooting gallery was not my idea of executing the mission. I wanted to move now to get to the southern crash site and collect our fellow Americans and destroy any sensitive equipment. Trying to stay mission focused, I successfully fought the too many other variables that danced inside my head because I knew the men still needed me.

As usual, air power was keeping this whole operation from disintegrating into further tragedy. Little Birds and Cobras danced in the night, seemingly everywhere. I began to memorize call signs and follow the traffic flow into and out of the northern and southern crash sites as I prepared for my eventual use of our greatest combat asset.

Contrary to TF Ranger's perception that the 10th Mountain's rescue column was just firing the area up, this was decidedly not a Divisional shoot-fest. Their seeming belief that our movement to their position was nothing more than a simple drive up from the airport is equally inaccurate. We fought our way into and out of their hunkered-down positions near Super 61, and that's what all the shooting was about!

As we closed on TF Ranger's location, the Somalis went quiet around the Ranger perimeter. Their silence was intentional, as they sought to use TF Ranger as the bait in a classic baited ambush. The real fight was going to be for access to that perimeter and, minus the "Lost Platoon," TF David was almost there.

CHAPTER 16

Southern Objective

After almost an hour of bouncing around the back of the Condor with the rest of the passengers, we finally got the "go" for CT Tiger's objective. I held on as we bounded over the curbs and anything else in our path on our way to the southern crash site of Super 64. Second Lt. Kenny Haynes led the way with his Condors as we broke from the remainder of the convoy. Colonel David and CT Bravo occupied Release Point Yankee to secure our exfiltration route.

Our white vehicles lumbered south down a route we had never been on in our tours around the city. We ended in a long line after a fairly quick ride from National Street. En route, I radioed a dismount order and directed the leadership to come to my vehicle when we halted. Thankfully the ride was quick, and as soon as we stopped I was reaching for the hatch release.

When I hit the open space outside the vehicle, the Somali night could only be described as delicious when compared to how stale and clingy the air had become within the cramped confines of our Condor. Cool air and a chill momentarily hit me. Closing the right side hatch, I looked at the hole created by the RPG that had impacted on my side access door. I wondered at the charred blackened hole with its melted tailings and scorched burn marks, knowing the passengers and I were both blessed and lucky to be alive.

Suddenly, we were dismounting under fire. In the blink of an eye, both of my lead vehicles took RPG fire from the higher elevations of the surrounding buildings to our front. One large, white building, three or four stories high, dominated the area and was filled with Somali gunmen. The incoming fire caused our first casualties of the night when two Malaysian Condor crewmembers were wounded.

I immediately reported our position and situation to Colonel David. A lesson learned from my report was not to mention words like "catastrophic." In my mind, the destruction and loss of our vehicles from a mechanized point of view was catastrophic. The crews were wounded and the vehicles could neither fight nor move. However, in the light infantry world, catastrophic means people, not equipment. Thus, my report caused Colonel David to think that I had lost the vehicles, complete with crews and passengers. Understandably, this filled him with unnecessary trepidation. Plain and simple, I should have reported better. Words have meanings, so be careful both with what you say over the radio and with how you say it!

As bad as it had rapidly become, my light infantrymen had already dismounted, which kept the initial casualty count from being a lot worse. Suppressive defensive fire cracked continuously into the night, with our red tracers pinging off buildings or diving deep into the black maws of window openings, while their green tracers searched the night for us.

We immediately cleared the wounded Malaysians from their vehicles and gathered behind the largest tree trunk I had seen in Somalia. On the left side of the road facing south, this monstrous ancient tree was easily 7 feet wide and provided the cover needed for gaining situational awareness, orientation, and our initial leader's rally where I provided instructions to my subordinates.

With the level of in- and outbound fires picking up and our voices nearly drowned out, I ordered the vehicles into more defensible positions on the western side of the road. The remaining Condors backed under trees, or placed themselves behind the already damaged lead Condors. Some moved under overhangs where they could watch the road and defend themselves better from RPG fire. I moved the AT Section up closer to provide better coverage of the area just to our south and the alleyways to our east, and to better protect the Condors. We simply couldn't lose any more vehicles or we'd be walking out.

Facing south, the platoon leaders, the first sergeant, Mace, and I all knew that the downed Black Hawk, Super 64, was about 100 meters to our right. We could just make out the labyrinthine shantytown that extended to our rear and as far as we could see on that side of the road. My Tigers were ready, and Mace and the other Delta operators were ready with the diamond-bladed saw. It was time to move.

I quickly gave the task, purpose, and order of march: 1st Platoon, with Mace's team, would secure the crash site; the HQ element would provide commo with battalion and the rest of the company and, as needed, call for helicopter gunship support; 3rd Platoon would stay linked with 1st and secure the return route to the dismount point; and 2nd Platoon would guard our vehicles and prevent any south-to-north crossing of National Street by anyone, thus stopping the Somalis from reinforcing the northern perimeter.

We still had an OH-58D on-call and shortly before we moved out, I called for them to sparkle our route to the crash site, the laser beam clearly visible with our NVGs. The beam efficiently guided Mace and 2nd Lieutenant Haynes's 1st Platoon west off the main road and into the tin shacks.

As I waited to follow them through the cave-like entrance into the shantytown, I looked up and saw the now-familiar trail of an RPG burning toward me from the large, white building. Reacting the only way I knew how, I rolled over backwards. Though the explosion rocked my prone body, thankfully I wasn't hit by any shrapnel. That backward roll saved my life, but the near misses were adding up.

I got up, brushed myself off, and headed into the maze with Randall and Alsbrooks. Almost immediately the world closed in on us. With absolutely no rhyme or reason to the arrangement of the tin shacks, a claustrophobic closeness gripped our senses. With the possibility of the enemy at any turn, trigger fingers were tight. Gunfire erupted in front of me as 1st Platoon made contact, and the din in the close confines within the tin shacks became overpowering. We kept moving fast, winding this way and that, following the man in front of us, firing when necessary as we cleared the neighborhood. I initially wore NVGs, but almost immediately took them off. In the tight confines of the shacks, my normal night vision proved to be a better than the green glow and white flash every time a weapon was fired.

I stayed close to 1st Platoon as we navigated to the crash site, winding in and around the shacks with our senses on overload. I also listened to the progress of the Task Force over the battalion net, which is how I got my first inkling that there was a "Lost Platoon," when Colonel David reported that there was a platoon about 100 meters south of CT Tiger's location and that they wanted to link up with us. "Okay," I thought, "what the hell are they doing down there?"

Without breaking stride, I factored in this new information as we continued to make progress toward our objective. Although focused on getting to Super 64, I was also receiving numerous radio calls from over-flying helicopters that a friendly pilot was on the ground in our area.

The perspective from the air was a lot different than on the ground. I answered every radio call that we would look for him, but needed more information than simply that he was down here. We desperately needed to know where he might be in relation to where we were.

Fighting through the shanties, we finally forced our way to the southern crash site and the bullet-riddled Black Hawk. We found the bird in an enclosed area surrounded by a tin wall. Quickly establishing a perimeter, we cleared all opposition in front of us and stopped all further attempts to keep us from our mission. The Somalis did not fare well.

The OH-58D that had helped guide us into the site went back to an overwatch orbit, taking with it the white noise of the rotors. Now the hard work began, the gut-wrenching, soul-searing, emotion-draining search for our countrymen. This was the mission at hand, the focus of our lives this day.

Super 64 lay diagonally across a small courtyard, pocked with holes from the earlier gunfight as the Super 64 crew and Delta sniper team tried to hold off the Somalis. Mace had a list of the guys that should have been at this site. Under sporadic fire, we began calling out the names that will haunt me forever: Frank . . . Cleveland . . . Field . . . Durant . . . Shughart

. . . Gordon. . . . Over and over, we shouted the names of these six men we did not know, because only Mace and his Delta RTOs had known them.

Using NVGs, we followed blood trails over 100 meters into the dangerous darkness. The feeling was horrible; there was nothing, no sign of life, no remains in or around the aircraft. There weren't even dog tags, just a deathly and unsettling absence of humanity that permeated the entire scene. The worst thoughts ran through my head: captured, tortured, desecrated; mindless savages doing the unspeakable. The need to act out, a hunger for revenge, was right on the tip of my soul.

With a keen and hardened focus, Mace guided us through the collection of sensitive items and the placement of the thermite grenades we had brought along to destroy what we could not retrieve. Some men stayed on the perimeter to engage the Somali fighters trying to get at us, while others worked with the men of Delta to complete the mission. Because there would be no attempt to recover the downed aircraft, we had to destroy it.

We stayed until Super 64 was completely engulfed in a thermite-induced inferno. As if drawn to the flames, Somali gunmen began converging on the site, and the sounds of their incoming near-misses began to come more frequently. I reported the actions at the objective to Colonel David.

When we left that smoldering aircraft, I was pissed. The mission to Super 64 was sickeningly anticlimactic. We had nothing to do but turn a multimillion-dollar helicopter into ash. There were no remains to recover, no survivors or wounded to attend to, and no knowledge of what might have happened to the men. The sense of futility was almost overwhelming. I wanted vengeance for this horrible day and for the night that was not yet over.

Realizing we could do no more, we began collapsing the tiny perimeter around the burning craft as the Tigers started exfiltrating along the route secured by 3rd Platoon. The night was still hostile, since the enemy now knew exactly where we were. As the Somalis began to concentrate on the Condors, 2nd Lieutenant Ryan's 2nd Platoon had their hands full trying to protect the APCs, keep the Somalis from attacking CT Bravo, and stop Somali reinforcements from crossing National Street from south to north.

As 1st Platoon made its way back to the original perimeter, eventually clearing the maze of tin shacks, I remained at the end of 3rd Platoon to ensure everyone was accounted for. On the way back, that placed me as the last man of the column, with Randall and Alsbrooks just in front of me.

It was then, hanging out on the far edge of the company patrol line, that I received a radio transmission from 2nd Lieutenant Hollis. I stopped where I was. He quickly explained that he was surrounded about 100 meters to our south, had wounded personnel, and needed to link up.

Stepping off the path, I asked Randall if he had a star cluster; of course he did, a green one. I then asked Hollis if he had a star cluster; he didn't, but he did have a red parachute flare. With a quick countdown, we fired our devices almost simultaneously. As Hollis's red flare streaked into the night sky, I determined that the distance between his marker and my green star cluster was not the 100 meters from our position that he had estimated, but was actually more like 700 to 1,000 meters! This had immediately become a problem that was not going to be easily solved.

With the road south of our position full of Somali gunmen trying to make their way to either our position or the northern crash site, and a stranded platoon needing immediate assistance, the night had just gotten significantly hotter and far more complex for Tiger 6. That would be me. Clearly, it had become "Take a deep breath; let it out" time.

Although our original mission was accomplished, the lack of recovered survivors or remains and the absence of any knowledge of our comrades' fates left us with a deflated sense of having done too little too late. Now we had a new mission with more lives at stake, as a junior lieutenant was trapped with his men in his own hell, their true situation unknown, and my own company perimeter was slowly being surrounded. Eventually, I knew, we would have to extract ourselves from our current position to provide support as the main body exfiltrated from the northern crash site, but we also had to do something now about Hollis's predicament.

In combat, the problem-solving challenges never cease.

Exhausted and seeking a momentary respite, I turned and slammed my back up against the tin shack that I had stopped near. Immediately, I felt the counterweight of a human being on the other side of the tin and heard both the muffled sound of a woman's squeal, accompanied by the universally soothing "shhh" sound of a mother. Instinctively, I knew that there were no males to deal with and that she had a child or children with her in that hut, and I envisioned her grabbing and calming them up against her legs.

We both stood perfectly still, each leaning on our respective sides of that tin wall, coupled, back to back, even as we were separated by only the corrugated tin. With senses acute, adrenaline surging, and even an instant of terror, I realized that our lives had become connected.

I would not kill her—but she did not know that.

I truly wanted her to know that I was one of the good guys. But I also understood that, from her perspective, on this night I was the boogeyman. And I hated it. I was not here to hurt her or her family. I was just a man with a couple of problems to solve and a mission to accomplish.

I turned and told Randall and Alsbrooks to keep up with 3rd Platoon. I didn't want any sudden reactions, mistakes, or accidents. Loyal as always, they turned and slowly departed down the path, glancing back to see what the hell I was doing.

The presence of that woman and the remnants of her little family fueled my awareness that I wasn't a savage and calmed me so thoroughly that I fully relaxed. Gathering myself, I stepped away from the wall and her counterweight, regained my balance, took one step, then two, and peered to my left at the small entryway on the side of the hut.

Nothing happened. No movement.

Perfect. I did not want the moment to be ruined, even though I had my finger full on the trigger of my M16. Slowly and confidently, I turned my back to that neighborhood and moved back to my men. We were done there, but we good guys still had more to do.

Though I never saw that Somali woman or the children I imagined were with her, I know she was there. Her presence made me feel human again, able to both care and to purge a vengeful heart. As I strode down that dark path back to whatever my future held, I wished her peace in this hellish place called Mogadishu.

CHAPTER 17

The Rescue

Standing in swirling cordite clouds in a dirt alley, I felt the loneliness of command tugging at my soul. For thirty seconds or so—an eternity in the middle of that night—I looked back over the shantytown maze, searching in the haze of the ongoing gun battle for the orange flash and shot that would kill me.

It didn't come.

I looked once again at the tin shack where my humanity had asserted itself. Calmly at ease with my role in this fight, I turned my back on death and, as if entering a new scene in a movie, walked through a hail of gunfire and RPG strikes into the company perimeter. Following in Randall's and Alsbrooks's footsteps, I moved to the makeshift command post behind that awesome huge tree and met the focused stares of battle-hardened men.

As wood chips flew from the tree and plaster chips flew from the surrounding walls, all eyes were on me and all ears were on the radio traffic. The company had accomplished its mission. Our role was to now remount our vehicles and fall back to a position at or near Checkpoint 207 from which we would cover the withdrawal under fire of the remainder of TF Colonel David. With Mace and his Delta RTOs still on hand, CT Tiger stood by, just an order away from reloading. I could sense the mounting anxiety as the men awaited my orders.

Only a few of my men had any idea that we had a trapped platoon well south of our current position. As I described the situation to the company headquarters, I watched the group take in the news, process the words, and steel themselves once again for yet another clash with the ever-probing enemy. Everyone seemed to search their souls, but the group's feedback was positive and resolute. *We* were going for Hollis, his men, and their Malaysian comrades.

It was time to get a SITREP from Hollis and to let the rest of the company know that we weren't leaving without that lost platoon. I called for all the key leaders to come to the company CP. Although this was not a group decision, I wanted to look everyone in the eye before we conducted the rescue.

When the leadership joined me, I explained everything I knew about our situation. A platoon from Alpha Company was in deep trouble to our south; we were not leaving until we got them out; CT Alpha was still heavily involved at the northern crash site accounting for everyone from TF Ranger and working desperately on the wounded; and Dragon 6 was still at the RP. I saw sideward glances and some "holy shit" looks from my most senior NCOs and platoon leaders. No doubt about it, we were looking the dragon square in the face.

I quickly formulated a plan of action and gave task and purpose to my platoon leaders. I told Ryan to continue protecting our vehicles and to keep any Somali fighters from making their way from south to north. We didn't want the Somalis attacking CT Alpha's withdrawal from the northern crash site. Initially, 1st and 3rd Platoons were to keep the perimeter secure and prepare to rescue the isolated platoon. Everyone needed to redistribute ammo and get ready for another fight.

Mounted or dismounted? That was the core question as I planned the operation to rescue Hollis and his platoon. Mounted, of course, had distinct advantages: It would be quicker, would provide impressive firepower, offered maximum physical protection (except at the pickup/turnaround point), and presented the fewest possible targets to the enemy. The downside was that each of those fewer targets was a helluva lot bigger—and easier to hit—than a single dismounted soldier, and popping one or two of those targets with RPGs would have catastrophic effects that could both stop the rescue effort completely and eliminate CT Tiger as a viable fighting force.

And dismounted? That would boil down to conducting an almost 1,000-meter running gun battle on foot through a heavily defended area just to fight our way to Hollis's location, with the likely attendant problem of taking significant casualties along the way, followed immediately by a do-over in the opposite direction to fight our way back out while simultaneously tending to both his and our own increasing casualties.

The decision was really a no-brainer. The best course of action was to go with the combination of speed, protection, and firepower that we had in our perimeter right now. I knew in my gut that those Condors were the key to success, but we needed to act quickly. The problem was that I didn't own the Condors, so I knew that I had to convince the Malaysian commander to support the rescue mission. Clearly, it was time to talk to Major Aziz.

Second Lt. Mark Hollis was in serious trouble. Already dealing with his own casualties from the destruction of his vehicles, his small force was running out of time as the Somalis continuously probed his perimeter with fire and maneuver. For the time being, however, he could only hunker down and wait for rescue from his deteriorating predicament, much as the Rangers and Delta were doing up in the northern objective area.

Weighing the options, I told him to stay put, thinking that I could at least reinforce his position with members of my company. But as the minutes continued to pass and radio traffic with the desperate but calm lieutenant remained sporadic, I realized that both Hollis and I had our hands full. While I had more men and held a better position, he had less than a full platoon, significant casualties, and occupied only a small compound. Thus, his predicament clearly outweighed mine, mandating that I take immediate action.

Calling over 1st Platoon Leader Kenny Haynes, I directed him to send a recon patrol south down the road to determine how far they could get without significant pushback. If possible, I wanted him to link up with Hollis and his men to reinforce their position until we could mount a larger rescue operation.

One thing was a certainty: I simply could not conduct a major rescue effort until the entire Task Force was ready to extract from the northern crash site. Moving CT Tiger from our current position would have opened the battalion's southern flank to an onslaught of Somalis that, in all likelihood, would have overwhelmed those at the RP, including my battalion commander. That, in turn, would have jeopardized the force holding the entire northern crash site perimeter, which already had its hands full fending off Somali probes, tending the wounded, and making the major effort to extract Super 61's pilot, CWO Cliff Wolcott.

Hollis needed to hang on just a bit longer.

In less than ten minutes, Staff Sergeant Tewes and his squad were on their way, hugging the shadows and searching for the enemy. I watched as the men vanished into the dark and over the horizon. Time ticked slowly and, with thoughts of those men never leaving my mind, I addressed the tasks at hand: contacting Hollis and fighting the company perimeter. Like bizarre background music, I could hear the *chunk-chunk-chunk* of suppressive fire from the Antitank Platoon's HMMWV-mounted M19 automatic grenade launchers. It seemed to me that time almost stood still as the minutes dragged on and on . . .

With Tewes moving, and without knowing Hollis's exact position, I radioed Hollis and directed him to begin moving north to shorten the distance between himself and Tewes's squad. Hollis acknowledged in one of our brief communication windows, followed orders, and gathered his men.

Hollis and two of his squad leaders, Sergeants Hollis (not related) and Maxwell, began organizing the men in his small perimeter so that Maxwell's engineers would be in the lead, followed by 2nd Lieutenant Hollis, his M-60 machine-gun team, the Malaysians, and finally Sergeant Hollis's squad. The wounded were comforted and readied for movement as the men organized and gathered themselves for a life-or-death northward push through the darkness.

Knowing their desperate situation, and with the din of rifle, machine-gun, and RPG fire buffeting us within the enclosed walls, I organized the company into a tighter defensive perimeter as near-misses sent puffs of dirt or plaster into the air. In response to Somali maneuvering, we began a close-in fight up an alley to our left, with me directing machine-gun fire while Mace and his RTOs fired their MP-5s. Shadows began to stack up waist high in the alley. God only knew how many Somalis we were facing; all I knew was that they just kept coming.

South of our perimeter, Tewes's recon squad had made it about 200 meters and was taking increasing fire from numerous enemy positions, especially from the tall, white building that had been giving us fits since we had dismounted. From our position, the view southward down the road showed what looked like a swarm of loud, angry fireflies searching for my men. Reluctantly, I determined that the recon squad would be unable to fight through to a linkup with Hollis's platoon; there was simply too much enemy small-arms and RPG fire. After a brief SITREP from Tewes, who could barely be heard over the noise of gunfire, I recalled his squad to our position.

After conducting a fighting withdrawal back to the company perimeter, Tewes reported that there seemed to be only one obvious route to Hollis. And, given the heavy concentration of Somalis along that route, a high casualty count was likely if the company attempted to negotiate that route dismounted. That confirmed my original assessment that a mounted movement was the most viable option.

Following Tewes's briefing, I walked over to the Malaysian commander's vehicle and slowly worked through a difficult exchange of pidgin English with Major Aziz. In essence, I asked if we could borrow a couple of his APCs to effect the rescue of Hollis's platoon. After a brief hesitation—and an obvious clear moment of understanding—Major Aziz picked up his hand mike and requested permission to assist us.

His battalion commander immediately denied the request.

Looking down at me, Major Aziz stoically reported that he was sorry, but he was not authorized to offer his vehicles to support us. Yet his demeanor showed that he had every intention of assisting us in whatever way he could. And that's when we shared a look that I will never forget, the kind of eloquent, Vulcan mind-meld connection between on-the-ground combat commanders that says "Higher just doesn't get it."

Clearly, we were in absolute accord. OUR men, both American and Malaysian, were down that road, outnumbered, some dead, some wounded, all in grave jeopardy and needing OUR help. And so we stood there, completely immersed in the very essence of leadership—the leader's duty to lead without regard for personal consequences.

Major Aziz tried again. Same answer.

Although we could understand the Malaysian battalion commander's reluctance to commit an entire company to a risky operation against an aggressive foe in view of the major losses they'd already suffered—four Condors that I was aware of—both Major Aziz and I were still shocked by his decision. When measured against my knowledge that Hollis's platoon and their Malay brothers—all of whom I now thought of as my own— were in serious trouble and needed immediate relief, my understanding of his reluctance did not translate to agreement with his decision.

Time continued its uncommonly slow passage through the most intense hours of my life. Randall once again handed me the hand mike from his radio: Hollis, again calling for help. I determined that, with or without the Malaysian Condors, we were going to get that platoon back. There was simply no way in hell that I was going to leave even a single soldier from Hollis's force to the tender mercies of the Somalis. If we had to claw our way to link up, so be it.

I went once again to ask for Major Aziz's vehicles. As I approached, it was obvious that he was talking heatedly with his battalion commander. Understanding that he didn't need me standing there, tapping my foot with a "Well . . . ?" look on my face, I left him to his business.

Meanwhile, Hollis, on my orders, had begun moving northward along the road. Getting him on the radio, I had explained to him that enemy resistance along the road was just too great to attempt a dismounted assault, and that we were still working on getting a rescue effort together.

At this point I relearned a lesson I had originally learned long before— NEVER ASSUME. Given the heavy volume of fires along the road that Hollis's APCs had initially traveled, I assumed he would understand not to go that way, and that, instead, he should first move west through the shantytown, then turn north. As fate would have it, however, Hollis opted to use the route he already knew as the most expedient—albeit dangerous— route to our position.

And it was during this movement north that a Somali gunman stepped out from an alley and unloaded his weapon into the lead squad in a spray-and-pray ambush. The Somali shot Sergeant Houston in the chest, Pfc. Ly in the back, and Staff Sergeant Maxwell in the knee. Immediately laying down suppressive fire, and with the remainder of the platoon racing ahead to gather the wounded, Sergeant Hollis courageously killed the Somali with grenades and precise rifle fire.

I didn't know it at the time, but 2nd Lieutenant Hollis's casualties now included two categorized as "litter priority," two "litter urgent," and eight "walking wounded," and his platoon, now effectively shut down, was still being engaged from an open area to the north of their position. In a now-desperate need for evacuation, he directed his RTO to contact me immediately with the platoon's new status, their location as best they could determine, and a request for immediate MEDEVAC and transport support.

More wounded; more complex problems. The soul gets tired . . .

Getting that call prompted me to reach for my hand mike as the thought "Fuck this" ran through my mind. I called airborne command and control and requested assistance from the best asset we had—overwhelming air power. And it was my intent to continue calling in Little Birds and Cobras until both sides of that street were smoking, ruined death zones.

Almost immediately after reference, location, and terminal guidance were transmitted, an absolute shit-storm landed on the Somalis. The overwhelming ferocity simply stunned the night. As aerial Gatling guns whirred and rockets began pounding the space between my company and Hollis's, whole buildings were destroyed. A new powder-and-cordite haze from the gun runs joined the pall that already hung over the city. The sheer power of the helicopters permeated our beings.

The essence of war links the resolute, the courageous, and those in need, and the fury-driven dance between friend and foe emphatically completes the circle of life. Meanwhile, I just called for more gun runs; and they came; and came . . .

With an intense awareness that I was about to risk my company and my life, I calmly walked back to the Headquarters area from Major Aziz's Condor and told the men to get up and ready, because we were going to get our men. I will never forget the look that passed between Mace and me. He knew, as did I, that death for many of us potentially lay just down that road. Still, he accepted my command and turned to talk with his

RTOs. Much to their credit, Mace and his Delta operators never hesitated about going with us.

As the helicopters made continuous gun runs, the world in front of us was torn asunder by thousands of bullets and rocket fire. The miniguns churned the earth and turned buildings into piles of rubble, while the synched rockets blew man and terrain to kingdom come. Standing there taking in the breathtaking view of our covering fire from above, I searched each man's eyes in that small perimeter. Aware of the meat grinder that lay ahead of us, we were all ready.

As if on cue, momentarily startling me, I heard a powerful shout above the din. Looking up, I saw Aziz motioning me over from the cupola of his Condor. I remember thinking to myself, "What now?" I had men to rescue. The last thing I needed was another "No."

What I got was a gift from God. Aziz had finally grown tired of listening to his battalion commander telling him to stay put while HIS MEN, fellow Malaysians, were seriously wounded and dying at Hollis's location. So, knowing that I had my company ready to move dismounted toward the stranded platoon, and fully recognizing that we would certainly sustain many casualties along the nearly 1,000-meter gauntlet of Somali fires to our south, Aziz did a remarkable and very brave thing: He disobeyed his battalion commander's direct order and, on his own authority, ordered his 3rd Platoon Leader, 2nd Lt. Muhammad Juraimy bin Aripin, to prepare his APCs for movement down the road to Hollis's position.

After readjusting the perimeter and reengaging the advancing Somalis, Aziz and I immediately worked out a very hasty plan. I would continue to direct covering fires during 2nd Lieutenant bin Aripin's movement and synchronize the recovery of Hollis's platoon. The details included movement to the platoon, marking, loading, fire coordination, and movement back to the company perimeter.

In a very quick radio call, I instructed Hollis to use M-203 parachute flares to mark the buildings of known enemy locations surrounding the extraction point. That, however, didn't initially go quite as intended. When Lieutenant Hollis directed Sergeant Hollis to flare-mark a particular building that held a heavy concentration of Somali fighters, Sergeant

Hollis immediately did so—but hit the wrong building, a twist that sealed that building's and its occupants' fate.

Well, a marked target is a marked target to a hungry AH-6 Little Bird, which immediately made a single pass and destroyed the incorrectly marked building with its miniguns and rockets. An exasperated 2nd Lieutenant Hollis emptied an entire magazine of 5.56mm tracer rounds to mark the correct target building, which then simply disappeared under the onslaught of the AH-6's second delivery of precision 7.62mm Gatling gun and 2.75-inch rocket fire. For the record, our aviators sure know how to put on a ferocious and breathtaking display of power!

At about 0410 hours, as bin Aripin's Condors began moving south, I called in eight or ten more AH-6 and AH-1F gun runs to keep the route cleared for the APCs. I am confident that the ensuing twenty to thirty minutes of precise and efficient aerial fire support kept the recovery APCs from meeting the same fate as the two that had previously been destroyed at Hollis's location. Any remaining Somalis must have been in shock at the overwhelming display of firepower.

Before they departed, I told Aziz to drive until he saw chemlights marking the road, pulling one out of my pocket to show him so he'd understand what to look for. He passed the word to the other Condors via his radio. I quickly coordinated with 2nd Lieutenant Hollis to mark the pickup location with the little wonders of modern alchemy, and Sergeant Hollis marked the road with green chemlights. Then both prepared to throw highly concentrated (HC) smoke grenades to cover the pickup area. 2nd Lieutenant Hollis's plan was to use the HC smokes once the APCs had moved to their position and turned around. This would lay a cloud of thick smoke to cover their dismounted movement to the vehicles, expected to be a slow process because of moving the gravely wounded.

Second Lieutenant bin Aripin's two Condors roared down the road, firing when needed to suppress any opposition, and arrived at the chemlight-marked extraction point just before 0430 hours. The language barrier immediately became a problem again, as Hollis's plan to turn the APCs around before his people boarded the vehicles was not immediately understood. After a momentary delay getting the vehicles to turn around,

one of the Malaysians finally understood what Hollis wanted and started
yelling in Malaysian to the drivers, who then quickly got the vehicles facing
in the correct direction—northward. It amounted to five minutes of sheer
terror for both the mounted crews expecting to be destroyed by RPGs and
the dismounted troops trying to get organized from uncovered positions.

Hollis's platoon mounted the vehicles as quickly as possible in the
swirling smoke during the daring APC recovery, and the vehicles then
drove as fast as possible back up the hill to our company perimeter. With
an inner sigh of relief from all involved, Hollis's platoon finally made it
back within friendly lines around 0445.

I reported our success to Dragon 6 and he immediately told me to
prep for extraction.

I ensured 100 percent accountability as we loaded Aziz's remaining
vehicles. It seemed to take forever, since we now had more wounded to take
care of and four fewer vehicles between Hollis's platoon and CT Charlie
than we had when we started the mission.

As the sun began to rise over the Indian Ocean and the rest of
Mogadishu began stirring from their khat-induced dreams, the vestige of
safety offered by the interlocking fires of the company's perimeter quickly
began to erode. Without the protection of dismounted troops facing out
to engage any adversaries, our somewhat disorganized mounted company
was far less secure. We were all well aware of how dangerous our situation
still was, and I believe everyone could envision a Condor's instant conver-
sion to a fireball by a single well-placed RPG.

Needless to say, tensions were high . . .

At about 0515 hours, I contacted Colonel David and reported that we
had 100 percent accountability, but that we were sitting ducks in our tin
cans and wanted to move immediately. When he granted my request and
told us to move out, we instantly began our planned withdrawal to
Strongpoint 207, a five-minute ride.

After ten minutes of movement, I realized that we'd gone too far. For
the extraction to work seamlessly, I knew that we had to stop at Strongpoint 207 to cover the remainder of the battalion's withdrawal from the
northern crash site. But the Malaysians were receiving conflicting instructions from their chain of command. When I strongly suggested stopping to

my driver (by pulling him down from his cupola by the pants leg), he merely pointed to his earpiece to indicate that he was only following orders.

By then, it was already too late, and I knew that we were not going to get those APCs turned around before they reached the stadium. Once again trapped in the belly of a beast, I listened to the Condors going through their gears, fully understanding that I was not in control and that my wisest course of action was to calm down and let the situation play out.

Colonel David, knowing that I was highly perturbed that our planned orderly withdrawal had vanished in a cloud of Malaysian Condor dust, simply told me to get to the soccer stadium and be prepared for consolidation and reorganization.

"Roger, out," I said, fully understanding that there was much more to accomplish to complete the process of getting the battalion, Delta, and the Ranger survivors back from harm's way.

I looked at my watch; it was 0530 hours, daybreak on 4 October. Mogadishu had stayed up all night. The party was still going on as the Tigers less than cheerfully rode onward toward the soccer stadium in the bellies of a line of fuming, white, metal monsters as they emerged from a night of death, destruction, misery, fear, heroism, adrenaline, and intense emotions into the peace of an early morning.

And against all odds, we were—I was—alive!

CHAPTER 18

The Soccer Stadium

With a sudden lurch that threw everyone forward, the Condor I was riding in abruptly stopped just outside of the Somali National Soccer Stadium. We were crushed inside the metal confines of the vehicle in all manner of body positions, the overcrowding caused by too many men in too few vehicles. It had been necessary to pack everyone into the vehicles to get them out of the objective area.

The stench of man sweat, blood, and adrenaline reeked in the limited breathable air within the vehicles. I was wedged between the vehicle commander's legs and Randall's radio, his whip antennae protruding against my helmet, his hand mike in my ear. Frustrated, mashed, and completely uncomfortable, I listened over the battalion net to the final extraction of Chief Wolcott's remains and CT Alpha's loading of the Rangers and Delta in preparation for their move to the soccer stadium. We squirmed until someone finally reached the crank handle, threw it, and levered the hatch open.

As soldiers spilled out of the vehicles, the wounded were eased with utmost care from the bowels of the metal monsters. Getting oriented was my first concern. My mind raced to assess the situation: new location; men and vehicles in disorder; mission still ongoing; accountability, as in looking each man in the eye; consolidation and reorganization; the rest of

TF David out there; edgy as the emotion of survival fought to take control; mission first; men always . . . Dammit, get it together, Mike!

"Fall in," I heard the first sergeant and platoon sergeants shout. In the increasing early morning sunlight under the ramparts of the soccer stadium, different languages began filling the air. The wounded were whisked away by foreign medical personnel, and my tired, hardened, serious men began the simple drill of getting into an organized formation.

Bam! Out of the blue came a bull of a man, an American soldier covered in the sweat and blood residue of war, weapon in hand, arms outstretched, gripping me in a bear hug and literally lifting me from the ground. "God, am I glad to see you, Sir!" I will never forget those first face-to-face words from 2nd Lt. Mark Hollis.

Startled as I was by his immediate presence, and after piecing together who he was, I was shaken from continuing thoughts about the mission long enough to be personal, human, and friendly again. He was so obviously grateful to be alive, and I was equally grateful to see him that way. He and his men had consumed the best I had in problem-solving, fire control, and leadership. And in this moment when a profound response was clearly called for, mine was pure B-movie dialogue: "You too, man." Corny, I know, but it is exactly how I felt.

What I thought on the inside as I stared at him made me realize I could have saved men for a living. With my mind still reeling from the night-long combat mission, my next words probably made me seem less than friendly. "Go take care of your men," I told him. Even today, I hope he understood that I was telling him to do what I thought was the most important thing in the world for him to be doing at that moment. Eye-to-eye, I believe he did. I shook his hand, the way warriors do, a strong and steady welcome back.

Watching my leaders begin to take accountability, my foremost thought was to go and take care of my men, and to make absolutely sure we hadn't left anyone downtown in all that madness. My dirty, sweaty Tigers were tired beyond measure, an after-effect of both the extended physical exertion and the adrenaline that had been rushing through their veins for hours on end. They also knew, as did I, that the mission was not yet over. Our battalion brothers and those we had come for, both living and dead, were still on the field of battle, and nothing short of their safe return to the stadium would right the situation.

As the senior NCOs attended to consolidation and reorganization tasks, I made a radio call to Dragon 6. A very quick conversation ensued. In essence, I asked if we, or at least our vehicles, were needed in any way. Colonel David decided to have us stay put.

Knowing that the colonel had his hands full, I bounced one more thought off him. I asked if I could run a mission to destroy the disabled Condors that were abandoned in and around the southern objective. I was sure they were full of sensitive items and that a TOW or Hellfire missile through each vehicle's roof would leave them ruined beyond any hope of recovery or use by the enemy. He agreed, and I spent the last few minutes before we entered the stadium directing the aerial missions that gutted the once-proud Condors of the MALBAT.

As the company formation broke up, I was assured that all were accounted for one final time. Staring into the early morning dawn, though, I realized that was not really the case. The men whose names we had repeatedly called into the unanswering night around Super 64 were not accounted for, nor was the pilot who had reportedly been on the ground in our initial objective area. Seemingly against all hope, I felt in my heart that we would find them.

Like specters, the Delta boys briefly appeared and then disappeared from Charlie Company's area as Mace and his RTOs quickly exited the Command Condor and left to link up with their own command. With my men beginning to enter the stadium, I looked for someone in charge. Almost gently, I was offered a cup of milked tea by a man dressed in a crisp Pakistani uniform, who then led me to an officer who was, in a manner of speaking, triaging the newcomers. Vehicles were sent to the sidelines and what we Americans would call the end zone. Walkers, whether wounded or just plain exhausted, were shown to stadium seating on our right.

The new sun bathed the interior white of the stadium with a warm, brilliant glow that was starkly contrasted by men so sweat-soaked that their mostly tan desert camouflage uniforms were the color of mud. The formerly brilliant white Condors, now covered with the grime of Mogadishu, reeked inside and out. Still deadly, the haunted hulks bore the effects of hard combat throughout the preceding night.

I joined my men in the stands and listened intently to the radio traffic from the northern objective. Near dawn, a HMMWV was used to rip apart Super 61, allowing Chief Wolcott's body to finally be recovered from the wedged aircraft. Capt. Drew Meyerowich directed the loading of the remains of those killed in action, the wounded, and any sensitive items into his Condors and any other vehicles available from the rescue convoy or CT Bravo.

Frustrated, I listened as those at the northern crash site ran out of vehicles to carry all of the men out. They were now attempting to pack nearly two full infantry companies, plus dead and wounded casualties retrieved at the site, plus sensitive items, into the same Condors that had already been packed full with a full complement of fighting men in their bellies when they had come to the fight just a few hours before.

Now the space requirement was almost doubled. Men were crammed into space occupied by the dead, the wounded, and those who had avoided bodily harm. Injured men still bled, still anguished for lost brothers in arms, and still fought to stay alive as the vehicles were packed to overflowing with Delta, Ranger, 10th Mountain, and Malaysian warriors. And firefights continued to erupt throughout the shrinking perimeter, as well as along the exfiltration route.

After Colonel David asked several times for an accurate head count and accountability check, Alpha and the remnants of TF Ranger slowly began the journey to the stadium, then picked up the pace. As the convoy made for the stadium, some soldiers had to run beside—and at times behind—the vehicles in order to keep up. This became known as the "Mogadishu Mile." Exhausted men, mounted and dismounted, had fought their way out of encirclement and arrived at the stadium sweaty, dust-coated, and raw from an epic battle. As the men filed by, I looked at them and knew that I was looking at a mirror image of myself. TF Ranger had fought hard to complete the mission and stay alive. TF David had fought equally hard to ensure they lived, thus preventing a disaster that would have echoed through the ages.

Banding in groups, the living took to the stadium seating. The lifeless, borne in body bags, were lined up behind Charlie Company's vehicles for positive identification, each bag gently opened in turn. I watched the solemn event as we retrieved our gear from the Condors we had ridden in, fought for, and, in the end, protected with our lives.

Death holds no curiosity for me. But the dark green bags, each with a double-strength zipper opened with such reverence, drew me to reflect on the likes of the men that we had not been able to rescue, the men who had given their all for those beside them, carrying out their mission despite the odds, despite the daylight, despite the ferocious nature of combat. As I slowly made my way among the fallen warriors, the thing I took away from that viewing was that even the most highly trained, brilliant, powerful, and near-perfect among us can be struck down.

I said a quick prayer for each man and was thankful that none of my men were counted among them.

Turning to walk back to my men, I watched the familiar white hair of Mace as he walked up to me and powerfully shook my hand. "That was pretty cool," he said, meaning the night of ferocity and pulling off the rescue of the lost platoon. I said thanks. Knowing that he didn't have any official reason to speak to me again, I appreciated the gesture, and count my time with him as "pretty cool," too.

Black Hawks began descending into the stadium far down the pitch to our right. One bird at a time began picking up loads of TF Ranger soldiers to cycle them to the airfield. The hammering of the blades brought ragged cheers as the choppers came and went, each aircraft bearing American heroes.

I went to find Colonel David, Major Ellerbe, the S-3, and Captain Meyerowich, eventually locating them at the colonel's HMMWV. What greeted me were, each in his own right, accomplished men. Dragon 6 had coordinated a huge, ad hoc, multinational combined arms task force that successfully executed a nearly impossible mission. Captain Meyerowich had found the living and gotten them out. And Ellerbe had stood his ground during a mortar attack, continuing to engage the attackers with his Beretta even after sustaining the million-dollar wound—a sliver of mortar fragment in his butt.

We were all sobered by the action and, as among the troops in the stands, our greetings were quiet and respectful, each man looking for some insight into what had just happened to us all. Living history, as opposed to reading about historic events, leaves one somewhat unsettled. You know you've just done something grand but are unable to take in the scope of it at the time. You just don't feel the history of the action, because real life overwhelms your senses in such a way that, while you will never forget the experience of it, you are left unable to describe the acts themselves, let alone the attendant emotions.

On reflection, I think that each member of this small group of edu-cated, highly trained professionals had, at one time or another, anticipated this rite of passage. Now that we had gone through it and even performed beyond our wildest dreams, we simply could not find the words. It's as if your tongue strives for them but the flood of vision after vision and act after act that fills your mind short-circuits your sense of speech; there is just too much to tell.

Colonel David told Captain Meyerowich and me to get with our men. I hadn't expected that we would be flown out like Delta and the Rangers, but that is exactly what was going to happen. Our battalion would be last in the queue, but at least we were going to be treated to a quick, helicopter-borne return to the University Complex.

I was informed that we would land at Jaybird LZ as soon as possible. I don't know how everyone else was feeling, but I was becoming numb. The heat of the early morning sun, the adrenaline drain, and the sheer exhaus-tion from the protracted physical and mental exertion was taking its toll.

As combat vehicles came and went inside the stadium, the aircraft came and went from the makeshift LZ in the middle of the soccer pitch; the roar of the survivors rose to a crescendo and slowly dwindled after each pickup. Soon, all that was left was a ground convoy ready to leave for the University Complex and a few remaining 10th Mountain Black Hawk loads. The last few of us, looking pretty weary, tried to make light of what had happened, but it was just too much. We all knew that this rescue was far greater than any of us could have imagined, but many of us were already mentally preparing to go back out if called to do so.

And, in my mind, it was clearly a matter of when, not if. This mission wasn't over until we got everyone back. I knew there were POWs or remains yet to recover. With the lights now on, we could press our advantage . . .

Amid its self-generated dust storm, my Black Hawk finally came in. Ducking our helmets into the rotor wash, my headquarters element and a few others climbed on board. The rotors bit the air and up we went over the city that we almost didn't make it out of. The fresh air felt marvelous and breathing it felt like heaven itself as clean Indian Ocean air scrubbed the dregs of the city from my lungs.

The bright, clear morning view contrasted so starkly with the dark confines of the back alleyways of Mogadishu. If you looked close enough, a lingering haze hung over the Black Sea. In and around the Bakara Market, people could be seen venturing wearily into the streets again, cautious after the deadly night before.

The ride was short and sweet, a deliberate point A to point B delivery. Jaybird LZ came into view, the Black Hawk hovered and threw up the usual rotor wash, and we hopped off. Quickly moving to the edge of the LZ with our heads down, we felt, rather than heard, the chopper drive into the air and head out for another load.

Even as our ears still rang from the night of firefights, the silence was deafening. We all looked at each other and realized that we actually were safely back in our own digs. Surrounded by my men, I headed for our company area.

This was the same road that we had whooped and hollered our way along after our first firefight on 13 September. Today, there was no hoopla. Tired, serious men simply made their way to the temporary home they had set up in this hellhole.

In a single night, Mogadishu had made the history books, and just the mention of the name would stir great feelings in each of us for the rest of our lives. Pride in our accomplishment was tempered by what it took to make it happen. Men—*my men*—were wounded and terribly missed already. TF Ranger and CT Alpha had it worse. They had lost friends and comrades, men they would never again run PT with, or swap jokes with, or share a personal concern or war story. Some of these men had made their own already legendary stories that night.

The company area was not the same. The boisterous, rowdy barracks area was now a quiet haven for introspection. Each man sought refuge in his own private space, belongings, and talismans. Pictures of loved ones were truly appreciated. Letters from home were reread, Bibles were opened, and Popsicle sticks were pulled from dingy cargo pockets.

We survived; others hadn't. It was a night in hell. Each man sought solace in the fact that he still breathed, had comrades to share his actions, and had a cot or homemade rack to call his own.

At around 0800 that morning the TV was turned on, and there we were on CNN's Headline News. Mogadishu was the lead story, and would be for days. Much to our chagrin, we saw the naked, battered, and mutilated bodies of TF Ranger being pulled through the streets by throngs of cheering Somalis. Seeing those great and proud men dishonored in such a way caused a part of my heart to remain forever cold.

We found out that Chief Durant was being held. I remember the stern look of those around me. Hardened men wanted to finish the mission and leave no man behind. At a word, we were ready to go right back out the gate.

When we returned, I told the XO, 1st Lieutenant MacDonald, to order 10 percent more ammo than we'd expended, per our SOP. His look told me that we would have an awful lot of ammunition to go back out with.

Making my way to the Battalion TOC, I asked Colonel David if we could call home. His reply, "Affirmative," was all it took. Everyone who wanted to was allowed to contact a loved one to let them know that their man was alive and that Tiger Company was in high spirits. When I made my call, Pam told me that the battalion wives were worried, but so damned proud of us. Because we didn't have cell phones back then, the call on the TA-312 was a necessarily short and sweet "I love you" to all of the kids, then back to the business of war.

Shortly after the call, I wrote a letter home that detailed our hard night and my feelings about it all, filling in the details that couldn't be conveyed in a short phone call. In just forty-eight hours we had gone from resting to full speed, from reaction force to rescuer, from soldiers to American heroes.

Such is the nature and privilege of leading America's sons and now daughters.

CHAPTER 19

Surreal Aftermath

A s I made my way through the company area in the hours following our return from the stadium, I noticed two things: introspection and preparedness. We had MIAs, meaning that we would conduct a mission to rescue or retrieve our fallen. It didn't matter that 2-14 Infantry had accountability of all its men; the fact was that Americans were unaccounted for, and that did not sit well with any of us.

Each of us could imagine being out there and alone, and it was not a great image to contemplate. In our culture, everyone is brought home, whether KIA, wounded, or captured. The men and I had watched as CNN developed the story and pieced together the details of the horrific night we had survived. All around me, men loaded magazines, filled canteens, exchanged NOD batteries, and grimly prepared to leave no man behind.

The company had a quiet focus, remembering the night, the fight, the sights, the sounds, and the exertion needed to do our job for seventeen hours straight. As a group, we were bearing down and preparing for what was surely to come. We all knew we were going back out, so the QRF was getting re-cocked.

But the order to execute never came. While we stayed ready, the policymakers were taking a different approach. Within forty-eight hours, reports came in that CW3 Michael Durant, the pilot of Super 64, had been captured alive and was being held at an undisclosed location. All the other missing had been accounted for, and their bodies were returned to checkpoints or brought to main compounds.

Chief Durant was badly wounded when Super 64 fell from the sky, injuring his back on impact, and then subsequently beaten and shot during his capture. Enduring eleven days of brutal captivity, he became the tragic face of the battle as the news media plastered his proof-of-life photos on television and on the covers of various news magazines.

We quickly realized that our rescue mission had become a frenzy of defeat and negativity. The video of our fallen being dragged through the streets with mocking and joyously savage Somalis dancing all around seemed to impart a spin on our battle that varied from heroism to tragedy and back again.

Hear this from one who was there: No matter what anyone says, we won that battle. Yes, we took casualties, and it did take longer than expected, but TF Ranger and TF David accomplished their assigned tasks and, ultimately, their missions. Much like Tet in Vietnam, American and U.N. forces had clearly and utterly defeated the enemy, only to have the government fold when they had the upper hand. Politicians pulled defeat from the mouth of victory, and yet another successful tactical action was reduced to a strategic defeat by policy decisions.

The USS *America* carrier battle group, including the USS *Guadalcanal* and its contingent of United States Marines, arrived off shore. The sight of the huge ships on the horizon was awesome and made you proud to be an American. Right there was tangible proof that if Aidid really wanted to party, we were ready. When the entire air wing screamed in over the city at what seemed like 50 feet, the writing was on the wall for Mogadishu. We were ready for a land offensive to clean up the riff raff around the Bakara Market. Or so we thought . . .

In just under two weeks, Michael Durant was back in the fold, recovering in Landstuhl, Germany, and rumors spread of millions of dollars paid to Aidid by our government to "not shoot at us."

Armor from the United States, in the form of a mechanized infantry company with M1 Abrams and M2 Bradley Fighting Vehicles from the

24th Infantry Division, arrived to finally augment U.S. forces in country. Additionally, the United Nations brought in an Indian armored battalion, with their distinctive white T-80 tanks and BMP-3 APCs, to augment the U.N. QRF.

As Delta and the Rangers began packing to leave, TF David went back to the training cycle and, much to our chagrin, the MSR protection detail. Daily life, in general, changed. As veterans of the greatest battle since the Vietnam War, we were awash in veneration. Senators, Congressmen, generals, colonels, everyone in our chain of command or those that wanted to be, and the news media all wanted to get the story of the night that would eventually gain the moniker "Black Hawk Down."

It was during this time that I met Sen. John Warner, whom I was told to report to at the brigade TOC. After meeting his staffers, he and I were introduced and spent a candid couple of hours together. During the meeting, he told me that he had flown the entire way from Virginia to Somalia just to see me because I was the only constituent from Virginia in the battalion. He wrote a very nice letter to my parents, which they cherish, telling them that we had met and that he was very proud of me and that I was doing just fine.

On 9 October, Aidid officially announced a "total ceasefire," and President Clinton barred us from any retaliation against Aidid or, for that matter, any Somalis. By 22 October, TF Ranger was gone from Somalia and the hunt for Aidid closed down for good. Even though there were individual incidents where Somalis were killed attacking Americans, no U.S. servicemen were killed after 6 October, when Sfc. Matt Rierson died when the TF Ranger hangar was mortared. In retrospect, TF David had ridden the wave of escalation to the inevitable conclusion of ground combat operations in Somalia. The remainder of the deployment was one of duty, ceremony, tradition, and practicality.

Our duty was maintained by "the cycle." TF 2-14 would conduct the missions we were given, whether in the bush, along MSR Tiger, as security at Sword Base, or operations in the mess hall on Thanksgiving, with the quiet pride of proven veterans. Like it or not, our lives had changed, even in-country. PT seemed easier, rounds downrange went cleaner, and sweat was gladly shed, because knowing what freedom truly meant had placed a warm glow in our breasts that remains to this day.

Ceremonies were held for our dead. Our wounded received Purple Hearts, and our infantryman received the coveted Combat Infantryman's Badge. We also began an intense "writex" to complete the recommendations for those whose actions warranted consideration for award of the Silver Star, the Bronze Star with Valor device, and the Army Commendation Medal with Valor device. Approved awards would be presented later in 1994.

Practicality reigned as we began preparations for overseas movement back to the United States. Recognizing that we'd soon be heading back to a Fort Drum winter, we set about getting the entire company qualified to 10th Mountain Division standards in marksmanship, the Army Physical Fitness Test, and completion of all road marches.

By mid-December, we could feel the mission coming to closure. As the cycle turned and our training days became fewer, I decided to take the company on one last trip to The Beach and a meeting with our Range 10 village friends. Knowing this would be our last trip so far south, I took in every sight, constantly making mental pictures of the Indian Ocean, its giant blue surface swaying to and fro; of hundreds of camels being driven along amidst the dust of centuries; of the glorious bush, with all its thorns; and of the vast bright azure of the African sky.

My favorite Somali village sits on a small rise overlooking the immensity of the deep ocean, just north of Marka. Its people are pleasant, lifelong workers. The men are lobstermen and the women provide everything else. The children are happy and, compared to the desperate survivors in Mogadishu, they are full of vim, vigor, and life. From these children, I gained an understanding of my position in Somalia and the grand scheme of things.

Shortly after our arrival, we positioned our vehicles facing out, appropriately spaced for interlocking fires and mutual support. In retrospect, this was unnecessary, as we had always been welcomed by the adults. And, as usual, a small crowd of the children almost immediately began to form. They were of all ages, male and female, wearing mostly clean clothes and exhibiting inquisitive demeanors. Shy at first, they initially remained within hand-grenade distance, but slowly began creeping forward, pushing one another as children do and faking scuffles to further close the distance.

Challenging, yet fearful, they approached to within a couple of arm lengths and began the searching eye movements that clearly signaled their unasked "What you got, mister?" questions.

Leery at first, the interactions were tentative on both sides. My HMMWV was particularly interesting because I was the leader. They inherently knew, because of the deference of my men and the various symbols, who I was. They also had a pecking order that was equally obvious to me. Older males ran everything, while younger males bossed females who stayed back, and the little ones were on their own.

But what now confronted me was that the village children were waiting to see what I would do. Would I shoo them away? Curse them? Respect them as people? Treat them as children? Respect their pecking order?

At first, it was a standoff, with the parents eagerly watching from afar to see my actions. Then the ice broke when I had the men in my vehicle begin passing out single MRE packages, then whole MREs.

As usual, the kids took advantage, pushing and grabbing just short of disrespect. Although always somewhat irritating, it could be written off as the way kids typically behaved. But what truly bothered me was the way the older kids pushed away the small ones. One little fellow in particular caught my eye by simply refusing to give up the fight, even as the older ones ran over him, pummeled him, roughly shoved him out of the way, and generally kept him from getting anything in the way of a handout.

After I'd seen enough, I stood in the back of my HMMWV. The crowd, including both my own men and the children, instantly froze. I looked them all in the eye, clearly showing displeasure that no one missed. Reaching to the back of the HMMWV, I pulled an entire case of MREs from under the seat. Then, I climbed down from the vehicle, everyone parting to let me pass as I walked straight to that dusty, sweaty, frustrated, yet totally feisty and determined little boy and presented him with the case of food.

I will never forget either the look of pride in his eyes, or the simple dignity of his straightened back and the zip in his step as he headed home to his parents with the prize. Nor will I forget the astonished look on the faces of those who had been fighting and quarrelling. The instant I showed respect to the young one, the others ceased to fight and patiently waited to gladly accept food, paper, pens, and whatever else we had.

For the duration of our stay, they never once stole from us or showed us any ill will. I know that I was watching life as it should be. I felt honored that they respected me, and that they respected my wishes by letting the little guy take his reward home in such a powerful display of human interaction.

Once set up in our defensive position along the coastal village, the company was welcomed on our return by the elders, who informed us that there would be a feast on our final evening following training. Strangely, they seemed to sense the finality of our visit. The leaders and I heartily agreed, and I told the men to make this last visit a relaxing and memorable one. Training turned out to be maintenance and security.

After my rounds of the company area, just before dusk, I walked up under my cliff-top perch, faced the sea, and sat down on my butt. Leaning back against my rucksack, I fell quietly into a most restful slumber amid the beginning rhythms of African drums, glowing firelight, a soft and cooling Indian Ocean breeze, the wafting aroma of boiled lobster, and the peace of knowing that I was protected by America's finest.

20/20 Hindsight

I wrote this book because I loved my men, was immensely privileged to lead them in combat, and because I love the men and women who will fill my shoes in years to come. Colonel David called us a "Supercharged Battalion," which he defined as one that gave all it had and 10 percent more. I believe him, always have. His guidance and training kept us alive. We trained hard to high standards and beyond, conducted required maintenance, and became brilliant at the basics. We had physical, tactical, personal, and moral discipline, were willing to go back again and again until we accomplished the mission, and never left a fallen comrade behind.

But most of all, we adapted. We trained over and over to adapt and overcome. We created simple, well-conceived plans, and we believed in initiative and trust. When you trust your subordinates and they trust you, anything can be accomplished. You must let the micromanagement go, give your men and women the mission, and let them surprise you with the ingenuity they employ to achieve the results you envisioned.

And they must always trust that you will have their back. Colonel David and his staff always had mine. Three times Tiger Company was challenged in close combat. In each of those chaotic experiences, the leadership rose to the occasion, adapted to the unanticipated, and didn't let bad luck stop them.

No military unit can specifically prepare for every possible battle scenario, and every leader faces unknowable elements. Consequently, you must always be prepared to adapt. But exactly how do you prepare for factors you never see coming?

You start by becoming brilliant at the basics: moving, shooting, and communicating. I don't care what century it is, either far in the past or far into the future; those that perform these three basic combat tasks better than their opponents will achieve victory. Victory, after all, is the only yardstick by which the military is measured, and the losers don't get to write the history.

Once the basics are set, build on them by:

- Using battle drills and crew drills to raise the bar to another level. Ensure roles and duties are known by every soldier, because the performance of well-trained teams is exponentially better than the individual performances of the team members.

- Learning targeted, complex, collective tasks, such as a company night assault of a trench live-fire. Because these exercises give all leaders so many things to do simultaneously, they are able to seamlessly jump to other mission tasks as evolving situations dictate. In other words, they learn the value of adaptability. It is this capacity for adaptation that allows accomplishment of each unit's overall performance of the full range of the core military operations: conventional, combined arms maneuver, irregular warfare, and stability.

- Balancing trust up and down the chain of command with aggressiveness, decisiveness, and confidence. These essential traits allow soldiers the freedom to quickly decide what is necessary to accomplish the mission.

- Ensuring that everyone understands the cultural aspects of the situation allows them to reach better conclusions and take appropriate action, knowing that their boss will both allow the action and absorb any fallout from genuine mistakes created by the chaos of battle.

- Understanding that inaction is worse than indecision. That's exactly why the axiom "Lead, follow, or get the hell out of the way" has stood the test of time for leaders down through the centuries.

No one thing, no single victory or accomplished mission, is more important than just making a good, solid decision. If you fail, fail valiantly, for if you fail, you fail your regiment, your division, your army, and your nation. Victory is essential to the warrior. It drives the ethos, the will. It drives history. Why do we know Leonidas and the 300? Because despite their seeming failure in a single battle—that magnificent Greek rear-guard was, after all, annihilated!—Thermopylae remains one of the greatest strategic victories in all of history.

America's fighting men and women are drawn from the very core of our society. Without them, we would not be the shining beacon of freedom that people worldwide see and aspire to be. Without them, there could be no democracy, only tyranny, anarchy, and the madness we faced in Mogadishu.

What did I learn personally from my experience in Somalia? I learned that no matter what type of unit you lead, you might find yourself in a combat environment where there are no front lines. Know that, in such circumstances, no matter what kind of warfighting function you fulfill, be it infantry, transportation, or military police, you must be expert in the controlled application of violence. Follow your instincts; they are probably right. God gave us that instinct for a reason, and it will likely be on overdrive in combat situations.

I also learned that life truly is situational, and that perception often is reality. Think on your feet. Be aware of and understand the situation around you, and do not hesitate to take the actions that the situation dictates.

Perception, while not necessarily truth, can often be manipulated to drive the situation. If, for example, someone thinks you are the baddest guy or gal on the block, they will either test you or leave you alone. Odds are they'll leave you alone. But once tested, your survival exponentially improves your odds for the next test. The same goes for how your organization looks and performs in everything from an inspection to a firefight.

How you are perceived matters. Remember that you never have a second chance to make a great first impression.

Think for those who are not able to think for themselves, either because they are already doing all that they can or because they are scared out of their minds. That is your job as a leader. Think through your own fear, and remember that courage is born of fear.

As emotionally difficult as this next reality is, you must always remember that casualties are an unfortunate by-product of our business. As leaders, we must recognize that the cumulative effects of rifle/helmet/boots ceremonies, speeches, and heartfelt trips to urgent care wards do take a toll. For your own well-being, as well as for the benefit of your soldiers and the unit as a whole, avail both yourself and those soldiers of the various forms of counseling and assistance that can help us all cope with these awesome psychological and emotional stresses.

At the same time, we cannot ever sacrifice victory and mission accomplishment for fear of casualties. Leaders must understand that a soldier's willingness to give his life for the mission hinges on his belief that competent leaders validly assessed the mission as being worth the lives it might cost.

Training doesn't stop in-theater. You must train ceaselessly, using your imagination to overcome the lack of ranges, obstacles, and electronic thingamajigs. To stay at your peak, you must design and build the best training infrastructure you can in-country and use it incessantly.

After Action Reports are not new to any military service. Understand that they are vital to learning and understanding your unit, especially after a combat action. Although your senses will likely already be overloaded, you can't let something slip by that was picked up by another team member, no matter what their rank.

You must pace yourself for the long haul. You can't get so excited in the first few days of a deployment that you burn out in month six of a twelve- or eighteen-month tour of duty. Stay focused; work out to burn off stress, and train, train, train. Most of your days will be routine, even boring. Without warning, though, some could become intense, life-threatening engagements that may or may not put you in the history books. Be prepared, and rest as often as possible, because you simply never know.

Keep a journal or diary. Without notes to go on, I could never have remembered most of my experiences during this extraordinary tour of duty. So be your own best record keeper.

And finally, if you do go in harm's way, God bless you, and Godspeed.

—*Lt. Col. Michael Lance Whetstone, USA (Ret.)*

Preparing a Company for Combat

I n 1994, Colonel David was asked to produce his lessons learned. In my opinion, those lessons and the training regimen he devised, shown below, are timeless. From personal participation, I know that his approach created a physically fit, highly motivated, competent, confident, and absolutely adaptive battalion that was thoroughly trained in the right stuff.

When I first conceived of this book, I immediately knew that including his wise guidance would enhance its value as a primer for effective command. However, what I wanted to do was to modify his writings so as to present his counsel from the company command perspective, rather than from the battalion command perspective of the original writing. Upon proposing this near-heresy to him, I was not at all surprised that he immediately and very graciously concurred and gave his permission.

What follows tries to retain nearly all of his words, but with company-level interpretations added by me and the other company commanders. Living and learning by and within his approach made us all into professional soldiers and created warriors with a core ethos that I genuinely believe saved us all.

What is related herein reflects the approach that C Company, 2nd Battalion, 14th Infantry, used before and during its tour in Somalia. These are not all-inclusive lists, and there are plenty of areas in which we probably could have done better. Cultural and counterinsurgency (COIN) aspects of the mission, for example, were sort of an ongoing learn-as-you-go issue throughout our deployment. Please keep in mind both the time and the context, and that these points and suggestions worked for all the companies, not just mine.

Physical Fitness

Light infantry operations place great stress on the human body. They involve prolonged exposure to the elements, broken sleep on rocky ground, bug bites, rashes, abrasions, contusions, and a ration cycle that is never guaranteed unless you carry them on your back. They also require foot movement over extended distances while carrying loads that would tire a pack mule.

At the completion of such movements, soldiers must still have reserves of both strength and stamina that will enable them to fight close, violent battles against a well-rested enemy. No matter how badly they may hurt, soldiers must be able to climb, crawl, and sprint long after their adrenaline is gone. Their lives and the lives of others depend on it.

Infantry operations, therefore, require a high state of individual and unit physical fitness. But physical fitness alone is not enough. Soldiers must also have the mental toughness to reach down inside themselves for that essential extra burst of strength or speed when their bodies are screaming No!

Physical fitness and mental toughness are inseparable and interdependent. One is of little use without the other. Together, they are required for every operation an infantry company will ever be called upon to execute. They are the essence of light infantry operations and, for this reason, are one of the company's core performance areas.

My initial assessment after assuming command of C Company was that we were in pretty good physical shape. We met all the required divisional standards for individual and unit physical training and, like many units, had a large number of soldiers who wholeheartedly embraced the value of physical fitness and took the initiative to maintain exceptional levels of conditioning. But we were not collectively aiming for the upper levels of physical performance. As a result, I believed we had not reached our potential in this area and could do much better.

As I talked with soldiers and analyzed the company's previous training, I realized that there was also room for improvement in the mental aspect of conditioning. As an intangible, mental toughness is virtually impossible to quantify or measure. But even if they can't define it, units that really are mentally tough know that they are.

This was the type of unit I wanted. Our soldiers had to know in their hearts that they were the toughest soldiers on the block. If the company couldn't go over, under, or around the wall, I wanted them to have the sheer grit to go *through* the damned thing. And when the tactical situation went to hell, I wanted them to have the strength of spirit to win through brute force of will.

When it came to physical fitness and mental toughness, the company was at the good stage, but I wanted that extra 10 percent needed to become high performers in this core area. To achieve that, we were going to have to adopt a training regimen that would stretch our physical and mental capacities in parallel.

There is no argument within the Army about the importance of the link between physical fitness and combat readiness. For all the right reasons, every division in the Army establishes individual and unit physical fitness standards that pretty closely mirror those of the other divisions. The minimum standards for 10th Mountain units, for example, are:

- Physical training conducted five days a week.
- Quarterly 4-mile run in athletic shoes in 35 minutes or less, normally conducted as a formation run. (This is also the XVIII Airborne Corps standard.)
- Semiannual 12-mile road march in 3 hours or less while wearing individual combat gear and a fighting load of 15 to 35 pounds.
- Semiannual Army Physical Fitness Test (APFT) with a minimum overall score of 225, with at least 60 in each event. An average score of 250 is established as a unit goal for PT excellence.

I believed that meeting the division's physical fitness standards was important to guarantee that our soldiers would have the physical and mental capacity to do everything we could reasonably expect to be called upon to do in combat. But in a light infantry company, where the highest state of physical fitness is essential to battlefield survivability and success, meeting the divisional standards is only an important first step. Light infantry soldiers have to be capable of doing more.

Five days a week of physical training was the right frequency, but we also had to ensure that we were doing the right things to put real teeth into our PT program. For a properly conditioned soldier, a 4-mile run in 36 minutes is no more challenging that a walk in the park. And if unit PT is properly planned and executed, individual fitness levels improve over time so that most soldiers, even on a bad day, can score higher than 265 on the APFT.

The 12-mile road march in 3 hours is a tough challenge that indicates overall conditioning. But while it does have its place in a unit PT program, it simply does not replicate all the physical endurance demands of light infantry operations. First, the prescribed loads for the march are much lighter than those normally carried by soldiers in the field. And second, meeting the 3-hour time limit requires soldiers to maintain a run-walk pace that is too fast to be sustained much farther than the finish line. As a result, the event falls short in developing any significant degree of mental toughness.

In my company, the process began as a leadership challenge to convince the chain of command that we should—and could—get more out of ourselves in this core performance area. I was confident that if physical fitness and mental toughness could be embedded as a core value of the company, then natural interaction and competition among the chain of command in our daily routine would lead us to the 10 percent performance improvement I wanted.

This approach had three important components. The physical fitness piece—built on an existing value system that is very noticeable in combat arms units—stressed carefully planned, balanced, and tough PT every day to improve overall physical conditioning. The mental toughness piece employed regularly scheduled grueling unit activities designed to force everyone through the physical and mental "wall" that is familiar to any marathon runner. And as the control piece that supported this demanding regimen, we held ourselves rigorously accountable to every regulatory tool at our disposal.

In garrison, PT was regarded as the company's most important unit activity of the day. We jealously guarded this time and rarely let other activities interfere. At each weekly training meeting, daily PT was briefed in detail down to platoon level. I looked closely for the proper mix of running distance and time, speed work, road marching, and strength development.

Although unit sports activities were highly encouraged, they were not allowed during PT hours. PT was a time of hard work for everyone, not a time to play games. When first announced, this philosophy was met with considerable resistance by the chain of command and engendered a lot of professional discussion. Eventually, though, all key leaders understood and fully supported my intent.

To model the behavior we wanted, the first sergeant and I did vigorous PT every day and made sure the company saw us doing it. We regularly spot-checked physical training to make sure it was being conducted as briefed. Impromptu After Action Reviews (AARs) at the end of PT sessions did a lot to help soldiers better understand the concept of what we were trying to achieve.

Battalion runs were conducted on Friday mornings every two or three weeks. Company 4-mile speed marches with 40-pound rucksack loads were conducted on all other Fridays to keep the soldiers' feet in condition. As the unit's physical condition improved, we began to use these runs to work on our mental conditioning as well. Gradually, we increased the length of the runs to 8 miles but, following extended periods in the field, would temporarily reduce them to 5 or 6 miles.

The fine-tuning achieved by establishing interest in all activities associated with PT and increasing the length of runs really got the ball rolling. The platoons had to conduct vigorous daily PT to avoid incurring the unwanted attention of the battalion commander during one of his unexpected visits. But even when I was not around, pride drove the platoons to maintain this rigor, because any deficiencies were bound to show up when the battalion rolled down the road for the next 8-miler. We had no fall-outs from C Company.

As a means of developing mental toughness, the 25-mile road march was one battalion activity that had a big payoff for all of the companies. We marched in full combat gear with a field load in our rucksacks and carrying all standard light infantry equipment. This was the infantryman's marathon. It did more to instill true mental toughness than any other single training event we conducted.

The goal was to execute one 25-mile march every quarter, but seven off-post deployments in twenty-five months limited us to doing it about twice a year. Nevertheless, we always had a 25-mile road march on the long-range planning calendar to keep our PT program focused on this high-performance challenge. With mile markers set out along the road-march route, a sustained pace of 17:30 per mile was set. The battalion took one thirty-minute and two twenty-minute rest halts during the nine hours it took to finish.

The soldiers could complete the first 20 miles on their conditioning alone, but the last 5 required guts and determination. Completing the march was a real badge of honor. When it was over, all of the soldiers knew they had accomplished something few other units would even attempt.

Every summer, 2-14 IN conducted Combat Olympics, a one-and-a-half-day blitz of full-contact, bone-crunching, intercompany competition based on both military and athletic competitions. This was not just organized athletics under a different name. It was a carefully constructed event intended to involve as many soldiers as possible in the competition.

Rules, uniform requirements, and schedules were worked out to the last detail. Any violation resulted in disqualification for the company team. To prevent team-stacking, multiple events were run simultaneously. Company internal organization was always extended to include every soldier. A weighted scoring system based on the scale of each event was used. At the end of the competition, trophies were presented in a battalion formation to individual, team, and company winners.

The Combat Olympics left just about everyone in 2-14 IN battered, bruised, and physically spent, but the soldiers thrived on the competition. The tougher and more physically punishing it could be, the better. Not surprisingly, the margins separating the individual, team, and unit winners from the runners-up were very slim, usually less than 10 percent.

2-14 IN also put on boxing smokers and participated in Fort Drum's intramural sports program. While these activities were done more for fun, they reinforced the values we were trying to embed in the unit—that physical conditioning and mental toughness are essential and inseparable components of being an infantryman.

Achieving high performance in physical fitness and mental toughness is a goal that is within reach for every unit. It took six or seven months of hard work before I realized that the company had risen from being merely good in this area to being at a higher level.

Obviously, coming from the temperate summer of upstate New York, our soldiers needed a high level of physical fitness to acclimatize quickly to Somalia's heat. Despite everything we had been doing in physical training, I was concerned that the company's performance would be degraded until the acclimatization process ran its course.

The weather could not have been more brutal. Temperatures rose above 90 degrees every day, with humidity levels between 80 and 100 percent. The effects of weather were exacerbated by our standard combat loads and the desert camouflage uniforms (DCUs) we wore in our role as the Quick Reaction Force. Yet I was pleasantly surprised to discover that neither the weather nor the high operational tempo significantly reduced the company's performance. Although the soldiers were being pushed hard, they remained physically strong and mentally alert. This told me that the company had arrived, and that we had gotten our 10 percent improvement. Better yet, as our soldiers observed other units that were not faring as well, they came to know it, too. We were clearly on the right track.

Throughout 2-14 IN's tour in Somalia, fatigue was a constant problem. The standard operational uniform consisted of either the heavy- or medium-weight DCU, load-carrying equipment, an M17A1 protective mask, a Kevlar helmet, Level II body armor, and the assigned individual or crew-served weapon.

The combined effects of uniform and weather for extended periods, particularly through the heat of the day, were enough to sap the strength of the fittest man. Environmental stress, interrupted sleep patterns, and diet also contributed to the cumulative effects of fatigue. A high level of physical fitness and mental toughness was therefore essential in combating this insidious and ever-present enemy.

Being quartered in the Mogadishu University compound gave the task force a relatively secure base of operations that allowed sustainment of our physical training program. Even with the demands of the mission, C Company conducted vigorous PT at least four times a week, sometimes more. Weight sets in the company area also gave the soldiers an opportunity to improve their upper-body strength on their own time. With few competing time demands other than the mission, individual and unit physical fitness actually improved during our tour. Before redeployment, the platoon APFT averages ranged between 265 and 285 points, up from the average of 255 we had before heading for Somalia.

All our attention to physical fitness and mental toughness, both at home station and in-theater, also had tremendous payoffs in every facet of the task force's Somalia experience. Without question, our high level of fitness improved force protection all around. The soldiers had the strength to stay in the proper and complete uniform, regardless of their physical discomfort, and any deviations from the prescribed uniform were based upon conscious decisions of the chain of command, not personal whim.

When soldiers rolled out of the compound for any mission, they were alert and dressed for combat, and they remained that way until their return. Their very appearance meant business and served as a silent deterrent to any hostility. Not a single one of our convoys or outposts was taken under enemy fire as a target of opportunity. I don't believe this was from chance. There had been too many other examples to the contrary in-theater.

Physical fitness and mental toughness also increased C Company's tactical capabilities. We did not have to slow the pace of operations to that of the slowest man, because all soldiers were able to keep up with the main body. This was clearly demonstrated on numerous occasions, but one in particular illustrates this point.

In the pre-dawn hours of 13 September 1993, the task force conducted an attack to clear two large compounds in Mogadishu. Dominating the objective area was a hospital that was densely populated with hundreds of noncombatants. Not surprisingly, this hospital also doubled as a major base of operations for the Somali National Alliance (SNA) militia.

As morning twilight gave way to sunrise, the 2-14 Infantry command group, with both B and C Companies, were completing actions on the objective and beginning withdrawal. Suddenly, we began receiving RPG and automatic weapons fire from the area of the hospital and its surrounding streets. What followed was a major firefight between the task force and the SNA militia that lasted almost five hours. Despite all planning and preparation, most such meeting engagements begin with some element of surprise, causing soldiers to experience a jolt of adrenaline that lasts about fifteen to twenty minutes. As their minds and bodies become adjusted to the situation, however, adrenaline-depleted soldiers often experience a deep fatigue. Veterans of close combat know best that unless soldiers are in top physical condition, they will have nothing left in reserve when the adrenaline runs out. Yet even with the cumulative effects of fatigue from loss of sleep, combat loads, heat, humidity, and adrenaline depletion, every soldier in the company had physical energy reserves when it mattered most, enabling them to use proper individual movement techniques over a 2-kilometer route while under continuous fire.

Likewise, the company's mental toughness, apparent in everything we did, was highlighted most dramatically on the night of 3 October 1993, when the task force was called out to extract ground elements of TF Ranger pinned down by the SNA militia at the site of the downed helicopter. At 1745, C Company, as the TF's QRC, and the battalion tactical command post left the Mogadishu airfield in an effort to break through to the Rangers, the entire element mounted on either HMMWVs or 5-ton trucks. Over the next ninety minutes, we encountered a series of almost simultaneous ambushes and found ourselves in a more intense fight than in any of our previous engagements. The SNA militia had effectively sealed off the area around the Rangers against any penetration by thin-skinned vehicles and inflicted three severe casualties on our company in the process.

Despite this setback, as quickly as another effort could be planned and coordinated the soldiers were ready to go. At 2300, a second effort was launched with a large force involving most of the TF. A Company and C Company were loaded into APCs provided by the Malaysian battalion, and a Pakistani tank platoon provided additional support. The ensuing seven and a half hours was a continuous fight of great intensity. This time, however, we were successful in breaking through to the Rangers and accomplishing the mission.

Sometimes, close combat boils down to a test of willpower between adversaries. Because I had seen our soldiers' perseverance and determination in training, I was confident that we had the mental resilience to bounce back quickly from our initial unsuccessful effort. Moreover, I was confident that our soldiers would have both the mental and physical staying power to see the task through to the end, even when the situation appeared grim. On both counts, the soldiers proved me right.

After everything we had done in training, any doubts I harbored about being unrealistic or unfair in the demands we placed on our soldiers were put to rest in Somalia. The exceptional physical fitness and mental toughness of the company in close combat spoke for itself. The soldiers, in later casual conversations in the mess hall or field, candidly thanked the leadership for insisting that the unit do the tough physical training that they felt kept them alive.

Combat Marksmanship

Marksmanship is the very essence of a light infantry company, the most fundamentally important individual combat skill for light infantrymen in a kinetic situation. When soldiers lack confidence in their buddies' ability to provide them with accurate covering fire, there is no fire and movement. And without fire and movement, the scheme of maneuver begins to disintegrate. No matter how well conceived a plan may be or how well it is coordinated and rehearsed, mission success depends upon solid marksmanship skills at the point of attack.

Close combat is a fight that is won or lost at squad and platoon level, where the impetus for fire and movement is found in the acts of individuals. Skill in marksmanship—and the confidence in one's weapon that comes with it—is the enabling tool that overrides a soldier's natural inclination to go to ground under fire. It can transform a group of otherwise passive individuals into aggressive squads and platoons with both the skill and the will to win.

To win such close fights, light infantrymen must be able to consistently acquire and hit difficult targets that are typically only partially exposed, are usually camouflaged, and are either stationary or moving, in both day and night operations. They must also be cross-trained on all platoon weapons so that they can confidently man key weapon systems in the event of crew casualties.

Confidence in marksmanship is also the most important mental ingredient commanders can give soldiers for overcoming their personal fear in combat. In close combat, where a soldier can often see his enemy, that fear is even more intense. Even if the enemy's physical form is not clearly visible, the flash of his weapon usually is, and the rounds can be heard snapping overhead.

It is a sobering experience to lie in the prone position with your face in the dirt as enemy fire impacts all around. Men you've never met and will never know are trying to kill you. The future is now, and is measured in terms of your ability to kill before being killed. For an instant, it seems strange and somehow wrong that the sum total of your life's experiences should come to this.

Fear is, therefore, a natural reaction. Its weight can slow or stop even the sturdiest of men. But when their marksmanship is developed to a high level, soldiers gain an intangible psychological edge that keeps paralysis from taking hold and gives them the capacity to act in the face of great danger.

For all of these reasons, when I took command of the company I viewed combat marksmanship as one of the essential core performance areas for light infantry operations. High performance in marksmanship would always give the company a key tactical advantage that, once acquired, would be ours to keep. This, I knew, was one area in which we could control our own fate.

Every division uses weapon qualification statistics as one of its primary tools for assessing combat readiness. Unquestionably important, individual qualification is rooted in each soldier's mastery of the fundamentals of marksmanship with his assigned individual or crew-served weapon. Only then will qualification tables provide a consistent standard against which to evaluate performance and measure progress.

Standard weapon qualification provides the start point for the development of combat marksmanship skills. To kill efficiently and effectively in combat, however, a light infantryman has to be a better shot than the marksmanship tables require him to be.

Weapon qualification is typically conducted on fixed ranges with clear fields of fire, using targets that move only up and down and that are usually clearly visible. Qualification isn't conducted as part of fire and movement and, except for the noise of the firing line, there are no distractions such as indirect fires, smoke, or gun runs by overflying attack helicopters. Most often, qualification involves firing only from the prone position only, and may not be conducted with sufficient frequency to keep skills truly sharp.

Faced with many competing demands for time and resources, units can sometimes be overwhelmed by the sheer crush of events. Unless they are careful, units may discover that they're spending most of their time on the range just keeping up with reportable weapon qualification requirements, rather than training soldiers in the essential skills required of combat marksmen. Marksmanship should be one of our major strengths, and focusing on weapon qualification alone won't develop high performance in combat marksmanship. To reach this high level, units must do more in their training.

To replicate what the soldiers will encounter on the battlefield, commanders must make conditions more challenging and realistic. And to provide soldiers with opportunities for steady improvement in their marksmanship skills, firing must be more frequent. These two steps will give soldiers both the skills and the will to overcome their natural fears in combat and to kill a determined enemy.

After assuming command, I initially assessed that C Company's marksmanship was in pretty good shape. Squads and platoons had achieved basic weapon proficiency across the board, and all training management standards had been met. Nevertheless, I knew that this was no guarantee that we would be able to perform at peak levels in combat and that, like any unit, we had room for improvement. This core performance area, therefore, became a focus of attention.

Combat marksmanship thus became another component in which we sought to gain a 10 percent improvement. By honing a variety of important battlefield shooting skills to a high level, our soldiers would acquire the skills needed to suppress their natural fears in combat and effectively engage enemy targets.

Any unit can make dramatic improvements in marksmanship. No hard sell is required. Noncommissioned officers and soldiers fully understand that their survival in combat is directly tied to their ability to shoot. This is one combat skill in which all light infantrymen want to excel.

My personal role in this process was simple. First, I made targetry and feedback on marksmanship a priority in all collective training, whether it was force-on-force or live fire. Second, I gave platoon leaders the freedom to use their initiative when conducting nonstandard marksmanship training on the range. These two adjustments were all that was required to put a series of actions into motion that would ultimately give us the 10 percent improvement we sought.

For all maneuver live-fire exercises, targetry was always a key item of interest to me. For live-fire exercises conducted at company level and below, it was one of the areas that required my personal approval during the platoon leaders' pre-execution briefings. I wanted to ensure that target arrays were realistic and that they accurately depicted enemy situational templates appropriate to the training scenario. I required that targets on the range be laid out as briefed and that correctable problems be fixed on the spot.

The same rules applied to any maneuver live-fire range run by the company. The company XO had to get my personal approval on the targetry plan at the concept briefing. Before execution, I walked the ground with either the company XO or the platoon leaders to confirm the plan and to make any necessary adjustments. In very short order the company figured out that I had a genuine interest in targetry, and that if they didn't have a good plan, their trip back to the drawing board would likely be accompanied by an impromptu class on the relationship between targetry and training realism.

Eventually, our targetry became downright sophisticated. We gradually replaced silhouettes with target mannequins (in the style of those at the Joint Readiness Training Center) that were constructed within the company. The company XO also coordinated with the battalion logistics officer for expendable uniforms and equipment to make our targets and objectives as lifelike as possible, and we even rigged moving dummy targets on a squad react-to-contact live-fire range.

Once we got started in the right direction, simple momentum eventually took over. Tricks and gimmicks for enhancing realism on the range became an area of constructive competition within the company, with the consequent payoff being higher-quality training for all of the soldiers.

To grade marksmanship, target hits were always counted on maneuver live-fire situational training exercises. Soldiers were allowed to see the effects of their weapons by walking over the objective as part of the After Action Review. Seeing a splintered mannequin whose uniform their fire had just torn to shreds helped them appreciate the deadly power they had at their fingertips.

Without exception, all force-on-force training was conducted with the soldiers wearing multiple-integrated laser engagement system (MILES) gear. While MILES is far from perfect, it helps get soldiers accustomed to shooting at moving targets and targets above ground level. It is also the best system available for honing individual movement techniques (IMTs) under fire. Most of our live-fire exercises were also conducted with MILES, and even in those exercises observer-controllers had the authority to score "kills" on soldiers who failed to execute IMTs according to standard.

The greatest advances in individual combat marksmanship training resulted from creativity and ingenuity at company level and below. These efforts made marksmanship challenging and, at the same time, sustained the soldiers' enthusiasm by making training fun. The following are a few examples of the techniques C Company employed:

- To give soldiers practice at hitting moving targets, we constructed simple 2x4 frames and hung plastic bottles or balloons from the cross-members. The wind was sufficient to cause target movement.
- In Somalia, we took target practice on water bottles thrown into the ocean, allowing natural wave action to move the targets. At night, chemlights were put inside the bottles for visibility and to give the soldiers immediate feedback on their hits.
- Timed squad marksmanship competitions were conducted, in which each squad was issued identical ammunition loads, then tasked to engage a 4x4 post vertically implanted in the ground. The objective

was to determine which squad could cut its post in half the fastest. Ties were settled on the basis of the fewest rounds expended.

- Marksmanship drills were devised for fire teams and squads during fire and movement by creating live-fire lanes where targets were randomly changed between iterations. The fire teams or squads with the most target hits were appropriately rewarded.

Because I wanted the chain of command to use imagination in seeking better ways to train, I did not standardize combat marksmanship training as a formal program. Instead, we shared information at weekly training meetings on training techniques that worked well—and those that didn't. I saw it as a perfectly legitimate use of time and resources for platoons to go out to the range and shoot, without turning it into a standard qualification range. And I didn't have to sell its importance to anyone.

Two training adjustments made achieving our 10 percent marksmanship improvement goal a reality. First, we made marksmanship a consistent priority in all collective training and established simple internal feedback mechanisms to assess our progress. And second, I left it to the chain of command to figure out the best way to improve individual combat marksmanship skills. Once they knew they were free to experiment, the non-commissioned officers really took over and ran the show, with dramatic results. The soldiers developed exceptional marksmanship skills and became extremely confident with their weapons. When the battalion subsequently conducted weapon qualification, about 75 percent of my soldiers fired Expert.

As intended, C Company, 2nd Battalion, 14th Infantry, had become a high-performing unit that could flat-out shoot. The proof of this was repeatedly demonstrated in all of the company's later combat operations in Somalia. Our focus on combat marksmanship enabled the company to deliver well-aimed, accurate fire during urban combat operations in Mogadishu. After squeezing the trigger, a soldier could see the enemy drop. If incoming fire came from the dark recesses of a room, that fire was quickly silenced by a 40mm round or a burst of machine-gun fire accurately placed through the window.

Most gratifying was that our soldiers were confident that they had the tools to beat the enemy in his own back yard, and that our side was the better force. Once a unit was in contact, the paralysis of fear never had a chance to take hold. In its place were confident soldiers, doing their jobs the way they had been trained.

The typical SNA militiaman was a poor marksman. Instead of using well-aimed shots, he preferred to spray areas with automatic weapon fire. While this technique was certainly an attention-getter, our soldiers could see that it was not an effective way to kill. By contrast, most of our fighting was conducted from point-blank range out to 200 meters, and on those occasions when the enemy exposed himself for a direct shot, our soldiers got immediate feedback by dropping him with well-aimed fire.

All of this gave my soldiers exceptional confidence, which was highly instrumental in maintaining momentum in the attack. They never hesitated to fire their weapons and were confident in the ability of their buddies on the right and left to deliver accurate covering fire. Squad and fire team leaders identified targets with tracers, and then eliminated the enemy. Fire and movement thus worked just like the book said it would, and it was high performance in individual combat marksmanship that made it possible.

My soldiers made each round count because our innovative training made them familiar with shooting at moving and partially exposed targets from a variety of firing positions. On the basis of post-battle reports from Headquarters, United Nations Operation in Somalia (UNOSOM), both the International Committee for the Red Cross and human intelligence sources determined that enemy casualties in each of the task force's engagements exceeded friendly casualties by factors of 10 to 20. This helped make the ammunition-intensive nature of urban fighting less operationally restrictive.

During engagements ranging from five to fourteen hours, our companies never ran out of ammunition. This meant that we never had to conduct an ammunition resupply under fire—the importance of which cannot be overstated. Our soldiers exercised the discipline to shoot only at targets they could clearly identify because their training taught them that well-aimed shots were far more effective that a heavy volume of poorly aimed fire.

Combat marksmanship is a skill in which soldiers and leaders truly want to achieve excellence, and its payoff in combat effectiveness cannot be emphasized enough.

Maneuver Live-Fire Training

While high performance in the core areas of physical fitness, mental toughness, and combat marksmanship did more than anything else to give our soldiers the skill and will to win in combat these alone are not enough. Why? Because battles are won or lost by units that have to effectively interact in well-rehearsed, mutually supportive maneuvers.

There is no substitute for realistic maneuver live-fire exercises to prepare soldiers and units for combat. Light infantry units must be able to integrate maneuver with all organic and supporting fires to kill the enemy at the point of attack and to accomplish the mission while sustaining the fewest possible casualties. This collective core performance area is the essence of light infantry operations. The best instrument a commander has for this training is a maneuver live-fire exercise.

Defeating an aggressive, organized enemy who is trying to kill you is no simple task. It requires multi-echelon choreography of incredible complexity, with squads and platoons playing the lead roles, and involves many things having to come together quickly at many levels. Leaders must figure out where the enemy is and what he's trying to do, and have the mental agility to determine whether existing plans will work or will need modification. Orders and fire control measures must be clearly communicated and understood by all concerned. Battle drills must be executed precisely, each moving piece must be closely supervised, and higher headquarters and supporting units must be informed every step of the way. And all this must take place amid the chaos of incoming fire, deafening noise, casualties, confusion, and fear.

As an institution, the Army fully acknowledges the value of live-fire training. Soldiers do, too. They understand the benefits of practicing in peacetime what they will be required to execute in combat and willingly do whatever it takes to make this happen. It's the type of training they joined the Army to do. They crave live-fire exercises because they get their adrenaline pumping. And it becomes addictive; the more they practice, the better they get, the more confident they become, and the more they want.

While it is impossible for units to completely replicate the conditions of combat in training, they can come close. When soldiers experience a realistic live-fire exercise, something wonderful happens. The awesome firepower of a light infantry platoon in the attack, fully supported by indirect fires and attack helicopters, makes soldiers believe they are part of a destructive machine. When these live fires are stepped up to company level, the effects are dramatically magnified. The air reverberates; the ground shakes; and every sight, sound, and smell tells the soldier it is the enemy who is in big trouble.

Maneuver live-fire exercises provide units with the best opportunity to scrimmage before game day. Simple live fires are the best vehicles with which to practice the Army's doctrinal playbook—squad and platoon battle drills. More complex live fires develop the situational awareness that leaders must have to call the correct audible signals. Constant repetition in training develops at all levels the confidence that allows quick responses to situational changes and seamless adaptation to commonly understood variations of standard plays.

Despite widespread appreciation for the value of live-fire training, units conduct it with differing levels of frequency and intensity. Clearly, there are risks involved, and no one wants a soldier to get hurt in training. Consequently, much detailed planning is required, and participating soldiers need to be at a high level of discipline and training. But if the leaders are committed, a battalion and its companies can safely do realistic live-fire exercises with relative frequency, to the soldiers' and units' great advantage.

After assuming command of C Company, I came to believe that supercharged infantry units built their collective training around a robust centerpiece of maneuver live-fire exercises. This belief developed while serving under Colonel David, who was committed to live-fire training, and it solidified during sequential rotations through the National Training Center at Fort Irwin, California, and the Joint Readiness Training Center at Fort Polk, Louisiana. In my opinion, the 2-14 IN stood head and shoulders above the other battalions, and realistic live-fire exercises in training were the principal reason. This early experience convinced me that getting an extra 10 percent in this core performance area could also make my company great.

Conducting realistic maneuver live fire is a major challenge for a company commander. It requires keen personal attention and persistence every step of the way. Delegating this task to subordinates with less experience probably will not get the job done. But if the company commander truly believes in their value, is genuinely committed to doing them, and focuses on his role as the primary collective trainer in the company, it is a bill he doesn't mind paying.

Because the Army so highly values live-fire training, an abundance of doctrinal reference material is already available to assist unit efforts to conduct meaningful maneuver live-fire exercises. One of the best single-source documents available is the Joint Readiness Training Center's Live-Fire Division's outstanding manual of detailed yet simple "how-to" instructions for improving the realism of live-fire training.

Because live fire is merely a condition of training, commanders should not deviate from the guidance outlined in Field Manual 25-101, Battle Focused Training, that addresses the necessary assessment and evaluation. Mission Training Plans (MTPs) contain excellent models to use in developing live-fire scenarios, along with appropriate training and evaluation outlines (TEOs) for all critical tasks and sub-tasks.

The Army's commitment to live-fire training can also be found in every divisional training regulation. These regulations typically outline recommended live-fire sustainment training, as exemplified by the 10th Mountain Division's guidelines for infantry units at battalion level and below:

- Battalion with combat support and combat service support slice: one combined arms live-fire exercise (CALFEX) every eighteen months.
- Company: One CALFEX, one fire control exercise (FCX), and one live-fire exercise (LFX) per year.
- Platoon: four LFXs per year.
- Squad: four LFXs per year.

This broad guidance gives subordinate commanders the flexibility they need to tailor their live-fire training scenarios and tasks to the areas that have been assessed as needing the most practice. Given the amount of discretionary training time a battalion has in a year, these sustainment training frequencies lead commanders toward internal live-fire programs with real substance. Indeed, if commanders followed the letter of this law, live-fire exercises would become the centerpiece of their collective training.

If all the appropriate bases are covered in planning and coordination, a battalion, brigade, or division commander will rarely say "No" to a live-fire exercise that makes sense. Each wants his subordinate commanders to aggressively pursue these exercises. But they can't—and shouldn't—do it for you, because this is one ball that is squarely in each battalion and company commanders' court.

Because time is such a precious commodity for every unit, commanders must judiciously use the limited amounts at their discretion. Making the tough decisions concerning the way their unit will train is one area in which company commanders wield enormous influence.

To make each day in the field count for my company, I wanted to ensure that as many of the component parts as possible were training on their known weaknesses. As a result, we concentrated on situational training exercises (STXs) for most of the collective training we conducted when our time was our own. As a condition of this training, live-fire was integrated at every opportunity. We executed countless maneuver live-fire STXs, both at our home station and in-theater, from fire team through company level, both day and night.

In combat, the company team is normally the smallest tactical formation given a mission that involves the task of attacking or defending. Platoons often conduct independent ambushes or reconnaissance operations, and squads conduct security patrols, but these tasks are usually performed in the context of the larger company mission of attack or defense. Consequently, the scenarios used in our maneuver live-fire STXs were derived from tasks on the company's mission essential task list (METL): either Core METL or Directed METL (CMETL or DMETL). *Note*: Times and doctrine have changed since my company command days. Because today's commanders must be prepared for the full range of military operations, situational tasks should include simultaneous offense, defense, and stabilization.

Of the tasks on the light infantry company METL, the battalion commander considered two to be the most important: the movement to contact hasty attack and the deliberate attack (night). By changing the elements of enemy and terrain in the METT-T analysis (mission, enemy, terrain, troops, and time), we were able to develop a wide variety of maneuver live-fire STX scenarios that required us to expand our repertoire of tactics, techniques, and procedures (TTPs).

An important self-imposed restriction for our live-fire training was that no unit could double as its own controlling headquarters for the task it was executing. This meant that training was always conducted at least one echelon down. Thus, the largest formation the battalion could train was the company. The beauty of training one level down is that units can conduct high-quality training that is resourced almost exclusively by the unit itself. For example, if the battalion was running company maneuver live-fire STXs, one company was in the execution mode, another picked up range support, and the third was free to conduct preparatory or remedial training.

To reinforce the combined arms aspects of the fight, at whatever level STXs were conducted, all next-higher level systems and supporting arms that would be present in combat had to be replicated. Leaders were given the same base operation or fragmentary order (with supporting annexes and graphics) that they would normally receive from their next higher headquarters.

For squad and platoon maneuver live-fire STXs, if the company did not have enough observer controllers (OCs), they were augmented with officers or NCOs from the battalion staff. The battalion commander was the senior OC for all company level live-fire STXs, assisted by the command sergeant major and a tailored cadre of staff officers and NCOs. In turn, I was the senior OC for all platoon level live-fire STXs, assisted by the first sergeant.

Although OCs doubled in a limited capacity as range safety officers, the focus of their safety charter extended only as far as ensuring that all fires stayed within the range safety fan. Silence from the OC implied consent. As in combat, all fire control within the range fan was the responsibility of the chain of command in the executing unit. This was an extremely important facet of the way our training was conducted. While there were risks involved, the level of detail in our planning and rehearsals made me confident that this structure would be enough to maintain the balance between safety and realism. As a result, it prevented our live-fire exercises from being "canned" events that were easily disrupted by too many safety considerations.

This procedure thus took the primary responsibility for safety off of the OC and placed it on the chain of command, where it belonged. I

credited this training innovation with being a significant systemic con-
tributor toward embedding internal company fire control SOPs down to
the lowest level.

Whether a live-fire STX was designed as a day or night operation, the
first iteration was always conducted as a daylight blank-fire, force-on-force
run using MILES. After the AAR, the senior OC then decided whether
another MILES iteration was needed or if it was safe to go "hot." For night
live-fire STXs, a daylight live-fire iteration was also conducted, and all signal and fire control aids to be used at night were rehearsed. After the AAR
for this iteration, the senior OC likewise made the call to go "hot" at night,
or to conduct another daylight run.

Before executing any maneuver live-fire STX, we planned and coordinated in considerable detail. The platoon leaders and I had to do our
homework before we were allowed to brief a live-fire exercise at a training
meeting as a scheduled event. First, we had to work out all the resourcing
issues with the S-3. If the exercise could be resourced, we had permission
to do further planning. I then had to personally brief the battalion commander on all facets of the training before any live-fire exercise was
approved for execution. I created operations graphics overlaid on range
fans, detailed objective sketches, and plans for targetry, safety, risk assessment, support, and evaluation. Once the battalion commander approved,
the range packet was given to the S-3 for final coordination at the training
support meeting.

While some might criticize this as micromanagement, we all saw these
briefings as an integral component of my mentoring the platoon leaders
and the battalion commander mentoring me. Because of the Army's policy
on the assignment of company-grade officers, most captains who come to
light units after their advanced course only have mechanized infantry
experience. Even officers who arrive in the battalion with Ranger qualification lack an appreciation for the level of detail it takes to plan and control light infantry operations at company level. Although they are quick
and ready learners, they simply do not yet have sufficient light infantry
experience, and they need to be taught many of the things more experienced light infantrymen take for granted.

The battalion commander viewed these mentorship sessions as the heart of commander's business and used them as professional tutorials. I followed suit to provide the platoon leaders quality time with me. The meetings were usually very informal one-on-one sessions over a cup of coffee, with lots of give and take. Our discussions usually went far beyond the specific live-fire STX they were trying to get approved. For example, we might also discuss how either the battalion commander or I wanted them to fight their units, and how the training expectations would be seamlessly applied in both directions.

Over time, we learned the battalion commander's ways and came to understand how he thought through operations, and he learned how we accomplished missions. The platoon leaders and I received the same benefits by following his example. We frequently hit on larger tactical problems within the battalion that needed resolution. Learning from past mistakes, these meetings were mutually beneficial. I never failed to come away from them without learning something new from the boss or my subordinates. Reflecting on my company command tour, I too, regard these meetings as the most important things I did.

Any echelon of command has the resources to create a high-quality training environment for the unit below. For training squads, platoons, and companies that are preparing for the challenges of combat, there is no better tool than the maneuver live-fire STX. An abundance of doctrinal material is available to support this effort, but it all starts with a commander who allows initiative and is willing to take training risks. He must be committed to doing these exercises the right way, be persistent in overcoming obstacles, and be unwilling to settle for anything less.

Having realistic maneuver live-fire STXs as the centerpiece of collective training was the critical factor that enabled us to defeat the enemy in all of our tactical engagements in Somalia. Squads, platoons, and companies were able to conduct fire and maneuver confidently, aggressively, and safely. Supporting direct fires were routinely placed within 5 meters of advancing soldiers, both day and night. This was not the result of luck. Live-fire exercises gave units the opportunity to perfect internal fire control SOPs that were clearly understood by all. In most respects, the fire and maneuver we executed in combat were done exactly as we routinely did them in training. Constant repetition made it seem natural. Given the intensity of close combat, this is not a lesson that can be learned on the spot once a unit is in contact with the enemy.

As the ground element of the United Nations Command's QRF in Somalia, the task force always had to be ready to respond to crisis situations. In such cases, our planning time was severely limited. Once the initial concept of the operation had been hastily sketched out with the company commanders, there was never enough time to make sure it was clearly understood at the lowest level. And, because situations were often unclear, we had to rely on our professional judgment to fine-tune our concept of the operation once we were in the objective area. Much of this was done on the fly.

The derivative benefits of extended maneuver live-fire training were most prominent in these operations. If the company had not focused so heavily on live fire, I do not believe our tactical execution would have been nearly as good in these situations. As a consequence, we could well have suffered fratricide or friendly-fire injuries on more than one occasion.

Maneuver live-fire training prepares soldiers and leaders for the combat environment. Because we concentrated on making our live fires as realistic as possible, leaders developed a keen battlefield awareness that made excessive radio transmissions unnecessary. Repetitive training in a variety of different situations also helped leaders visualize what was happening at lower levels.

The intensive training also fostered confidence that lower echelons were doing the right things, even in the absence of radio traffic, which greatly simplified command and control. Concise orders told subordinates what to do without wasting time discussing how to do it. Without superfluous traffic, the net was clear for reporting. And most importantly, it freed the platoon leaders and me to focus on our most critical personal tasks.

When confronted with changes in the tactical situation, we could think through the action/reaction/counteraction cycle. As a result, we avoided having to make knee-jerk decisions. On more than one occasion, having the freedom to think kept us from making snap decisions in the heat of battle that, in hindsight, may not have achieved their intended aim and may well have been very costly.

None of this could have occurred without realistic maneuver live-fire training. An old lesson, relearned yet again, is that units will perform in combat exactly the way they are trained. Conducting these exercises was the best thing we did to prepare our soldiers and leaders for the conditions of combat.

Because of its live-fire training, my company, and the task force as a whole, achieved overwhelming tactical success in our first engagement in-country, and we only got better afterward. While our soldiers and leaders maintained a healthy respect for the enemy, we had no doubt as to which was the superior force and which would win in any firefight. The unit was truly an aggressive team with supreme confidence in their abilities. Because they felt they could not be physically defeated, they were never mentally defeated either.

All of these factors played a big part on 3 and 4 October 1993 in the few short hours following our first, unsuccessful attempt to rescue the Rangers. Every soldier had clearly heard the din of fighting above the city since the battle began earlier in the day. Ears strained as radios crackled with emotional situation reports that were barely audible above the noise of incoming and outgoing fire. There had already been many U.S. casualties, and as long as the battle raged, there were bound to be more. No one believed it would be an easy fight, and we all knew that the night would be long.

In the darkness, a couple of soldiers held flashlights aloft, and the orders group crowded in on all sides as we were talked through a simple concept of operations from a map stretched over the hood of a vehicle. In the background was all the discordant noise of a unit trying to make something complex and difficult happen very quickly. Helicopters raced low overhead. Executive officers and platoon leaders scurried around, positioning APCs, tanks, and trucks from various units into march order formation. The shouts of first sergeants, platoon sergeants, and squad leaders moving men and equipment filled the air.

When the orders group broke its huddle, there was not enough time for any detailed brief-back. Nevertheless, I was confident that I understood both the plan and the battalion commander's intent. This understanding, however, would be less clear at the platoon, squad, and individual soldier levels, where there would be, at best, only a rough idea of the situation, mission, and fire control measures. The situation compelled us to rely on both the TTPs we had first developed in live-fire training and our own recent combat experience to carry us through.

Soon after the task force left the staging area, it began receiving intense RPG and automatic weapons fire, as it had earlier in the day. With most of our soldiers now riding in more survivable APCs, however, we were able to fight our way through to the vicinity of our objectives, where our soldiers dismounted their APCs and carried the fight on foot.

Our hastily developed plan survived enemy contact with only minor modifications. Even though they did not understand the full situation, squads and platoons executed their pieces of the operation exactly as planned. And although there were several grim moments before the mission was accomplished, the end result did not surprise me. What these men were asked to do that night was, in many ways, merely a variation of what they had done so often in training. And, most notably, even in that chaos, the entire task force did not suffer a single fratricide or friendly fire injury during the successful linkup with and extraction of the Rangers.

Extensive live-fire exercises in training were the key to that success. In every interview after the experience in Somalia, the soldiers and leaders of the task force confirmed what we already knew: In their minds, what best prepared them for combat was the extensive live-fire training the unit had conducted as a matter of routine, both at Fort Drum and in-theater.

Combat Leadership

A battalion and its companies make up the Army's basic family unit. Although soldiers may identify with their division or brigade, they bond with their company and battalion; ask a soldier what unit he's in, and the odds are that he'll respond with the company and battalion designation first. It therefore falls to the battalion and company commanders to be the Army's caretakers of this family unit. Because of this extremely close-knit unit organization, a battalion commander is able to directly influence the lives of hundreds of soldiers, and company commanders influence scores of soldiers.

Command at battalion and below demands intimacy. The commander's personal influence on everyone and everything in the unit affects all facets of unit life. There is little that escapes his personal attention. Indeed, it could be argued convincingly that the personal influence that commanders at battalion and company levels have on their units is unequalled at any other level in the Army. As a consequence, either at battalion or company, all units reflect the standards, commitment, and priorities of their commander.

Because of his position as the foremost leader in the organization, a commander is the unit's primary behavioral role model. What he does or fails to do is always in plain view of his subordinates and becomes the subject of much discussion. The responsibility of command, therefore, carries enormous weight and emphasizes the importance of doing the right thing.

The combined effects of position and organization force a commander to focus not only on accomplishing the mission but also on how it is accomplished. The long-term health and well-being of his unit depend on his ability to balance this dual focus.

These factors are, of course, every bit as relevant—and probably more so—when a unit is deployed to a theater of operation. Once a unit is deployed, soldiers and units live together twenty-four hours a day, seven days a week. Anything that was working well before deployment requires constant maintenance to sustain, and things that were not working so well typically get worse.

In an operational theater, the mission often becomes all-consuming. The commander, therefore, must make a concerted effort to maintain his focus on all the other areas that are important to the unit. But since every operational deployment has an end date, once that date arrives the unit must immediately begin preparing for its next mission. The leadership challenge of command, then, is to finish the first race on a horse that is ready to run the next one.

For these reasons, when the 2-14 IN was alerted for deployment to Somalia, I felt it was important not to limit our focus to the operational domain. When it came to the mission, I was confident that everything we had done in training would serve us well, but the leaders also had to focus on the human dimension.

What follows are combat leadership lessons learned from our experience in Somalia—before the battle, during the battle, and after the battle. I will highlight the elements that, in hindsight, I consider the most relevant. Taken together, these are intended to provide a picture of the way we tried to sustain the long-term well-being of the company.

During an officer professional development class before our deployment, the battalion commander provided a handout with his intent. (See the "Going to War: Officer Professional Development" handout below). I linked my intent to his, and reinforced in the minds of the company's officers and NCOs the idea that they had to take a long-term view of the operation. On the basis of the training we had conducted and our past performance, I had no doubt that the company would accomplish its mission to a high standard. For the health and well-being of the unit, however, the manner in which we accomplished that mission was also extremely important, and the roles the officers and NCOs would play in the process were critical. We would, of course, be tactically and technically prepared to dominate any situation. But it was essential that we also be ethically and morally sound: someone's worst enemy or best friend. Combat is a cruel and brutal expression of man's competitiveness. We would prevail in combat, but we were going to be good while doing so, both literally and ethically.

I thought that, as the mission wore on, it might be easy for officers to lose their long-term focus or to become complacent in their duties. Therefore, I felt it was important to establish a common reference point of expectations up front. Although my discussion was focused at the platoon and squad leader levels, this before-the-battle effort was equally applicable to all of the company's officers and NCOs.

The major lessons that follow were derived from personal experience in the many combat operations the company executed during its tour in Somalia. While most of them are not new, they are, nonetheless, still valid:

- Deploy well forward. Your tactical presence instills confidence beyond measure.
- You are not indispensable. If you become a casualty, someone else will step in to take your place. The Army has many qualified people who can do the job.

- Your personal leadership counts. Your personal behavior in tough situations shapes and guides the actions of others.
- Listen to the battle around you. What you do *not* hear is sometimes as important as what you do. Do not rely solely on radio reports. Your experience in training exercises gives you the best feeling for what's occurring on the ground when reports tell you differently.
- Think. If you're not, neither is anyone else. Think action, reaction, and counteraction. Any decision made in haste will cause needless losses in men and materiel.
- All leaders must stay cool and clear-headed under fire. This takes concentrated effort that always starts with you.
- Your subordinate leaders need reassurance. Sometimes this takes a gentle form, sometimes not. Everyone knows that accomplishing the mission is the way home. These leaders truly want to do the right thing, but fear and confusion sometimes get in the way.
- Don't allow knee-jerk reactions when soldiers are killed or wounded. This is an unfortunate element of our business, and it will happen despite your every effort. Accepting this fact and living with it are difficult.
- Give subordinates the time and space to develop the situation. They have a difficult job to do. Don't badger them with unnecessary reporting requirements. Waiting is the hardest part, particularly when you know your men are dying.
- Remember the Regiment. Many have stood in your shoes before. Don't allow your actions to stain the Colors. After we are gone, the Regiment lives on.

The following lessons learned after the battle are designed to help a commander take stock of himself and his unit as they prepare for the next battle:

- Learn from what you and the unit did, and continue seeking organizational improvement. Do this even if it means changing your personal ways. Actively enforce the AAR process so that good ideas are not stifled at lower levels.
- Keep routine decision-making decentralized, and save the important decisions for yourself. Your staff and subordinate leaders need

room to take the initiative and work out problems on their own. The better they can do this, the better they can serve you.

- Be tolerant of honest mistakes. Everyone is under stress and trying to do his best. So long as mistakes don't cause casualties or impede mission accomplishment, they probably aren't that important.

- Pace yourself for the long haul. Your unit needs a commander who is physically and mentally fresh. Get regular sleep and maintain a regimen of physical training, hygiene, and relaxation. If you don't maintain your balance, neither will your unit.

- Don't let the operational tempo make you lose sight of everything else. Lots of other things still demand your attention—awards, punishments, promotions, rear detachment, family support group, maintenance, mess hall. They are all your responsibility; don't ignore them.

- Stay visible and approachable to soldiers. Management by walking around helps keep your finger on the pulse.

- Make every effort to keep rumors in check, both at home and in-theater. Write a monthly newsletter to dependents. Send videos to the family support group. Routinely meet with subordinates to dispel groundless rumors.

- Maintain your perspective and sense of humor. Not everything is serious. If you don't laugh very often, chances are no one else does either. And units that don't laugh, even at themselves, have big problems.

It is almost impossible to overstate the effect a commander has on his unit. While accomplishing the mission will always be his paramount consideration, it cannot be the commander's only consideration. Fulfilling his role as caretaker of the Army's basic family unit demands a balanced approach to command. For sustained operations, the company must maintain its health over the long term. Therefore, it is essential to keep an eye on how the company accomplishes the mission.

The following is the handout Colonel David gave all of us before we left for Somalia:

Going to War:
Officer Professional Development Handout

As officers, you are the standard-bearers of the Army's institutional values. Soldiers and noncommissioned officers will take their cues from what you do or say, and from what you do not do or say. Seek excellence in all things, and never let a fault or error pass by you uncorrected.

Have trust and confidence in your chain of command. Once a decision is made, vigorously support it 100 percent. If you hear grumbling in the ranks, put a stop to it immediately. Never do anything to foster the notion that "higher" is screwed up. Remember, you are somebody's "higher," too.

Performance counseling does not stop once the unit arrives in-theater. On the contrary, it is more frequent. Performance counseling remains our best available tool for modifying individual behavior that affects unit performance. This task is not delegated below squad leader level. Platoon leaders review every counseling in their platoon. Your notebook becomes your bible.

Training does not stop in-theater. You must always have a series of mission-related training scenarios ready to go. Most training will be "opportunity" training. Accept the fact that you will not be popular when you force your unit to do this.

Pre-combat and post-combat checks are standing operating procedure (SOP) in every mission. This task is never delegated below squad leader level.

AARs are conducted upon completion of every mission. Lessons learned are incorporated into SOPs immediately.

The ultimate form of troop welfare is bringing everyone back home alive with all equipment operative.

Establish personal goals for self-improvement, both mental and physical, on this deployment. Encourage your subordinates to do the same.

Pray regularly and get to know your God. Encourage your subordinates to do the same. There are no atheists in foxholes.

Keep a diary. It is a good aid to your professional growth. Encourage your subordinates to do the same.

Maintain your balance and sense of humor. Do not get "stressed out." If you do, you will lose the trust and confidence of your soldiers. Understand the difference between losing your temper and showing your temper.

Allow no deviations from the prescribed uniform, ever. Deviations must be conscious decisions by the chain of command based on an analysis of METT-T (Mission, Equipment, Terrain, Troops—Time), not personal whims.

All soldiers perform personal hygiene daily, shaving and brushing teeth at the very least. Squad leaders check; platoon leaders and platoon sergeants verify. No exceptions.

Physical training is conducted daily in accordance with METT-T. Develop a program of standard isometric and manual resistance exercises.

Do not let good performance go unrewarded or poor performance go uncorrected.

Encourage constructive feedback from subordinates on ways to do things better, and then send recommendations up through the chain of command. The best solutions often come from the bottom up.

See that weapons and ammunition are cleaned at every opportunity.

Take charge of all Government property in sight. There is always something that needs to be checked or verified.

Stop rumors immediately and ruthlessly. Do not allow the morale of your unit to rise and fall on the basis of the latest rumor. If you don't hear it from the chain of command, it's not true.

We are a combat organization, expert in the controlled application of violence. Follow your instincts; they are probably right. The chain of command will support you. Maintain patient aggressiveness in your platoon.

Conclusion

ny unit in the Army can be truly great, whether it's a combat, combat
support, or combat service support unit. By focusing on high
performance in several fundamental areas that are critical for success
in combat, a commander can significantly increase the overall capability of
his unit.

The principles outlined in the Army's doctrine and training system
work. They have shaped an Army that is the world's best. The levels of individual and unit performance throughout the Army are solid. Consequently,
most units are pretty good by any measure, but there is always room for
improvement.

Every unit has several fundamental areas of individual and collective
endeavor that are critical to anything the unit will ever be called upon to do
in combat, regardless of the conditions. These areas are the essential char-
acteristics that define the unit. I call them unit core performance areas.

Commanders can achieve high performance in their core areas with
only a small increase in effort, about 10 percent. But getting this 10 percent requires commanders to maintain a long-term focus on their core
performance areas that does not change in the face of competing demands.
Core performance areas must constantly be integrated as sub-tasks or

conditions in everything the unit does. They must then be reinforced at every opportunity by all the institutional weight the chain of command can bring to bear.

Based on Colonel David's command guidance, the core performance areas for C Company, 2-14 IN, were physical fitness, mental toughness, and combat marksmanship. Through extensive realistic maneuver live-fire exercises, we maintained a constant focus in these areas, both at our home station and in-theater. Our aim was to find the extra 10 percent that would make us high performers in each of them. Achieving that did not require a major overhaul of the unit. The key was thoughtful, finely tuned adjustments in what the unit trained on and in the way training was conducted.

When a unit achieves high performance in its core areas, it gets an additional payoff of tremendous proportions. Because the core performance areas are at the heart and soul of the unit, their combined action powers performance in other important areas as well. The result is a super-charged unit with far greater capabilities.

Adopting this philosophy in training paved the way for C Company, 2-14 IN's superb performance in all of its combat operations in Somalia. The company got more than its extra 10 percent in each of its core performance areas from every soldier. As a result, it was, indeed, a high-energy, high-performance outfit across the board.

BIBLIOGRAPHY

Baumann, Robert F., Lawrence A. Yates, and Versalle F. Washington. *"My Clan Against the World": US and Coalition Forces in Somalia, 1992–1994.* Fort Leavenworth, KS: Combat Studies Institute Press, 2003.

David, William C. Paper, "Developing a Supercharged Battalion."

Ecklund, Marshall V., and Michael A. McNerney. *Personnel Recovery Operations for Special Operations Forces in Urban Environments: Modeling Successful Overt and Clandestine Methods of Recovery.* Monterey, CA: Naval Postgraduate School, 2004.

Ferry, Charles P. "Mogadishu, October 1993: Personal Account of a Rifle Company XO," *Infantry* (September–October 1994).

Hollis, Mark. "Platoon Under Fire," *Infantry* (January–April 1998).